Roger Enrico
and Jesse Kornbluth

THE OTHER GUY BLINKED

AND OTHER DISPATCHES FROM THE COLA WARS

BANTAM BOOKS
TORONTO · NEW YORK · LONDON · SYDNEY · AUCKLAND

THE OTHER GUY BLINKED
A Bantam Book
Bantam hardcover edition / November 1986
Bantam paperback edition / January 1988
Previously published as THE OTHER GUY BLINKED:
HOW PEPSI WON THE COLA WARS

Library of Congress Cataloging-in-Publication Data

Enrico, Roger.
  The other guy blinked.

  1. Pepsi-Cola Company. 2. Coca-Cola Company.
3. Soft drink industry—United States. I. Kornbluth,
Jesse. II. Title.
HD9349.S634P464 1986   338.7'66362'0973   86-17485
ISBN 0-553-26632-2

Published simultaneously in the United States and Canada

Bantam Books are published by Bantam Books, Inc. Its trademark,
consisting of the words "Bantam Books" and the portrayal of a rooster, is
Registered in U.S. Patent and Trademark Office and in other countries.
Marca Registrada. Bantam Books, Inc., 666 Fifth Avenue, New York,
New York 10103.

PRINTED IN THE UNITED STATES OF AMERICA
KR   0 9 8 7 6 5 4 3 2 1

CONTENTS

ACKNOWLEDGMENTS

How does a person run a company like Pepsi-Cola USA and find time to write a book?

The answer is: with a lot of help.

In my case, I was fortunate that some of the most dedicated and talented people imaginable got personally involved, not only by giving advice and counsel but by taking on a great deal of the work.

The first was Joe McCann, PepsiCo's vice president of corporate affairs. During much of the time the events in this book were taking place, Joe was my energetic and effective public relations chief. As such, he actively participated in—and, not infrequently, was the catalyst for—the most important initiatives of Pepsi-Cola USA. It's right in character that this book is his idea, and that he has contributed his insights, writing talent, and critical review to it.

Also at PepsiCo, former Chairman Don Kendall and our current Chairman Wayne Calloway supported this unusual, noncorporate project from the beginning—adding another to the long list of reasons why I owe them so much.

Along with Joe McCann, Pete Reader gave me sound advice on getting the book started. Their wisdom and the recommendation of David Fisher led me to Bantam Books.

At Bantam, Louis Wolfe, Alberto Vitale, Linda Grey, Stuart Applebaum, Stephen Rubin, and Peter Guzzardi responded enthusiastically and decisively. Their belief that the Bantam team could publish *The Other Guy Blinked* in a fraction of the time normally required to produce a book gave me the energy and courage to proceed.

Bantam Senior Editor Peter Guzzardi deserves unending thanks for prodding that was invariably good-humored, editing that was sensitive when there was little time for sensitivity, and an uncanny ability to keep numerous drafts of the manuscript in his head without confusion.

Literary agent Kathy Robbins also made a vital contribution by recommending my coauthor, Jesse Kornbluth—without whom this book would still be an idea floating in Joe McCann's fertile mind. That Jesse and I each claim the other wrote his favorite parts of this book says everything about our collaboration.

My secretary, Patti Giordano, got the manuscript into my MacIntosh computer with speed, accuracy, and a constant curiosity about what was coming next—a bracing reaction from someone who already knew the story.

My good friend, scuba instructor, and creative genius, Alan Pottasch, was invaluable in his encouragement and input, as were Pepsi USA executives John Almash, Richard Blossom, Dan Clark, Becky Madeira, Bennett Nussbaum, Ken Ross, and Jim Stanley. Outside the company, special thanks are also due Rockbill, Inc. President Jay Coleman; Frito-Lay Senior Vice President Jim O'Neal; Carol Dreyfus and Scott Ellsworth at the Smithsonian Institute; Edward Kosner, Editor and Publisher of New York Magazine; A.O. Smith; Pearl, Sam, and Richard Kornbluth; and Annette Tapert.

The editorial and production team at Bantam labored mightily to meet our hair-raising deadlines. My gratitude to Alison Acker, Barbara Cohen, Betsy Cenedella, Sara Goodman, Jim Plumeri, Donna Ruvituso, Lucille Salvino, and many others along the way.

It was a special pleasure to be reunited with former Pepsi colleague Jack Hoeft, now president of Bantam's Sales and Marketing Division. It's gratifying to see that the marketing lessons learned in one business can be applied to another.

Finally, my wife and son put up with a lot of tension, cold dinners, and lost weekends as I struggled to put this account of the cola wars on paper. I can never thank Rosemary and Aaron enough.

Well, maybe I can—if I promise never to try writing a book while running a company again.

I do.

THE
OTHER GUY
BLINKED

CHAPTER 1

"The Surest Move Ever Made"

Once upon a time, in a simpler and more innocent world, you could order a Coca-Cola without being asked, "Which one?" This book explains why that world is no more. It also explains why, after the Coca-Cola Company launched New Coke with such fanfare in the spring of 1985, it brought its original formula back less than ninety days later. And it explains why, thanks in part to Coke's schizophrenic summer, the unthinkable occurred—Pepsi-Cola became America's favorite soft drink.

Businessmen who purport to know the inside story of two companies that are intense rivals are, in my experience, either trafficking in information that's been deviously acquired or they're dabbling in fiction. Let me reassure you at the outset—I'm not known for underhanded tactics or for my skill as a novelist.

What, then, qualifies me to tell this multifaceted, two-company story?

Two things. First is that I'm president and chief executive officer of the Pepsi-Cola Company. The second has to do with a series of decisions my associates and I made. I believe those decisions were as significant for the men at Coca-Cola headquarters in Atlanta, Georgia, as they were for our associates at Pepsi. It sounds brazen, I know, but I really think this: Along with the gentlemen in Atlanta, my Pepsi associates and I invented New Coke.

This remarkable story begins years ago, before I became president of Pepsi. At that time, Pepsi was gaining ground rapidly on Coke with an advertising campaign built around a head-to-head taste test called the Pepsi Challenge. Stung by Pepsi's success, the executives of the Coca-Cola Company decided to hold a taste test of their own—a Coke Challenge. The tasters were Coke employees. The tasting took place at Coke headquarters in Atlanta.

According to *The Wall Street Journal*, Pepsi won. Not by much, but we won.

A few months after I took over at Pepsi—on November 11, 1983, my thirty-ninth birthday—I signed the most expensive celebrity advertising contract in history: $5 million for the privilege of making two commercials and sponsoring a tour featuring a talented but shy young man who sang in a high-pitched voice and danced backwards. A lot of people thought I was nuts. Many wrote to say so. And even I began to think they might be right.

The next big event in what has come to be known as the Cola Wars occurred on April 23, 1985, when Coca-Cola made what its executives described as "the most important announcement in the company's ninety-nine-year history." Gone was the product which had made Coca-Cola famous—and which had made billions in profits. In its stead, we would forever have "New Coke," a product which, said Coke's eloquent chairman, Roberto C. Goizueta, was "rounder . . . smoother . . . more harmonious, yet bolder."

Nearly everyone thought Coke was nuts. Tens of thousands wrote to say so. And I knew damn well they were right.

Now the Pepsi Challenge, the signing of Michael Jackson to make commercials for Pepsi-Cola, and New Coke are not three unrelated events. As you'll see in these pages, one follows from another just as surely as soft drink sales go up in summer.

But history, even the history of the soft drink business, isn't ever a simple connect-the-dots affair. Relatively insignificant events often set much larger forces in motion.

Nowhere is this clearer than in military history. World War I "started" with the assassination of the Archduke Franz Ferdinand of Austria-Hungary and his wife. World War II "started" with the invasion of Poland. Large-scale American involvement in Vietnam "started" with the purported shelling of an American ship in the Gulf of Tonkin.

By comparison, of course, the battles that Pepsi-Cola and Coke fight in the Cola Wars are trivial. There are no final defeats.

The ammunition we fire at one another is often damn silly stuff. But for all that, our battles are very real.

Tens of billions of dollars are at stake. And "market share"—the sales performance of a soft drink compared to others in its category. And something intangible, but no less important: pride. That last reason is, in this story, perhaps the most important ingredient.

I can understand why the proud and frustrated executives of the Coca-Cola company—men who'd been told by everyone *except* consumers that they were selling the best soft drink in the nation—would want to respond to the Pepsi Challenge and our Michael Jackson commercials.

Still, when I'm asked, "Okay, but why did they respond with the world-class blunder that was New Coke?" people are often surprised by my answer. They assume I'm going to launch right into an account of the wonders of Pepsi—a self-serving, not entirely credible monologue about our superior taste, superior advertising, and, by immodest extension, superior management. That's not my style.

But in order to tell you how Pepsi won the Cola Wars—and, contrary to all expectation, has kept on winning them—I have to do something that's even less my style. That is, I have to ignore Pepsi for a while and talk solely about a subject which, as you'll see, is fascinating for very different reasons: the Coca-Cola Company.

On March 7, 1985—little more than a month before Coke changed its formula—a ninety-five-year-old man died quietly in an Atlanta hospital. His name was Robert Woodruff, and he was one of the soft drink industry's two giants. (The other is Donald Kendall—but you'll hear more about him later.)

Power came to Woodruff in 1923, when he became president of the Coca-Cola Company. He held that title until 1965, when he retired. In that year he became a member of the company's board of directors and the chairman of the board's finance committee. In 1981 he became chairman emeritus. When he finally resigned from the board in 1984, Robert Woodruff had served Coke for sixty-one years.

I never met Robert Woodruff, but I've read enough about him—and admired his handiwork—to have some sense of his complex, often contradictory character. On one hand he was a quiet, almost invisible executive who cherished anonymity and took his ego satisfaction from Coke's evergrowing profit statements.

In Atlanta you'd never guess he was the head of the world's largest soft drink empire: He lived in a house that one of his junior executives might well have purchased. If his four other residences were more lavish—his 4,600-acre ranch in Wyoming and his 47,000-acre plantation in Georgia were certainly not modest—few people from Atlanta saw them.

To the citizens of his hometown he was "Mr. Bob," and he was known for his charity. He donated millions to his favorite causes—$200 million to Emory University alone. And though few knew it, he was interested in religion; a minister sent him specially prepared written sermons that spoke of moral problems in terms of syrup and carbonated water.

Robert Woodruff loved his privacy—and he was well positioned to guarantee it. At the old Coke headquarters he had a special elevator built to whisk him to his office. Adjoining that office was a kitchen, with a full staff that catered only to him. He didn't much like to leave this sanctum, so he encouraged Atlanta's most prominent citizens to visit him there and even gave some of them office keys to facilitate their visits.

For all that, Woodruff was a man who never hesitated to use his power. It was often said that the division of influence in Atlanta was fifty-fifty—Woodruff had half the power in town, and everybody else, taken together, had the other half. His management style only *looked* so low-profile as to be subliminal. True, he rarely gave a direct order, almost never signed a document. But that was because he never needed to. One word from Mr. Bob—at any hour of the day or night—and his people jumped.

Because Mr. Bob was childless, he treated his company like his child. And no one has ever suggested that he wanted his precious offspring to be anything but a reflection of its father. As a result, Coca-Cola became, over the years, more and more successful and less and less innovative.

But then, Coke didn't need to innovate. For Robert Woodruff was a man with a single perception so brilliant that it needed no revision.

He wanted a Coke sign on every corner. He wanted bottles of Coke in every store. His aim, quite simply, was to put a Coke within arm's reach of every possible customer.

That ideal—the foundation of the Coca-Cola empire—has

become the foundation of all soft drink companies. It has never been improved upon.

Robert Woodruff had something else going for him which, in his view, needed no updating. It was called "Merchandise 7X," and it was the formula for Coca-Cola syrup.

Merchandise 7X has long been one of the best-kept secrets in the world. Coke was so protective of it that, when India demanded that they disclose the formula to its government, Coke closed its business in that hot and thirsty country of 850 million souls.

Mr. Woodruff was right to pull Coke out of India. For Merchandise 7X was not just a mixture of sugar and flavoring—it was an alchemical concoction. And the soft drink it produced was not just a thirst-quencher. It was the one unchanging taste in a world that changed more rapidly than anyone would have wished.

In the years before large jets and low fares allowed Americans to travel in huge numbers, the world outside our borders seemed big and inhospitable to many of us. To find yourself in North Africa, therefore, and to see the familiar Coke sign was almost as satisfying as a return ticket to the USA. Even here at home, Coke had immense power to tap into our emotions. A Coke emblem on a warehouse in Iowa, its colors faded by the heat of innumerable summers, could take any American back to his childhood.

But those feelings didn't just lead to nostalgia or fantasy. Because of Robert Woodruff's single-mindedness, those heart-tugging Coke signs—in North Africa, and Iowa, and places much more remote—usually led to a Coke machine. And when that cold green bottle slid down the chute, it took a Coke drinker back to high school football games and first cars and Sunday picnics.

In 1938 a legendary Kansas newspaper editor named William Allen White was photographed on his seventieth birthday. He chose to have that picture taken at the Coke dispenser at his favorite soda fountain. "Coca-Cola is," he explained, "the sublimated essence of all that America stands for."

White understood. Drink a Coke and you were transfusing yourself—taking in a little bit of the soul of America. Coke was the American Dream in a bottle.

Robert Woodruff also understood this. That is, I think, one reason Woodruff didn't swagger and boast. He had no reason to. He knew who he was: Coke's caretaker.

* * *

Under Woodruff's stewardship, the Coca-Cola Company made billions and billions of dollars. But no man rules forever. Inevitably, Mr. Woodruff's place was taken by men who—though professing allegiance to his ideals—had their own agenda.

In 1979, Brian Dyson became president of Coke USA. Dyson is tall and thin and super-fit. He competes in triathalons and, I'm told, writes poetry and short stories. I believe that. Born in Argentina and educated in England, he isn't the sort of guy you imagine hanging around bottling plants in his spare time.

When Dyson took over, Coke USA was a sleepy division that had, for almost a decade, been badly kicked around by the Pepsi upstarts. Some of this was the result of some very aggressive marketing on Pepsi's part. And a lot of it was the result of the Pepsi Challenge.

When the Pepsi Challenge was invented in Dallas, Texas, in 1974, that city was nearly exclusive Coke territory. If people who lived there didn't drink Coke, they drank Dr Pepper, which had its headquarters in Dallas. Pepsi ran a distant third—and it was having trouble fighting off discount soft drinks.

In desperation, PBG—the Pepsi Bottling Group, which is the division that runs our company-owned bottling plants—asked Alan Pottasch, the father of Pepsi advertising, to develop a special ad campaign for the Dallas market.

Blind taste tests that pitted Pepsi against Coke were run. Not only did Pepsi win these tests, but Coke drinkers said things like "Hey, I've been drinking Coke all my life. You mean I *really* prefer Pepsi? I can't believe this!"

"What are you going to do now?" the testers asked.

"Guess I'm gonna drink Pepsi," the lifelong Coke drinkers said.

In 1975, after the results of these tests were confirmed by an independent consumer research firm, Pepsi filmed them and started running these real-life dialogues as commercials. A number of everyday people became television stars in their hometown. Meanwhile, Pepsi's numbers went through the roof. Sales shot up in Dallas—and they stayed up.

Soon, the Pepsi Challenge was expanded to 80 percent of the country—and there seemed to be no end of people who were happily surprised to learn that the drink they preferred wasn't Coke.

By 1977, Pepsi was outselling Coke in supermarkets across America and gaining market share elsewhere. Yes, Coke still ruled supreme—its overwhelming dominance in vending machines and restaurants and its ubiquity abroad made that certain—but during the seventies Coke's business was powered more by past achievements than by the vision and energy of its executives.

Brian Dyson, the native Argentine, was made president of Coke USA to change all of that, to get Coke moving again. But though he had racked up an impressive string of accomplishments in Coca-Cola's international division in Mexico and South America, he was much less familiar with the American market. So his first few years were devoted to studying and learning—and developing a strategy that would breathe some life into a dormant company.

In 1981, Roberto Goizueta, then forty-seven, became chairman of the Coca-Cola Company. His predecessor, Paul Austin, had once won a case-loading contest in a bottling plant. It's difficult to imagine Goizueta—who was born and raised an aristocrat in pre-Castro Cuba and educated at Yale—doing that.

Goizueta started his career with Coke's international division as a chemical engineer. By 1977 he was head of the technical operations department at Coke headquarters in Atlanta. In that year, researchers secretly began working on the formula for Diet Coke—the first diet cola that the Coca-Cola Company would decide was good enough to carry the world's most famous brand name. There was no way, in diet-conscious America, that such a drink could fail. Everyone connected to Diet Coke's early development knew the company was looking at one of the consumer products industry's greatest successes.

Everyone, that is, except the top management of the Coca-Cola Company. "Coke," they believed, meant Coca-Cola—the product in those little green bottles. It was sacrosanct, not to be tampered with. So, in the late 1970s, Diet Coke was quietly shelved.

When he took over in 1981, Roberto Goizueta was determined to change the rules of the game and create a modernized Coca-Cola Company. Nothing was to be sacrosanct—Diet Coke *would* be introduced.

And more. Goizueta looked over the balance sheet and saw a ton of money in the pot. He chose to spend it and, for the first time in Coke's modern history, take on some debt. So Coke bought Columbia Pictures for about $700 million. And then

Goizueta looked around to see what changes he could make in the soft drink business.

First, he restructured the company to get rid of the deadwood—mostly third-generation bottlers who were so wealthy you couldn't get them off the golf course. Then he did some headhunting. Guess where he looked?

At McCann-Erickson, Coke's advertising agency, the account was turned over to John Bergin, who, in the many years he'd been at BBDO, had been important to the creation of the "Pepsi Generation" commercials. How well did Bergin know Pepsi? Well, let's put it this way: He used to write speeches for Don Kendall, PepsiCo's chairman.

He also hired Sergio Zyman, late of Pepsi, to be Coke's vice-president of marketing. He hired a slew of junior-executive types, recruiting them both from Pepsi USA and from Pepsi bottlers. He lured away former Pepsi bottlers—Larry Smith and Marv Herb, among others—with lucrative deals, setting them up in Coke franchises. And, later, he hired Ed Mellett, the president of Pepsi's food service division, to fill one of Coke's many nebulous executive positions.

With all those former Pepsi people—and a new corporate spirit based on a quick-action philosophy known as "ready-fire-aim"—Coke woke up.

The empire was ready to strike back.

How does a company move to regain the initiative? One way is through astute marketing. Sure, Coke was an old brand—in 1986, exactly one hundred years old.

So what? In the food and beverage business there's no such thing as a product life cycle. There are no old brands—only old marketers who are unable to breathe new life into the products they're supposed to market.

A whole host of first-class marketing companies have kept their old brands vibrant and contemporary. General Mills has done this, repeatedly and brilliantly, with Wheaties. Here is a product America grew up on. Hundreds of millions of people knew it as the Breakfast of Champions. Now, Wheaties are "What the Big Boys Eat." Same product—with very minor improvements, none of them taste-related—but pitched to attract a changed consumer-base.

Coke might have done something like that. But it seems Coke executives just couldn't figure out how to reposition their product without trading in its Mom's-apple-pie appeal. So they looked to another way of taking the initiative—introducing new products.

It took a while to do the formulations and testing, so it was not until 1982 that Coke's new or improved drinks began to appear. In the next three years, Coke repositioned or changed six of its eight brands. There's no question that's a very ambitious schedule—particularly for a former turtle.

But I would never have guessed that effort would eventually include their flagship brand. Changing products people consume a lot of—and are intimately familiar with—is risky business. The marketing graveyard is littered with the bones of formerly great brands—and formerly great executives—who have disregarded that fact.

Once, years before I joined PepsiCo's Frito-Lay division, sales of Fritos corn chips suddenly took a dive. Frito-Lay hired consultants, did all kinds of analyses, changed the advertising, and then discovered that some geniuses had played around—but only just a little—with the recipe.

When Frito-Lay top management discovered that, the original recipe was restored in two seconds flat. And when I got to Frito-Lay, this story was told to me—with a moral attached. The moral?

"Don't f—— with Fritos."

The meaning is clear: When you have a gold standard—a product so well-loved that when people think of your company, it's the very first thing that comes to mind—for God's sake, cherish it.

I never forgot that moral. Despite—or perhaps because of—the profanity, the alliteration has a memorable quality.

As the empire gathered its forces and prepared to launch its new or repositioned soft drinks, Coke executives discovered that they had a problem. A very happy problem, they thought.

During the experiments that led to Diet Coke, Coke executives say their researchers just happened—by accident—onto a better recipe for regular Coke which just happened to taste less harsh than Merchandise 7X.

The researchers brought it to the executives. The executives went into swoons and raptures. But what should they do? Give it to the consumer—change the formula for Coke—or put it in a closet?

I say the Coke executives had a problem, all right, but that wasn't it. More likely the problem was: How in hell were they going to tell Mr. Woodruff that they were screwing around with Merchandise 7X?

And what *were* they going to say when he cried out, "Change the formula? My God, boys, that would be like Procter and Gamble putting out a bar of Ivory Soap that *sinks!*"

When in doubt, do research.

Coke says that it hired, among other researchers, Patrick Caddell, the pollster who came to prominence during Jimmy Carter's run for the presidency in 1976.

Coke says that 200,000 people taste-tested the new Coke formula over a three-year period. Coke says this polling cost the company $4 million. It was, Coke says, the most exhaustive and expensive research program in its history.

It probably was, but they didn't do their homework. They just did tests in which consumers tasted small amounts of unidentified products. In those tests, Coke says, 55 percent of the people tested preferred New Coke. When the researchers informed consumers that they were tasting two varieties of Coca-Cola, the preference for New Coke, they say, went up to 61 percent.

Well, it probably did, in the one-sip consumer tests they apparently relied on. But it seems they didn't do any extended home-use tests—tests that would have put quarts and quarts of New Coke into consumers' homes to assess the drink's appeal over time.

Nor did they do any test marketing—actually putting the new formula live into one or two cities to judge consumer reaction before committing to changing their product throughout the country.

And when Coca-Cola asked people to judge Cokes A and B in all those blind sip tests, they never told consumers that voting for New Coke was a vote for *killing* Old Coke.

Now why didn't Coke do home-use tests? Why no test markets? And why didn't Coke tell people a vote for New Coke meant euthanasia for Merchandise 7X?

Could it have been that their marketing executives would have learned more than they really wanted to know? Perhaps—just perhaps. Because my guess is that all they really wanted to know was whether they could legitimately claim, on network television, that a small cupful of Coke tastes at least as good as a thimbleful of Pepsi. That way, they could force the Pepsi Challenge off the air.

Somehow, I can't picture Goizueta and Dyson *rushing* to pass the results of their blind sip tests on to Mr. Woodruff. If they did, don't you think he might have had a pretty obvious question for them?

"What did consumers say when you told them that if enough people voted for the new formula, we'd take the one they know and love off the market?"

Somehow, I can see Roberto Goizueta and Brian Dyson looking down at their shoes like guilty schoolboys at that question. And I can see them suddenly remembering an urgent appointment elsewhere.

And I can hear Mr. Woodruff cursing as they beat a hasty retreat.

"Two hundred thousand taste tests, $4 million spent—and *nobody* figured out that our loyal users are going to be upset with us? What did the home-use tests show? What? We didn't do any? What's *wrong* with that research department of ours? What's wrong with our marketing department? Come back here, boys, and tell me. . . . what the hell is *wrong* with you?"

The irony is that Coke management didn't need to change the formula of Coca-Cola to get the Pepsi Challenge off the air. Because in 1983, there was a changing of the guard at Pepsi too. At the ripe age of thirty-eight, I became—much to my surprise—president and CEO of Pepsi-Cola USA, the domestic soft drink division of PepsiCo. I was determined to revolutionize our advertising—and, a few months after taking over, I killed the Pepsi Challenge.

When they got wind of that, the Coke brass probably breathed easier. And they probably had a good laugh when I signed our bank-breaking contract with Michael Jackson.

Now you might ask: If that's so, why did they go ahead with New Coke?

Well, early in 1984, we released the Jackson commercials. Over the following twelve months, 97 percent of the American public watched them at least a dozen times. The Jackson commercials generated immense publicity for Pepsi—and focused vast attention on our "Choice of a New Generation" advertising campaign.

The advertising won just about every possible award. It pushed our sales to record levels. In the end, it made history for Pepsi.

It's my contention that those commercials also made history

for Coke. For if Michael Jackson had not moonwalked and spun and flashed his magic glove—and sung Pepsi lyrics to the tune of his greatest hit—I really don't think that the Coca-Cola Company would have made the colossal blunder that was New Coke.

In my view, Michael Jackson created New Coke just as surely as Roberto Goizueta and Brian Dyson did. I think Coke just couldn't stand the publicity we were getting. I think the way our "Choice of a New Generation" campaign made them look old and out-of-date. And our ability to sustain the "New Generation" campaign by flowing from Michael Jackson to our just-as-popular Lionel Richie commercials—and a pointed and funny tweak at Coke called "Archeology"—put our Atlanta competitors around the bend.

As you'll see in these pages, they don't thrive in that zone. As you'll see here, they get very, *very* peeved at us.

We've never understood this. At Pepsi, we *like* the Cola Wars. We know they're good for business—for *all* soft drink brands.

You see, when the public gets interested in the Pepsi–Coke competition, often Pepsi doesn't win at Coke's expense and Coke doesn't win at Pepsi's. Everybody in the business wins.

Consumer interest swells the market. The more fun we provide, the more people buy our products—*all* our products.

The catch is, the Cola Wars *must* be fun. If it ever looks as if one company is on the ropes—as if it's been dealt such a run of bad fortune that it won't recover—the air will go out of the game faster than the fizz leaves an open can of soda.

The warfare must be perceived as a continuing battle without blood. All the interest lies in keeping the public curious: "Okay, Pepsi did *that* today—what do you think Coke will do tomorrow?"

In short, without Coke, Pepsi would have a tough time being an original and lively competitor. The more successful they are, the sharper we have to be.

Which is fine with us: There aren't many people anywhere who have the chance to run a business in which one of the prime objectives is to create some innocent fun. We love being the scrappy underdogs in the industry—and we couldn't be if the boys in Atlanta threw in the towel.

I don't sense, however, that my counterparts at Coke headquarters feel quite that lighthearted about our competition.

At Coke, the manhood of their key executives seems to be on the line all the time.

On the other hand, no other executives I can think of have presided over a self-created disaster of the magnitude of New Coke.

Well, maybe not *wholly* self-created. According to Roberto Goizueta, he *did* get around to telling Robert Woodruff that he was changing the Coke formula. And, Goizueta says, Mr. Woodruff gave that decision his blessing.

Now, just *when* do you think Goizueta got around to breaking the news to Coke's patriarch? According to Goizueta, he did it shortly before Coke's ninety-five-year-old patriarch died.

A month later, at the press conference announcing New Coke, Goizueta called his decision "the surest move ever made." "The only thing I'm sorry for is that Mr. Woodruff isn't here," Goizueta said. "Mr. Woodruff is the one who loved to paraphrase Oscar Wilde: 'The world belongs to the discontented.'"

Later that day, a reporter asked me whether I believed Goizueta really told Robert Woodruff he was scrapping Merchandise 7X. "Well, *The New York Times* reported that Woodruff went into the hospital ten days before he died," I said. "And Roberto claims he told him in . . ."

"No, no, you're not getting my drift," the reporter said. "Did Mr. Woodruff tell Goizueta to go ahead as a final blessing—or did he expire *because* Goizueta told him he was changing the formula of Coke?"

Well, of course I had no answer to that. As far as I know, the only witnesses to that conversation were Woodruff, Goizueta, and God. But another quotation from Oscar Wilde does come to mind. "The only duty we owe history," Wilde said, "is to rewrite it."

I'm happy with history as it happened. I *know* that my counterparts in Atlanta would love to rewrite the rest of the New Coke story.

Unfortunately for them, that bit of history was America's most watched and most discussed news story of the summer of 1985. We made sure of that by taking out a full-page newspaper ad the morning of the Coke press conference.

In this ad, I hailed the Coke reformulation as a resounding victory for Pepsi—and, because victory always calls for celebration, I gave Pepsi employees a day off. America cheered that.

A week later we had a commercial on the air that tweaked

Coke for betraying its loyal consumers. America cheered that too.

Coke had lost control of the agenda. It now had only one chance to regain it—when New Coke reached the stores. But the formula that killed Merchandise 7X—and, supposedly, beat Pepsi in all those expensive taste tests—succeeded only in turning off the American public. New Coke lasted as Coke's flagship less than ninety days.

In July, humbled Coca-Cola executives announced to an amazed world that despite New Coke's "great success," they were bringing back the old Merchandise 7X formula—now rechristened as "Classic" Coke.

Pepsi now had two Cokes to compete against. One was the Edsel of the '80s. The other was a product we'd beaten for years—in more than 20 million Pepsi Challenges, in retail stores, and most everywhere else in America where consumers had a choice between the two brands. Good news, I thought.

But the best news, as I look back on that wild summer, is that the Cola Wars heated up again. And after eighty-seven years of going at it eyeball to eyeball, the impossible actually occurred: The other guy blinked.

If we can keep him blinking, what you're about to read will explain the beginnings of one of the more amazing upsets in American business history.

CHAPTER 2

For Those Who Think Young

Americans don't drink fifty gallons of soft drinks apiece each year because they have to. Water's a lot cheaper and booze gives a better kick.

But you choose soft drinks—more often, these days, than you pour yourselves a glass of water or any other beverage— because soft drinks have become part of American life.

And because companies like Pepsi and people like me spend a great deal of time and energy to encourage you. We do this with print advertising. With coupons in newspapers. With signs at stadiums and billboards on highways. With eye-catching displays in supermarkets and convenience stores. With catchy jingles in radio ads. And we do it with television commercials.

These days, television commercials have become more and more important. How important? This year Pepsi will spend about $150 million to promote Pepsi, Diet Pepsi, Pepsi Free, Mountain Dew, and Slice on television. Coke will outspend us by $50 million—they'll put around $200 million behind the television promotion of their brands. An enormous amount of money.

If we're going to win the Cola Wars, we have to be smarter in a lot of ways. Mostly, though, we have to be shrewder, faster, more attuned than Coke in the place where you see us most: on television. So we don't spend those millions casually.

We spend them so carefully—and agonize so much over the creation of these commercials—that it may seem, in these pages, as if Pepsi is a company that creates advertising, and oh, by the way, we make soft drinks too.

There's a reason for that. It's not that advertising—the show business side of soft drinks—is glamorous fizz and all the other elements of the business are, by contrast, flat. It's that imagery is critical to our success.

Imagery is how we define ourselves—and then how we present ourselves to you. After making sure that our products are as good as we know how to make them, sharpening our image is the most important thing we do.

In other businesses, imagery isn't always so important. But the distinctions between soft drinks—between different varieties of carbonated flavored waters—are not universally appreciated. Pepsi may, as we claim, taste better than Coke, but millions of Americans seem to find other things in their lives a lot more pressing than choosing a favorite soft drink.

That's why it's so important for us to give Pepsi an image that could never be confused with Coke's. For twenty years, therefore, we've positioned Pepsi as the "leading edge" soft drink and called our consumers the "Pepsi Generation." And, for twenty years, we've used this Pepsi Generation campaign to reach out not just to the young but to all people who look *forward*, who are curious about the *next* thing, who want *more* out of life.

We like that message because we're forward-looking people ourselves, and, of course, because the leading edge is a very good place to be. If we're new and bold and challenging and a lot of fun, what's left for the other guy?

The past. Nostalgia. Rock-ribbed American values. Small towns, parades, picnics. All good stuff—we use some of it ourselves—but deadly in the soft drink business if that's your dominant image. So if we maintain our leading-edge imagery, Coke gets boxed in. That's not awful for the short term—there are still lots of people in Coke's America. But their numbers aren't growing.

That makes for a certain anxiety. And for a very understandable desire to break out of the box.

It makes for experiments conducted under stressful conditions. It can make for mistakes.

It did lead to New Coke.

For most of the eighty-eight years that Pepsi has been competing with Coke, however, the Pepsi-Cola Company wasn't successful enough to inspire Coke blunders—or even to give Coca-Cola executives the jitters. Like Coke, Pepsi was invented in the South by a pharmacist. And, like Coke, Pepsi was originally heralded as a cure. But Coke's thirteen-year head start, some astute decisions by Coke executives, and some bad ones by Pepsi's owners combined to give Coke such a commanding lead that, until recently, Coke never mentioned Pepsi by name.

Caleb Bradham, a North Carolina pharmacist, concocted Pepsi-Cola in the 1890s as a cure for dyspepsia. In 1902, Bradham applied for a trademark, issued ninety-seven shares of stock, and began selling Pepsi syrup in earnest. From the beginning Bradham understood that marketing would be the key to Pepsi-Cola's prosperity; in his first year of business he spent $1,900 on advertising, a huge sum when you consider that he sold only 8,000 gallons of syrup.

Bradham's advertisements worked. In 1905 he built Pepsi's first bottling plant. Soon he needed three more. By 1907 he was selling 100,000 gallons a year; two years later, he hired a New York advertising agency.

Pepsi's troubles began at the end of World War I, when sugar prices soared from 5 cents a pound to 22 cents. Fearful that the price would climb still higher, Bradham bought huge amounts— and then watched helplessly as the price skidded to 3 cents a pound in 1920. By 1922 the company was insolvent; a year later it went bankrupt, and Bradham returned to his pharmacy.

Roy Megargel, a Wall Street broker, stepped in and reorganized the company. He was no more successful than Bradham. From 1923 to 1928 the company lost money each year, and each year, Megargel poured his own money in to keep it going. When the crash of 1929 made that impossible, Pepsi, early in 1931, went bankrupt a second time.

At this low point, Charles Guth, president of the Loft candy company, bought the trademark. Guth was a supersalesman— and a monomaniac. He didn't like the taste of Pepsi, so he had the formula changed. Disdainful of the public's preference for Coca-Cola, he banished Coke from Loft's soda fountains; sales skidded, but Guth held firm. By 1933, Guth's bravado was a hollow shell. He was so humbled he actually sent an emissary to Atlanta to offer the Pepsi-Cola Company to Coke. But so low were Pepsi's prospects that Coke declined to bid for the company.

In desperation, Guth began another series of experiments. The availability of cheap, used 12-ounce beer bottles led him to double the serving size of a Pepsi—and, at 10 cents, charge twice as much. Naturally, consumers balked. So Guth decided to offer the 12-ounce bottle for 5 cents. With all the other colas on the market selling 6-ounce bottles for that price, Guth had finally given consumers their first good reason to buy Pepsi. In 1936, Pepsi had a $2 million net profit; two years later, profits were $4.2 million.

But prosperity and Pepsi were not, in those years, destined to know each other very well or very long. A salary cut at Loft turned that company's employees into a mob. Guth resigned, initiating an equally heated fight over ownership of Pepsi-Cola. In 1938, Walter Mack became president. And Mack, who considered advertising the keystone of the soft drink business, turned Pepsi into a modern marketing company.

By 1940 a comic strip featuring the Pepsi-Cola cops, "Pepsi" and "Pete," was appearing in 205 Sunday newspapers. Pepsi ads were running in 77 magazines. That summer, 8 planes logged 145,000 miles in a coast-to-coast skywriting campaign that had all America craning its neck. (When one pilot forgot the second *P* in Pepsi while flying over Brooklyn, the company received 11,000 irate phone calls in two hours.)

But the company's biggest marketing coup in 1940 was a jingle sung to the tune of "John Peel." It had no introduction, no announcer, no celebrity endorsement. Just this:

Pepsi-Cola hits the spot.
Twelve full ounces, that's a lot.
Twice as much for a nickel, too.
Pepsi-Cola is the drink for you.

Initially, Pepsi bought time for this fifteen-second commercial on four radio stations. Then America went wild for it: by year's end it had played for free 300,000 times on 500 stations. And because Americans wanted to hear still more of it, the company made 1,500 copies for jukeboxes. Amazingly enough, people were quite willing to pay a nickel for a song about a drink that cost a nickel. Orders kept flooding in. In the end, 100,000 copies went out. Fame, and prosperity, had come to Pepsi.

World War II changed everything. Robert Woodruff promised to put a Coke in the hands of every American soldier. This inspired the government to exempt Coke—but, somehow, not Pepsi—from sugar rationing. The government also built almost a hundred Coke bottling plants overseas, enabling Coke to supply American soldiers with 95 percent of the soft drinks they consumed during the war. And when the war ended, Coke not only had millions of grateful servicemen as consumers, it also had the makings of a worldwide bottling network, courtesy of Uncle Sam.

Pepsi, by contrast, came out of the war as the prisoner of its "twice as much for a nickel, too" slogan. That line positioned Pepsi as a bargain drink—an ideal pitch during the Depression, considerably less effective later. When the soldiers came home and the postwar boom began, no one much wanted to be reminded of hard times. Pepsi was, people thought, a drink you had in the kitchen. If you were going to serve it in the living room, you poured it into a Coke bottle first. Few did. Pepsi profits plunged from $6.3 million in 1946 to $2.1 million in 1949; the stock price during that period fell from $40 a share to $8.

Pepsi's declining fortunes weren't reversed until Al Steele became president in 1949. Steele was a remarkable and bold leader. He'd worked in the furniture business, he'd run a circus, been advertising director of Standard Oil of Indiana, and vice president of marketing at Coke. There, in 1948, he had the misfortune to preside over an annual convention memorable for the complete breakdown of the microphones. Without amplification, the elaborate and inspiring skits Steele had prepared looked like nothing but crazed charades.

At Pepsi, Steele was hardly chastened. He took long vacations, arrived at the office when he felt like it and when abroad, thought nothing of sending the company plane to pick up his favorite brand of cigarettes. But from the very beginning he was beloved by the bottlers. In a famous speech, he told them: "The time has come for you to stop driving around in lousy Fords. I'm gonna put you in Cadillacs."

This attitude was a terrific shot in the arm for the bottlers. You see, bottlers don't have some temporary right to distribute Pepsi. They own their territories. They also own their bottling plants and their route trucks and their vending machines. Pepsi owns the trademarks and the formulas. Pepsi creates the marketing and the products. And Pepsi produces the flavor concentrate the bottlers buy to manufacture the actual soft drinks. All told, the bottlers make a huge capital investment in their business—and they want it returned in the form of a growing market value for their franchise. When Al Steele took over, at one of the company's low points, that wasn't happening. Just the opposite—Pepsi franchises were so unprofitable they almost couldn't be given away.

Al Steele changed all that. He introduced a stylish bottle,

started a marketing department, positioned Pepsi as a lighter, less caloric refresher, and married Joan Crawford. And something else: He got Pepsi bottlers to gut their savings accounts and mortgage their homes and build their businesses. As a result, by 1959 there were more than two hundred Pepsi bottling plants that weren't even dreamed of a decade earlier. Domestic sales were up by 200 percent, profits by 700 percent.

In the process, Pepsi became—at last—a significant challenge to Coke.

The last campaign that Pepsi did before BBDO became our agency in 1963 was called "The Sociables." It was a very high-society campaign, with gray-haired men in crewcuts dancing with their taffeta-gowned wives. In one commercial, there were two top-hatted people in front of an art museum. The Pepsi was in silver bowls. Butlers were poised to serve. In yet another spot, Joan Crawford's daughters sat at a table with their poodles. In each commercial the music was the same. While a small jazz band played, a female singer offered these lyrics:

Be Sociable, look smart.
Keep up to date with Pep-si.
Drink light, refreshing Pep-si.
Stay young and fair and debonair,
Be Sociable, have a Pepsi!

This might have been a great campaign for a status-driven product like Perrier, but it was a major miscalculation for Pepsi. The bottlers were not much enamored of this campaign. Nor was the public.

Al Steele, whose marriage to Joan Crawford had made him much more status-conscious, was one of its few supporters. In 1959, with earnings dipping and a price increase for concentrate in the offing, Steele embarked on a nine-city, six-week "Ad-O-Rama." His goal: to get the franchise bottlers to invest more heavily in this advertising campaign. Steele was, by all accounts, brilliant on this tour—impassioned, forceful, convincing. By its end, he was clearly in command of the company. Three days later he suffered a massive heart attack and died. With him died "The Sociables."

When BBDO was asked to pitch for the Pepsi account, the first thing the agency did was to poll heavy cola drinkers. "Are the people in these ads people you'd like to be your friends?"

they asked. The heavy cola drinkers took one look at The Sociables before breaking into Bronx cheers. The fact is, BBDO learned, most people in this country don't look up to socialites. The people who were drinking Pepsi in these ads were folks that the people who really drink Pepsi wouldn't be caught dead with—and vice versa.

BBDO then did some age research. Cola drinkers were asked how old they were. Then they were asked how old they felt and how old they'd like to be. The agency found that young people tended to want to be a little older, old people a little younger. Twenty-three-year-olds, however, didn't want to change a thing. "The Sociables" was aimed at thirty-year-olds.

Clearly, the shrewd thing to do was think younger.

If the men and women who run advertising agencies are honest, they will tell you that companies get the advertising they deserve. Great campaigns, then, are no accident. They are inspired—in marketing businesses, anyway—by a single individual: the CEO.

In 1963, Pepsi had the good fortune to get as its president the second of the two giants of the soft drink business, Donald M. Kendall.

Even then, Kendall was a legend within the company. The son of a dairy farmer, he'd spent his childhood in Sequim, Washington, milking cows, working in a logging camp, and operating bulldozers. In World War II he was a much-decorated navy pilot in the Pacific. Then, in 1947, he came east—to work as a fountain syrup salesman for Pepsi. A decade later he was national sales manager.

What made him a legend was not just his rise from syrup salesman but his ability to sell Pepsi in the most unlikely place of all: the Soviet Union. For in 1959, when he was running Pepsi's international division, Kendall transformed the American National Exhibition in Moscow into a stage for the advancement of a single capitalist product. Vice President Richard Nixon was there too. And the customer? Soviet Premier Nikita Khrushchev.

Thanks to some artful footwork, Kendall persuaded Khrushchev to stop at the Pepsi booth to taste two kinds of Pepsi— one bottled in America, the other in Russia. That Khrushchev preferred the Russian Pepsi wasn't the point. What mattered were the photographs of a Pepsi-refreshed Khrushchev that went around the world. "Khrushchev Learns To Be Sociable," the captions read. They might have added, "And Don Kendall Proves He's a Brilliant Diplomat."

Four years later, at forty-one, Don Kendall was named president of Pepsi.

Between 1963 and 1986, when he retired, Kendall took a mildly prosperous but definitely second-string soft drink company and turned it into a corporation ranked number 41—Coca-Cola is 44—on the Fortune 500 list.

The vehicle for this accomplishment was a merger—of Pepsi and the snack food company Frito-Lay—that he and Herman Lay engineered in 1965. That merger gave birth to PepsiCo, Inc., with Lay assuming the chairmanship and Kendall becoming president and CEO. In 1970, when Lay retired, Kendall became chairman.

Back in 1965 Don Kendall knew that a shrewd merger was not enough to build a great organization. But he had a vision, and a compelling premise: he would create the biggest small company in the world, a corporation where talented people would truly make the difference and entrepreneurship would thrive.

To create the climate that would attract the kind of people his vision called for, he moved PepsiCo headquarters from a beautiful but small building on Park Avenue in New York City to the Westchester county town of Purchase, about twenty miles north of the city. The offices, designed by Edward Durrell Stone, were set on 122 acres landscaped by the renowned Russell Page. On the rolling lawns, Don Kendall set large sculptures—by Henry Moore, Alexander Calder, Isamu Noguchi, and David Smith, among others—that he chose himself. And he initiated one of the first employee physical fitness programs in the country, constructing a fully equipped and staffed facility for the purpose.

Then, having recruited top-notch talent and having given his associates this idyllic setting to work in, Kendall went out—as the Pepsi salesman he still considered himself to be—to build Pepsi's businesses around the world.

With his white hair, bushy eyebrows, vested suits, forceful leadership, and powerful admirers in capitals as ideologically diverse as Washington, Moscow, and Peking, Don Kendall did just that.

By 1986, when he turned PepsiCo over to Wayne Calloway, the corporation—now including Pizza Hut and Taco Bell restaurants in addition to its soft drink and snack food businesses—had sales of almost $9 billion. That was a sales volume eighteen times greater than in 1965, the year PepsiCo was created.

In 1962, the year before Don Kendall became president of Pepsi, BBDO had used its cola-drinker age research as the foundation for their Pepsi campaign.

"Now It's Pepsi, for Those Who Think Young" was the slogan.

And for the first time, a Pepsi slogan was viewed and heard more frequently on television than it was seen in print advertising or listened to on radio. The age of electronic sound and motion had arrived, and the noted photographer Irving Penn was hired to shoot the commercials.

The music for the commercials may have been from the 1920s, but Eddie Cantor's "Makin' Whoopee"—with the smoky-voiced Joanie Somers singing seductive new lyrics—made no one who remembered it feel old.

How could Don Kendall, in his first year as president of Pepsi, top that? Mostly by challenging BBDO to go further. His orders were simple. The commercials had to emphasize real people. They had to be visually compelling. And they had to have a great musical hook.

And with that, the stage was set for the creation of the longest-running, most successful advertising campaign of its kind.

For Alan Pottasch, Kendall's new advertising director, this was the kind of challenge you relish. For a young writer named Phil Dusenberry it would become a chance to incorporate some of the film techniques he was learning from English movies. And for a creative director like John Bergin, it was a chance to orchestrate a word here, an idea there, until BBDO had one unforgettable phrase: "Come Alive—You're in the Pepsi Generation."

"Come Alive" was a perfect idea for television. There would be a few seconds of serenity and lilting music . . . and then all hell would break loose. High-speed film in lightweight cameras, late-afternoon sunlight enhanced by backlighting—these had never really been used together in television commercials. And the cameras would be trained on sports cars, motorcycles, helicopters, and athletes. The result would be intense and visual. But would it sell Pepsi? Or would the public laugh at that long theme line?

For that matter, who'd consider himself part of a generation named after a soft drink?

BBDO did something else before presenting this campaign to Don Kendall. The agency chose a jingle written by Sid Ramin. Ramin had never written a jingle before. He had, however, won an Academy Award for his arrangements of Leonard Bernstein's *West Side Story.*

Alan Pottasch endorsed the concept, the slogan, and the music. But it was Don Kendall's vote that counted.

And Kendall's vote was a resounding *yes.*

"The most killing moment in history was when Don Kendall heard that music," John Bergin recalls. "In that moment, Don Kendall became the father of the Pepsi Generation."

The Pepsi Generation commercials, with their emphasis on consumer life-styles and up-to-the-minute film techniques, were a great hit with the public. But they lasted in pure form exactly two years.

After the creation of PepsiCo in 1965, Don Kendall's responsibilities became more corporate. A talented former bottler took his place running the Pepsi-Cola business. And like a number of bottlers at that time, the new president distrusted advertising that didn't feature the product.

So the ad campaign became "Taste That Beats the Others Cold (Pepsi Pours It On)." And the advertising turned away from the non-actors who had been the stars of the Pepsi Generation commercials. Now the hero was, once again, a bottle of Pepsi. The music was vibrant, the images flashed across the screen in interesting ways, but the feeling—and the consumer response— just wasn't the same.

Research showed that the thing consumers remembered most about Pepsi advertising was not "Taste That Beats the Others Cold," but the theme of the commercials that had been taken off the air nearly two years earlier: the Pepsi Generation.

Don Kendall soon realized that a mistake had been made. In 1969 that mistake was corrected. And the creative team made the best Pepsi Generation commercials of all: "You've Got a Lot to Live . . . and Pepsi's Got a Lot to Give."

When Don Kendall became chairman of PepsiCo in 1970, Andy Pearson became PepsiCo's president. By definition, Pearson had direct responsibility for the day-to-day operations of the company. But he really wasn't what you'd call an "operating guy"; he'd never run a business before. Before coming to Pepsi, he was the resident marketing guru at McKinsey, the highly regarded consulting firm. Now his ambition was to make PepsiCo *the* blue-chip marketing company.

To help in this effort, he recruited a strong ally. Vic Bonomo had been head of the Maxwell House division at General Foods. When Bonomo became president of Pepsi-Cola, he and Pearson recognized that becoming a blue-chip marketing company would take a great deal more than desire—they'd need to build a marketing team from the ground up. That meant an unpleasant but necessary replacement of many of the key executives on the organizational chart.

One of the new talents Pearson and Bonomo uncovered was a vice president of marketing. And John Sculley quickly demonstrated that he was no second banana. At thirty-two, Sculley was pictured on the cover of a *Business Week* issue that asked the question: "Is the Product Management System Dead?" John's well-articulated ideas formed the basis of that article. From that day on, this shy but seemingly contradictory man—at times a thinker, remote and cool; at times a teacher, open and warm; at times a firebrand, with a genuine sense of the dramatic when onstage—became among the best-known and most respected marketers in the consumer products business.

The Bonomo years were years of unprecedented growth. Starting in October of 1971—with the single exception of one two-month slack period—Pepsi enjoyed seventy-two straight months of market share growth. By 1974, the Pepsi-Cola brand had pulled even with Coke in food stores. In 1977, Pepsi pulled ahead—permanently.

Two years before that momentous event, John Sculley's PepsiCo career path took a turn away from soft drinks. Just after brand Pepsi passed Coke, though, Vic Bonomo moved up to take on broader corporate responsibilities, and Sculley made a triumphant return to Pepsi—as the youngest president in Pepsi history. He was then thirty-seven years old.

In the middle '70s, I'd worked—briefly—for John Sculley at PepsiCo Foods International, the company's overseas snackfood arm. In 1980, when I came to Purchase to be senior vice president of sales and marketing for company-owned bottling plants, I saw a lot more of him. Our chemistry was strong. In 1982, John asked me to be his executive vice president.

I attacked the job with my usual obsessiveness. I focused immediately on the change we were then contemplating—and soon would implement—from sugar to high-fructose corn syrup as the sweetener for Pepsi. I began the development of a new line of fruit-juice-added soft drinks. And, though I was the newest member of Sculley's team, I began to get involved with Pepsi advertising.

Green as I was, I could see that we were confused—and with good reason. For five years we had racked up good sales increases as the Pepsi Challenge became a bigger and bigger building block in our marketing strategy. The sixth year, 1982, wasn't so terrific. Our sales increased, but not at the rate we were used to.

And as the Challenge had grown in importance, it was squeezing out our Pepsi Generation advertising. Fewer and fewer of our media dollars were being invested in imagery. Our message was becoming solely "Pepsi Tastes Better Than Coke." It was a powerful, compelling message, but it certainly wasn't new. And from my years in consumer products marketing, I'd come to believe that there are three things American consumers won't forgive: product quality that doesn't measure up, untruthful advertising—and being bored.

We clearly had no problem with the first two, but boredom was an imminent possibility, as it frequently is when marketers are afraid to move away from a tried-and-true advertising formula—which is to say, when creativity is feared instead of being encouraged and embraced.

There were other problems with the Pepsi Challenge. The biggest was that everyone—except, seemingly, John Sculley, the guy who counted most—had a strong opinion about it. No two were alike. And so, in addition to the usual black/white split, there were bountiful patches of gray.

Harry Hersh liked the Challenge. Harry's the president of PepCom, a large and important Pepsi franchisee. On the other hand, when you looked to the bottlers—who, by this time, mostly didn't like the Challenge—you really couldn't point to Harry. He used to work for Pepsi-Cola Company. The Challenge was his brainchild.

Andy Pearson, never one to be accused of gray thinking, believed the Challenge was the long-lost Holy Grail. So did my predecessor, Jack Pingel, who was largely responsible for merchandising it to life.

Don Kendall only tolerated the Challenge. He saw it as a short-lived promotional campaign that had lived—with some justification—a lot longer than he expected. But he never intended for it to replace Pepsi Generation thematic advertising.

Alan Pottasch was also in that camp. And Alan, by then, was

the dean of consumer products advertising executives. Alan has never acted like a dean—he flies his own plane, is an ace scuba diver, and owns a home in the Cayman Islands, where he longs to spend more time and someday start a scuba-diving school. But Alan's other interests have never intruded on his business life. He likes nothing better than making advertising that has the potential to blast open the business.

It didn't matter, therefore, that Alan had created the Pepsi Challenge commercials. Now he believed they'd outlived their usefulness—all they were doing was advertising Pepsi *and* Coke.

So Pepsi was, as 1982 ended, ripe for a change in its ad campaign. What we needed were the two elements that make for all great advertising: a person willing to take the big risk that such a change demands, and an idea so potent that it would capture the imagination of the American public.

But at that time, good ideas for an all-important new image for Pepsi were in short supply.

And no one seemed willing to take big risks.

CHAPTER 3

Learning to Lead

How did I get to be president of one of America's great companies?

Good question. I certainly didn't have it as a goal. I wanted to be an actor. So much for long-range planning and goal setting!

Most of my life before age twenty-one would suggest that corporate management was not a very promising direction. I was not the "practical" sort.

My father, an intelligent, pragmatic, and hard-working man, wondered a lot about me during my early childhood. Usually he had no difficulty forming very strong opinions about things. But about me, he was mystified. Though he won't admit it today, I'm sure he considered the possibility that he had a flake for a son.

I wasn't one to leap at the chance to do physical work and I didn't care much for sports. That's no big deal if you are living in Paris, but in Chisholm, Minnesota, the small town where I grew up, that's a major problem.

Chisholm is part of Minnesota's Mesabi Iron Range—mining country where people make it with the power of their muscles and sweat of their brows. It was a great place to grow up in, but it's not known for producing actors. I did manage to snag the lead in several school plays, but by the time I got to high school, no Hollywood scouts had yet come to see me, so I got interested in the closest thing to acting there is: politics.

I was a volunteer in JFK's presidential campaign, got myself elected class president—and began to discover it was fun to run things. If my father was less than impressed, he was cheered by the fact that I also finally learned to enjoy working. As luck would have it, my first job was in the local soft drink bottling plant.

If my mother was less concerned about me, it wasn't because she knew it was all going to turn out well. She was one of those great Italian mothers who's just very protective of her kids. It didn't matter to her that I wasn't as practical as most people in town. I was her offspring, so along with my brother and sister, I was automatically terrific.

After high school I didn't know where I wanted to go. I longed to get out and see the world, but we didn't have that kind of money and my summer jobs hadn't exactly put a fortune in my wallet. So when I applied to colleges I picked ones that were close. And because I got a scholarship at St. John's University in Collegeville, Minnesota, I decided to go there.

As it happened, I had taken the National Merit Scholarship exam early in my senior year. When I didn't win a scholarship and received only something called a Letter of Commendation, I threw it in a drawer and forgot about it. Late in the spring, however, some thoughtful individual who worked for the National Merit Scholarship program figured there was something to be said for all the thousands of kids in the country who hadn't won one of their scholarships but had earned a Letter of Commendation.

That person sent their names to small colleges that had scholarship money going begging. Some of those colleges were trying to diversify their student bodies. And to them, a kid in Minnesota who scored high enough on the National Merit Scholarship exam to get a Letter of Commendation—even if he didn't play football or hockey—wasn't such a disaster.

Suddenly I knew what it was to be a star. Every week a stack of mail arrived offering me full scholarships. In June, I got a letter from Babson College in Wellesley, Massachusetts, a suburb of Boston.

The day the Babson letter came with its offer of a scholarship, I also got an orientation book from St. John's. It promised lights out at eleven P.M., freedom to leave campus one weekend a month, and other good stuff. I thought: Forget *this*—and hurried off to the library to see if Babson really existed. Only then did I discover it was a business administration college.

At the time, I had no idea what a business administration college was. But then I didn't really care—it could have been a school devoted to astronomy. All I cared about was that it was more than a thousand miles farther into the great big world than Collegeville, Minnesota.

You see, somehow or somewhere—I really don't know why—I had gotten the idea that the best thing to do in life is to experience as many different things as you can. To avoid overprogramming yourself, to go a bit with the flow of opportunities and pursue a variety of interests.

And as I think about it today, that's one of the most important things for young people with big ambitions in business to learn. The most successful executives don't follow narrow career paths, carefully laid-out steppingstones to the top. More often, they've allowed themselves the opportunity to learn and grow in a more natural—even if seemingly haphazard—fashion. They've had lots of different goals in their careers, lots of different jobs. Not necessarily with different companies, but at least in different functions within a company.

They are better marketing executives because they've worked, say, in personnel or manufacturing. They're better manufacturing executives because they've done a bit of marketing. And they are better corporation chief executive officers because they have a broad view of the business, of life, and of people.

So—as is the case with most successful executives I know or have read about—my willingness to take a chance, to try my hand at a lot of different things, is probably the primary reason an Italian kid from a small town in Minnesota got the opportunity to be president of Pepsi-Cola. That, and the fact that I was lucky enough to work for and learn from several terrific people who were more than willing to be my mentors.

As you'll see, I often found myself in the strangest places—and I was often the guy who seemed out of place. Like, for example, a small-town kid who wanted to be an actor, then a politician, enrolling in a business administration college in Boston.

Being out of place can be scary. At Babson, a supportive faculty worked hard to give me confidence in myself. Still, I was so damned scared I studied like crazy and got a 3.97 average my first term. Amazingly enough, my father began to think there was hope for me.

I raced through college in three years, so busy running a fraternity and the student court and editing the yearbook that I never really decided what I'd do afterward. I was good with numbers—not advanced math, just plain old simple numbers—

but I really wanted to do something that was more people-oriented. I decided on Personnel, thinking at least from that vantage point I'd get an opportunity to learn what people actually did in a corporation—and determine later just what field might be best for me.

I was eager to get back to Minnesota and see Rosemary Margo, my girlfriend from high school, so I applied to a number of companies in Minneapolis. General Mills hired me and set me to work writing up job descriptions. The writing was pure tedium. Finding out what people really did was fascinating.

But the Vietnam War began heating up and my Selective Service Board was beginning to look my way, so I had to make a choice: the military or graduate school. Nearly everyone I worked with at General Mills had an M.B.A. and since it was rapidly becoming clear to me that an advanced degree would be a definite asset in any business career, I applied to Babson's M.B.A. school. I got accepted, but I never went.

Instead—in another of my departures from the stepping-stones of a logical career path—I responded to the slogan "Join the Navy and See the World," and enlisted in the Navy Officer Candidate program, thinking nothing more than how much fun it would be to steer a ship across the seas.

Much to my disappointment, the first thing the navy did, upon discovering I couldn't tell the difference between red and green, was steer *me*—far away from the bridge of their ships. They sent me to Supply Officer School for six months. Then, in the summer of 1967, they got around to asking me what I wanted to do.

"I'm going to be in business for a lifetime when I get out," I said. "The last thing I want to do now is keep the books. Give me a job that has as little as possible to do with all this supply stuff."

"All right, smartass," the detail officer replied. "How do you feel about Vietnam?"

"As long as I don't have to use anything I learned here."

"You got it."

What the hell, I thought: I'm in the navy, and the navy's business is to fight wars. And though no one I know wants war, when there's one going on, I figure you can't be in the service and not go where the cash register's ringing. In 1967 it was definitely ringing in Vietnam. Besides, I'll admit to heart-fluttering patriotism—at the time, I thought we were in the right.

* * *

My mentor in Vietnam was Lieutenant Commander Bill Aldenderfer. He was in charge of fuel operations for I-Corps, the northernmost part of South Vietnam. Few of his predecessors had lasted more than six months: If they didn't ask to be relieved, the navy replaced them.

This was understandable. The job was immensely difficult. Each week you had to get several million gallons of fuel from tens of different and notoriously unreliable sources. Then, with the help of an incredibly unreliable communications system, you had to send it to seemingly hundreds of different destinations.

That was on good days.

On bad days—between artillery, mortars, rockets, Viet Cong sabotage, typhoons, and an occasional stupid accident—it was hell to move anything anywhere.

I was one of three guys selected for what Bill liked to call his Fuel Operations Commandos. Bill was a Naval Academy grad who, if all this had happened in 1985 instead of 1967, might have been described as the Supply Corps version of Rambo.

Half the time he acted like a teenager. Half the time he got you to work eighteen-hour days. But 100 percent of the time he made sure of one thing: Nobody ever ran out of fuel.

He couldn't have done this if he had gone strictly by the book. So he didn't. And under his leadership we all became incredibly resourceful. We'd get pilots to fly fuel into remote jungle bases by loading huge rubber bladders onto their airplanes—sometimes in a barter-type exchange for things they wanted, sometimes by appealing to their can-do attitude, and all the time by ignoring the paperwork.

Bill taught me to take chances, and to get the job done—no matter what. Once, when I was an ensign and Bill was away, I decided we needed another underwater pipeline so that we could offload more ships at one time. Now, installing such a facility requires an immense amount of materiel: miles of pipe, valves, pumps. Unconcerned with the magnitude of the task, I sent out an "operation immediate" message—which is just short of announcing the start of nuclear war—to Hawaii, requesting materiel. A day later, a captain called from Pearl Harbor.

"What's your rank, Enrico?" he demanded.

"Ensign, sir."

There was a lot of swearing on his end. "Who signed this frigging thing?" he asked when it stopped.

"I did."

"Do you know what you're doing?"

"Yes, sir," I said. "I sure do."

He paused. Then: "Well, do you want it flown out—or is a ship okay?"

"What does it take to fly it here?"

"Forty-two planes, son."

"No, no," I said. "A ship's fine."

In retrospect, I suppose you can see the seeds of a pattern here: Aldenderfer taught Enrico to do anything to deliver precious liquids to his consumers.

In support of that thesis, consider another of these pre-Pepsi escapades. It occurred in 1968, just after the Tet offensive, when the First Air Cavalry moved into the northern part of South Vietnam. These guys had more helicopters than the entire Marine Corps—they were going to need a lot of fuel.

I was sent to a desolate piece of sand called Cua Viet, just a few miles south of the DMZ. My mission was to see if I could do anything to help the First Air Cav get fuel for their hundreds of helicopters stationed not far away.

The pilots were like suburban teenagers—they parked their choppers next to their tents as if they were hot rods.

Their colonel was just as wild. "We don't need anything," he said. "We don't want any help. We fly our fuel in, slung below our Hueys."

"Yes, sir, but you *burn* a lot of fuel flying it in. We could do it easier and save you time and trouble."

"How?"

"We'll build a pipeline—from our storage tanks to your base."

The colonel snorted. I pressed on.

"It's only sixty-five miles," I said.

"By the time you do it, the war will be over."

"No, sir, we could do it in sixty days."

"How?"

"We'll get the Seabees to do it."

"Sure you will."

So I went off to Da Nang, and Bill and I went to see the admiral. He hated the idea. "The VC will blow it up," the admiral said.

"Yes, sir, they very likely will," I said. "But we'll build the pipeline with temporary assault pipe. It's made for that. They blow a section up, we can easily replace it the next morning."

Sixty days later, we had my pipeline.

The VC blew it up. We replaced the pipe. Then they blew up

the big, expensive, and not-so-easily-replaced control valves along the line.

The admiral learned, once again, not to rely on the judgment of junior officers.

I learned to listen to admirals.

The colonel went back to flying in his fuel.

Because I'd volunteered for Vietnam, I could pick my next tour anywhere in the world. I sneaked a second R&R leave, met Rosemary in Hawaii, and got married. After I had finished my Vietnam tour of duty a few months later, we moved to Gaeta, Italy, a small town halfway between Rome and Naples. I had a calmer job on board the Sixth Fleet flagship, running the laundry, barbershop, and store. Hardly exciting after Vietnam, but it was a fun year and it gave me time to think about the leadership principles I had observed while in Southeast Asia—principles that would have important applications in my business career.

I discovered from Bill Aldenderfer that you've got to spend a lot of time learning what your job is really all about.

I discovered from the admiral that listening to what other people have to say is critical.

I discovered from both of them that you're in a position to take chances only after you've done those two things. In fact, then you're *smart* to take chances, because if you have reasonable intelligence, your judgment will be right more times than not.

And I discovered from the entire sad and frustrating American experience of the Vietnam War that it's dangerous to believe in your own infallability.

In 1970, I returned to General Mills, this time in brand management. In my last incarnation there, I'd written job descriptions of people who did this work and I'd come to discover that I liked it; in a consumer-products company, it's where the action is.

What is brand management?

Well, it's a management system that became popular in the late 1950s, largely through the efforts of Procter & Gamble. It enables big consumer-products companies that sell lots of individual brands to act like small companies with only one brand to sell. In the middle of it all, almost like small company presidents, are the brand managers—coordinating, leading, and controlling. There's a Tide brand manager, a Crest brand manager, and so on.

Outside the company, the titles often sound hilarious. Imagine calling your father with the exciting news you've just been appointed "Charmin Toilet Tissue Brand Manager." But to an earnest young marketing person, responsibility for Charmin is as important as running the world. He'll nurture it, coddle it, make sure it gets attention from the bureaucracy and the sales force. And he'll know his career will very likely rise—or fall—with Charmin's sales and profits.

Corporate cynics view brand managers as overeducated, snot-nosed kids who overintellectualize everything, accomplish nothing, do all the talking and none of the listening—and get promoted on a weekly basis.

Sometimes they're right.

Good brand managers, though, research the market to find out what will attract consumers to their product. Then they connect all that to advertising, pricing, and promotion tactics to build the brand. And most of all, they plot a strategic direction for their business.

When things work right, the brand manager is the hub of the business. Because he or she is a central coordinator of information. And information is everything.

If that sounds overstated, it's not. The brand manager gets power through information. The more information, the more power.

That's true, really, in any function of a business. Personnel, manufacturing, public relations—it makes no difference. Getting command of the facts is how people make an impact on what happens.

Good junior managers understand this and actively seek out information. Bad ones never quite catch on. They concentrate instead on building fatter organizations under them, and getting control of bigger expense budgets. They see those things as representing power in a company. And with that narrow field of vision they often skim the surface of issues—maybe even play politics with the boss. In due time—almost every time—they get overshadowed by the really good young person who understands that he or she must dig deeper and *know* more about any given issue than anyone else in the room.

It is not, you see, a matter of stripes.

It's a matter of facts.

And with the facts in hand, that person can then become an entrepreneur, a general manager without the title—a champion.

What does a champion do in a corporation? Well, a champion is someone who runs through the halls shouting, "Follow me, guys." And if he says it persuasively enough, with enough substance—guess what? People follow.

Then he's really the manager of *everything* related to the cause he's championing. Because if people follow him, who cares what the organization chart says? Clearly, this person is in charge. He (or she) has usurped the bureaucracy.

If this seems job-endangering, it isn't. You just have to remind yourself that the bureaucracy doesn't want to *do* anything. It's just sitting there, administering. It is, quite literally, *waiting* for someone to come running down the halls shouting, "Follow me." It *requires* this person. Without him, without her—nothing will happen.

No champions, no growth.

The first person who taught me these things was Steve Chase, my marketing director at General Mills. I'm forever indebted to him, because he took me on despite the fact that I was about the only person in the company without an M.B.A.— up to then a *required* admission ticket for a seat in the brand management arena.

I loved working in marketing, and I loved General Mills. It was and is a great company with terrific people and a lot of integrity.

It didn't matter that I was low man on the pole, as was my product line: OABs, or "Other Advertised Brands." I wasn't even upset that OABs were misnamed—they really weren't advertised much at all.

We had Red Band flour, which was sold only in the Carolinas. We had Betty Crocker pancake mix, then sold mainly in northern California. We had Wondra flour and we had La Piña flour, sold in Hispanic markets in southern California.

With products like these, in a company as big as General Mills, nobody pays much attention to you. But I worked hard and, nine months into my career, got a promotion to the big time: Wheaties, the Breakfast of Champions and the home of marketing kings.

Pumped up by my first promotion, I dug into the job of being ASSISTANT BRAND MANAGER OF WHEATIES. My wife, Rosemary, was suitably impressed, as were my father and mother and brother and sister and the small army of relatives they managed to tell about it.

After six weeks I was still riding high, but one small detail started to nag at me: My paychecks didn't show a raise in salary.

One day I mentioned this to my boss. Soon he dragged me into his boss's office.

"Yes, you were promoted," I was told by this model of executive excellence, "but we'll give you a raise when we damn well feel like it."

With that, the balloon burst. To be honest, my first thought was: Screw you.

Then, after a few weeks, I concluded that it didn't make much sense to stay at General Mills. I was the only junior guy in marketing who didn't have an M.B.A. I thought this had to have something to do with the way I was being treated. And soon enough, I knew, it was going to affect my energy and enthusiasm. If I kept on festering, I decided, they'd justifiably end up firing me.

I thought about talking all this over with Steve Chase, the guy who took a chance by bringing me into marketing in the first place. But—put it down to emotional immaturity—I didn't. Instead, I decided to leave.

Despite my negative feelings about what had happened, the hard part was finding a job—and a company—as good as or better than marketing at General Mills.

I sent my résumé to all the headhunters I could find in the Yellow Pages. Thankfully, I got a feeler from Frito-Lay, a division of PepsiCo, in Dallas, Texas. I went right home to see Rosemary. Her reaction echoed my own: "That's where they shot Kennedy. Forget it."

But I'd never been to Texas, so I went down to Dallas and looked around. Much to my surprise I discovered that, in 1971, both Dallas and Frito-Lay were poised for a boom; the energy and excitement were electric. When I returned to Minnesota, I told my boss I was leaving.

In minutes I was in the office of Cal Blodgett, the division general manager for all "Big G" breakfast cereals.

"I'll admit Frito-Lay's a wonderful company, but we don't want you to do this," Cal said. "I'd like you to reconsider—and if you do go and it doesn't work out, give me a call. You can come right back."

I left, but I filed what he said. Not because I was planning to come back—it was just that he handled the situation in such a classy way that, if I ever got myself into a position of responsibility, I'd want to tell my people that. And, over the years, I have. Nobody's taken me up on it. But word gets around.

I also filed something else. I promised not to treat anyone who worked for me in the callous and insensitive way "the boss's boss" had treated me. Sometimes, in the heat of battle when things are going wrong, I know I haven't always held to that promise, but at least I've learned to be ashamed of that fact.

Occasionally it really does take extra effort to remember to treat your people with dignity, sensitivity, even a little love. But it works—for the people, for the business, for yourself.

Frito-Lay has often been heralded as one of the best-run companies in the country. That's because it pays very close attention to the consumer, and to the details of running a highly complex business with forty or so manufacturing plants, several hundred distribution centers, and a delivery system that has more than 10,000 route salesmen bringing its products directly to the 300,000 retail outlets that sell them. Frito-Lay does these things so well that in 1986 its sales were edging up on the $3 billion mark. It is—by far—the largest contributor to PepsiCo's bottom line.

It does, however, have a tendency to pick juvenile-sounding brand names for its products. I started my PepsiCo career at Frito-Lay as an associate brand manager on—get this—an onion-flavored snack called Funyuns. My boss ran a much bigger brand named Cheetos. Somewhere in the stratosphere was the guy in charge of Fritos.

But aside from its name, there were serious things wrong with Funyuns. The product had survived lengthy test marketing. Frito-Lay had then rolled it out nationally. Now, six months had passed. For reasons unknown, sales were rapidly heading south.

"When sales drop off like this, it's usually that somebody's changed something," my marketing director, Jim Groebe, said. "The advertising, the package design—or it could even be a change in the product. Dig into everything, but especially those things."

So I went around to all the people responsible for every element of the business. I couldn't find anything wrong.

Then a curious thing happened. My boss, the brand manager, came to me. "Can you believe this?" he said, "I picked up the phone this morning and I've got some damned little old lady *consumer* complaining on the other end."

"What did she say?"

"That she used to eat Funyuns, but she doesn't anymore—

they taste burned. I don't know what the hell she was talking about."

Neither did I, so I went on with my analysis. And I found a correlation: Funyuns sales turned down about the same time Frito-Lay introduced another new product, this one a potato snack with the intelligent-sounding name of Munchos. I took this news to my boss. It seemed noteworthy to him as well, so he passed me on to the VP of marketing. He brought the VP of sales in on it, and soon enough, people were telling me to get ready to present my findings to Harold Lilley, then president of Frito-Lay.

This is one of the great things about Frito-Lay and PepsiCo. The guy who does the grunt work on an issue carries the ball all the way to the top. No lateraling by memo up the line, with a decision passed down from on high for the troops to execute. But I didn't appreciate the importance of this at the time. With less than a month's experience on the job, a brand heading toward apparent disaster, and my first meeting with the president, fear was the only emotion possible.

Fear, mostly, of Harold Lilley. For Lilley was a big, burly executive, smart as hell though not intellectual, a real "street guy" whose gut instincts on issues and the direction the business should take were more on the mark than all the tiresome analyses done by junior guys like me.

Lilley sits down and points at the table. "What's that?" he asks.

It's my presentation deck—inches thick.

"Jesus Christ! The *brand* isn't this big."

I figure: Well, let's go. And I flip over the cover. There's a big table of numbers—just what he doesn't want to see. Beside each table I've put a circle.

"What the hell is that circle for?"

"Well, sir, the period when Munchos was introduced in that part of the U.S."

"Are you going to tell me that *Munchos* is the cause of Funyuns' sales going down?"

"Well, sir, there *is* a pretty strong correlation."

He looks at the chart. Then he looks at me.

"Boy, *you* can believe that Harvard bullshit if you want to, but *I* know what's wrong with that product—we should never have changed the formula."

Eyebrows go up. Nobody knows what he's talking about, but everybody backs away from the table. I begin to feel I'm alone with Lilley. Dead silence. And I think: I'm here less than a month. I've left a good job at General Mills because I don't have an M.B.A. This guy thinks I've got one from Harvard—and he obviously doesn't like it!

In the softest, most pleasant voice I can muster, I say, "The formula was changed?"

"Well, we didn't tell any of you guys," Lilley booms back, "but the Food and Drug Administration was taking another look at the coloring we used in Funyuns, red dye number two. So we thought it would be a good idea to take it out of the product, just in case they decided there was a problem. We put a little sugar in so when the product is fried, it caramelizes a bit and keeps the reddish tint."

Right. And he hadn't told the manufacturing people who are taught to fry until the color's right. And they fried them too long and the sugar burned.

And though Harold Lilley really was, I discovered later, a sensational leader, he liked to keep information to himself unless he felt people needed to know. Somehow that did not include marketing kids. Operations was for *real* men.

Something like a product formula change?

Only the consumers—like the little old lady who made that phone call—were allowed to know.

The meeting ended and I honestly believed I was going to get canned. Finally I mustered up enough courage to go into Jim Groebe's office and ask if my departure was imminent.

"Are you kidding? You did great," Jim said. "We found the answer, didn't we? Who in the hell cares how we got there? Just go get the formula changed back and have some fun with this product we just brought back from the dead."

Three months after my presentation to Lilley, I was promoted. (Apparently he didn't *totally* dislike Harvard M.B.A.'s.) Now I was brand manager on Cheetos. In less than a year I was asked to move up to the stratosphere—brand manager of Fritos corn chips. Another year and I was marketing director, responsible for several hundred million dollars' worth of business.

A meteoric rise in the world of brand management.

Credit being in a fast-growing company more interested in people who got results than in tenure—and bosses more interested in developing people with potential than in protecting their backsides.

And also credit the fact that I didn't spend my time in the office shuffling paper. You can't learn a damned thing if you spend all day in your own chair. Instead, I'd spent a lot of time in the field with the Frito-Lay sales and manufacturing people—particularly with Jim O'Neal, now Frito-Lay's senior vice president of operations, then merely the smartest, most knowledgeable guy in the whole company. And what I got out of those visits was teaching me a lot more about my business.

By that I don't just mean the numbers and procedures, but how the business is built. What sustains its growth. Why consumers buy its products. How they're made, merchandised, sold.

You see, in the beginning of your career, the whole purpose of working in a corporation isn't to make profit for the business. Sure, you've got to do that if you're going to be successful and get promoted and have your ideas listened to—but that's not why you're there. You're there to learn. And the people above you and around you are there to teach.

Viewed that way, what was happening with my career at Frito-Lay couldn't possibly pay off right away. It was an investment for both of us. So I told myself: Okay, this company makes something and sells something, and it doesn't do either of those things at headquarters.

And so I went out in the field to watch and listen. And when the plum jobs opened up, I got the promotions. Because when the chips were down, so to speak, I was the guy who had the most credibility.

One of my heroes at Frito-Lay was Jimmy Sappington, the father of its justly famous route-sales system. Jimmy wrote his own speeches, so painstakingly that he spent an hour of preparation time for each minute he spent onstage. His performances showed it. As vice president of sales, he'd come up to the podium only at the end of a rousing sales meeting. Suddenly all the lights would dim. And he'd walk back and forth on the stage, saying nothing.

It would get very quiet—and then he'd stop, turn, look at the audience, and say, "What a *company*!" And then he'd walk some more, and stop, and say, "What a *team*!" After about five minutes of this, you'd be ready to follow him anywhere.

I loved Jimmy Sappington. He was the absolutely last guy I wanted to disagree with.

Came the 1975 Frito-Lay midyear operating review, and it fell to Jimmy and the fellow who managed our Tokyo office and me to review our business in Japan for the benefit of Frito-Lay and PepsiCo top management.

Two years earlier I'd been asked to help out with our marketing in that country. I had made several trips to Tokyo, and we tried just about every gimmick that we used to market our products in the United States. But nothing was working particularly well there. It was a good time to talk about changes.

The night before the meeting, the Tokyo general manager and I had dinner. As we talked, we came to the conclusion that in our attempt to duplicate Frito-Lay's great success in the American market, we'd spent all our time and money trying to build the same formidable distribution system we had in the United States. But in Japan, it didn't count. Our competitors distributed through established Japanese food wholesalers, which were more than adequate to do the job. What's worse, competing snack companies could in this way quickly get their products into literally hundreds of thousands of retail outlets, while we were limited to the ten thousand or so stores we could get to on our small fleet of route trucks.

At dinner, I encourage the Tokyo general manager to tell Jimmy we should change direction—use the Japanese wholesale distribution system and put our time and money behind bringing products to the market instead of route trucks.

"Are you crazy?" he replies. "I can't do that."

"Why?"

"After all this time and money? Me tell that to the father of the Frito-Lay route-sales system? I'll be history before the day is over."

"Okay," I say. "I'll tell him. I'll do that part of the presentation. You give him the operations report and tell him what works; then I'll come on with the bad news."

The next morning we go into Jimmy's office. Through the windows I can see that the sun is already beating down hard. It's going to be one of those hot Dallas July days. I think: Let's hope the heat stays on the outside of the building.

Jimmy's there with some aides, people who have grown up in his system. The Tokyo manager begins his report. He finishes. The temperature in the room is still comfortable. My turn.

I start talking about why we should abandon route sales in Japan. And I don't stop. Because I can *feel* everybody in the room thinking: *This guy's got some* guts.

And then—now I can *see* it—they're thinking: What's gonna happen to him when he *finishes?*

And I'm beginning to see it from their angle, so I have no great desire to finish. Finally I run out of ways to say that we've been worshiping the wrong gods in Japan.

"Well, I've been thinking the same thing for some time," Jimmy says. "I just don't know how we're going to tell Harold Lilley that. You know Harold. He believes the sun rises and sets on our route-sales system."

General amazement ensues.

I press on. "As long as we're reexamining route sales, I think we have to relook our whole business approach in Japan," I say. "Frankly, I think we should be in a joint venture, instead of on our own. We really have no idea what we're doing over there. And we'll never get this thing off the ground if we don't team up with a good Japanese company that can show us what to do on their turf."

Suddenly there is general agreement that yes, this is just what we ought to do. Let's tell top management just that. In fact: "Enrico, *you* tell them!"

The more they're patting me on the back, the more I can see that their arms are getting longer and longer. By the end of the meeting everybody's putting about twenty miles between himself and the marketing kid.

Now it's time to go in and present our recommendations to the main men: Harold Lilley, PepsiCo Chairman Don Kendall, PepsiCo President Andy Pearson, people like that. And in the back of the room at this presentation is John Sculley. As far as I know, he's head of marketing for Pepsi. He has no reason to be here.

But I quickly forget about Sculley. The back and sides of the room are jammed with more than twenty people, all nervously paging through their presentation scripts and all dressed in their "sincere" suits—that special, conservative clothing kept safe in closets for formal presentations like these.

I wonder: What are they all so worried about? I'm the one who should be worried. The Frito-Lay business is in great shape—their presentations will be fine. I've got to give the bad news on Japan—and hell, I just realized I don't even *have* a script!

At the conference table is the audience: THE CHAIRMAN. Don Kendall's large frame towers over the table even while he's sitting in his chair. His white hair and bushy eyebrows make him stand out from everyone else in the darkened room.

The Tokyo general manager begins his presentation. Did I say presentation? It's more like the news reports the day after Pearl Harbor—bad news followed by more bad news.

And Don Kendall is not known as an aficionado of bad news. His attitude is: Don't stand there and tell me, for an hour and a half, how screwed up everything is. Tell me what you're going to do about it.

But he says nothing.

Finally it happens. Kendall addresses the Tokyo manager—who's lived in Japan for years and was hired for his affinity with the Japanese. "Damn it, what's wrong?" Kendall asks. "*Why* isn't it working?"

"The route-sales system doesn't work well there."

"Why?"

"The Japanese don't like to be route salesmen."

"What?!"

"Well, you know—they're all college-educated over there. And, you know, Japanese don't like to work that hard at this sort of thing. They all want to be white-collar types—not get their hands dirty. They'd rather go home early."

The pregnant pause lasts an excruciatingly long time.

From the silence in the darkened room, the guy with white hair and bushy eyebrows says one word: "Bull!"

There is no mistaking what Kendall thinks of all this.

And now it's my turn. I walk to the podium. My legs get heavier and heavier. My depression increases with every step.

I plunge ahead anyway, talking about the Japanese wholesale distribution system, about joint ventures, about our Japanese competitors, about bringing new products to that market. And I ever so carefully cushion things a bit by saying maybe we ought to put together a task force to find out if any of this connects with reality. Because right now, of course, these are just hypotheses.

That makes some sense to Lilley. Kendall says nothing. We get out of the meeting alive.

The next morning Sculley comes up to my office and tells me he's about to become president of PepsiCo Foods International. Japan will be shifted from Frito-Lay to his division. He wonders if I can fill him in a bit more.

I've got a two-drawer file cabinet filled with stuff about Japan. We spend damn near the whole day together. Then he goes off.

It's not long before Frank Peck, then Frito-Lay's senior VP of sales and marketing, calls me in. "John's decided to form the Japan task force you suggested," he says. "Can you go to Japan for a few weeks?"

"Sure."

A week later Frank calls me in again. "If you were offered the job of president in Japan," he says, "would you take it?"

"Yeah, I would—but I don't know about my wife."

"Why don't you ask her?"

"She's in Minnesota, visiting her parents."

"Well, I suggest you get on a plane, because there's a good chance they're going to offer you this job and you ought to know what you're going to do."

I know Rosemary will not want to leave Dallas and the new home we've just purchased, but I fly up to Minnesota. I don't tell her I'm coming. Instead, I go directly to my parents' house, three blocks from Rosemary's family. And I have my mother call and invite Rosemary for dinner.

Rosemary walks in and sees me. Tears of anger well up.

"Where are we moving to?"

I start to smile nervously.

"Oh, no—not Japan!"

On the plane I've prepared a flip-chart presentation for her with the advantages and disadvantages all lined up. And now I take it out and go into my pitch: Our son, Aaron, is four years old. In Japan we can raise him with no distractions. We'll consolidate our family. We'll all become much closer than we otherwise would. And it will be a great life experience.

The downside: If, after six months, we see it isn't like that, we'll come back. If the company can't handle that, I'll get another job. We won't starve.

Rosemary listens quietly, saying nothing. I finish.

"We'll go," she finally says, "but it's bad enough that you come up here without saying anything and then spring this on me. But what really makes me mad is *this*. Pluses and minuses and *charts* not just for you, but for Aaron, for me. We can do our own, you know."

After *that*, I did.

I went off to Tokyo as a member of John Sculley's task force, where, in September of 1975, I was offered the job of president of PepsiCo Foods Japan, reporting directly to John in Purchase, New York, some eight thousand miles away. A few months later, we began negotiations with a Japanese company to form a joint venture.

But the following spring, in the midst of these negotiations, Sculley called me home to tell me to stop negotiating for the joint venture. He had a plan to buy a bigger snack company in Canada. I'd have an important role in it, so now he'd like me to sell our Japanese company for whatever I could get for it.

I argued that he hadn't actually bought the Canadian company yet—it was just a plan. And added: "It costs us virtually nothing to stay in Japan. Let's try the joint venture. If it doesn't work out, then we'll close up shop."

Sculley was not swayed. I went back to Tokyo and told our potential joint venture partners we'd changed our minds—now we wanted to sell them the company. After all the months of negotiation for a joint venture, this blew them away.

A few weeks later I received a message that Don Kendall was coming to Japan. He'd be staying at the American ambassador's residence, and seeing the Japanese prime minister, foreign minister, economic minister, and me.

Me?

Yes, to discuss the Japanese joint venture, it seemed.

"Doesn't he know we're not going to have a joint venture?" I ask of John Sculley when I get him on the long-distance line.

"I don't know," Sculley responds. "I think Andy Pearson may have bucked him a copy of the memo I wrote."

"John, for all we know he may have thrown it in the wastepaper basket. Could you talk to him before he leaves to come out here? So he'll at least know your point of view."

"Yes," Sculley says. "I suppose I should."

He and Andy Pearson go to Kendall's office.

"Don," Pearson says, "I want to talk about the Japanese snack food company."

"Yes?"

"Did you get the copy of John's memo I sent you?"

"Yes."

"What do you think?"

"Threw it away."

"Well, let's talk about it."

"Talk all you want," Kendall says, "but we're not getting out of Japan. I know it hasn't had much success yet, but it's not costing us any real money to be there. And if we can't stick it out in countries like Japan, we'll never have much of an international business."

Sculley calls me back. Kendall's heard his point of view. He's heard Andy's. Now, John tells me, Kendall wants to hear mine.

"Why," Kendall asks upon his arrival in Tokyo, "have you changed your mind about doing a joint venture here?"

"Well, I haven't changed *my* mind," I tell him, carefully selecting my words. "But given the facts as I presented them to John Sculley, he and Andy think we're better off getting out."

"What facts are those?"

"It is a risky business proposition," I say. "Most American food companies are losing money here. Procter and Gamble, General Foods, General Mills—they're all having a rough time of it. Still, as I see it, we've got a reasonable chance for success. The snack market's about ready to take off. We could be positioned to ride the crest, if we can link up with a first-rate Japanese marketing company. And it will cost us only three million dollars—well, maybe five—to play."

"I get the feeling you aren't on the same side of the fence as John and Andy," Kendall says.

"Well, I said the same things to them I'm saying to you. I can understand how they'd decide to sell—and I recognize it's a corporate decision. But, as for me, I think PepsiCo is easily big enough to take risks like this. I'd stay."

"None of those risks bother *me*," he says. "Go do your joint venture."

Back in my office after our meeting, I think: Oh, God, I've really done it this time. Stuck in the middle, with Sculley and Andy Pearson, the president of PepsiCo, on one side—and the chairman of the board on the other.

And I'm just beginning to get that tight, squeezing feeling in my chest when my secretary comes in to tell me Andy Pearson's on the line. I pick up the phone. He's already talked to Don. Odd, he doesn't seem upset at all.

"Look," Andy says, "I don't want you to feel uncomfortable about this."

Uncomfortable? Me? No, I'm always in a cold sweat like this.

"Don and I have disagreements all the time," he continues. "That's why we complement each other so well. Why don't you look at it this way: It's like having a mistress, and your wife approves. So don't worry about it, just do your best."

I'll never forget that call. It's the kind of thing you remember forever. Here was Pearson, after being shot down by his boss, more concerned about how I felt than with his own ego.

That's another lesson in executive behavior to be filed away and retrieved when you're the one with problems.

Now it was time to go back to our prospective Japanese partners, the Fujiya Company, with another flip-flop. My good friend and consultant in Japan, Bud Ingoldsby, devised a semiplausible story line for us to follow.

Bud's been in Japan since the early '60s. He started the first real consumer-research company there and later sold it for a nice profit. Along the way, sake, sushi, and nearly everything else Japanese got into his blood, so he stayed to consult with people like me who believed they could crack the Japanese market.

Bud's story line was simple: good cop, bad cop. Kendall, the good cop, was well-known and respected in Japan. They knew him as a great internationalist. I felt guilty about it—particularly after his considerate telephone call—but I agreed that Pearson had to be the bad cop. The faceless technocrat whose computerized analysis says: Shut the business down.

So this is what we told the Japanese: "Kendall has stormed into town and he's mad as hell. He believes in Japan, and by God, he wants this joint venture done."

And it was basically the truth, if a bit melodramatic.

And the Japanese said, "Kendall is a very good man."

And, sixty days later, we had a deal.

Of course the Japanese didn't give a damn about any of this maneuvering. They were just waiting for the inscrutable Americans to get their act together.

The person we negotiated the deal with was Mr. Goro Fujii, a quick-minded, very wise, and very patient man. We went off together to sign all the documents at PepsiCo headquarters on an appropriately auspicious day selected from a little book Mr. Fujii pulled from his pocket. The evening of the signing, at a dinner in his honor at Kendall's home, he spent a great deal of time talking with Andy Pearson.

Later, Mr. Fujii pulled me aside and said, "Your Mr. Pearson is a brilliant and gracious man. I don't see how his thinking could have been so incorrect on our company."

"Yes," I said, "it is hard to understand. We must see to it that he has an opportunity to become educated on Japan."

Then I quietly slipped into the backyard for some air.

A few months later, the new joint venture, Fujiya-Frito-Lay, opened for business. I was its first president. Like many new companies, it faltered in the beginning. But a few years later it came to life under the leadership of Mr. Ohi, who had come from the Fujiya company to be my second in command. He was an experienced and thoughtful man, and I never would have guessed that, as my eventual successor, he would introduce—

and be successful with, would you believe—an octopus-flavored corn puff.

I didn't get to see that oddity become a hit. Long before Mr. Ohi introduced his octopus corn puff, I was in Brazil, working as the Pepsi-Cola International area vice-president.

When Rosemary and I told our son, Aaron, who was then six years old, that we might move from Japan to Brazil, he asked, "Have I ever been there?" We said he hadn't. "Well, then that's where I want to go," he said. "And after that, I want to go to Africa."

It seemed—much to Rosemary's dismay—that I was having quite an influence on him.

Andy Pearson had other reasons for me to take the job. As he explained it, Japan couldn't tell him much about me because it was so difficult for Western executives to understand the Japanese market. I could be brilliant and the business could flop, or I could be the dumbest executive ever to come down the pike and the business could succeed. In Brazil, he believed, I'd be in a business where my efforts would make a measurable difference. And Pepsi could tell what I really had going for me.

What I had going for me, when I settled in Rio in 1977, was a very good idea of where Berlitz classes were held. About everything else—the language, the soft drink business, South America—I was woefully ignorant.

Once again I was out of place. And I spent the first six months telling everybody I met just that.

"I really don't know anything about Brazil"—or Argentina, or Chile, or Paraguay, or Uruguay, or Bolivia, all of which were my responsibility—"and I don't know much about the soft drink business. I don't know . . ."

Not surprisingly, with such clear direction, my staff did pretty much what it wanted.

Particularly my suave, dark, and handsome manager in Brazil, Sergio Zyman.

Zyman was born and raised in Mexico. He was well educated—he spoke a half-dozen languages fluently—and for two years he had been the marketing director for Pepsi in Brazil under my predecessor, Ted Glover.

Because Ted had left Brazil a few months earlier to take up a new assignment, Sergio was pretty much running the operation when I arrived on the scene in June of 1977.

Zyman clearly liked things that way. He enjoyed having

power—and he exercised it with such relish that, many years later, he was tagged by his associates with a nickname: "The Aya-cola."

One way to take power from a boss is to co-opt him—make him so dependent on you that there's nothing much he can do without your pulling the strings. And in my state of self-proclaimed ignorance, I was an easy mark. "Don't worry," he'd say. "I can handle that." And before I could ask a question—much less agree to a course of action—he'd be on the move. Still, I wasn't born quite yesterday, so I soon figured out what was going on.

I've always been most comfortable actively running things under my command, so I had a sense that things between me and Sergio were going to get worse before they got better.

Just before Christmas, Rosemary and I gave a party, and though neither our Portuguese nor our Spanish was passable yet, we hit it off with one of Sergio's subordinates. As it happened, he and his wife were going to spend the holidays near Montevideo, and coincidentally, Rosemary and I had to be in Buenos Aires. As the two cities are barely half an hour away from each other by air, I suggested our new friends fly over for an evening. They agreed.

The day we're to meet, I work out of our Buenos Aires office. Just as I'm about to leave, here—out of nowhere—comes Zyman. "Hey, how you doing, boss?" he says.

"Sergio, what are you doing here? You're supposed to be in Rio."

"Oh, I had to come down to negotiate a fast deal—on some bottles," he says.

Bottles? Well, maybe, but I figure that Christmas shopping in Buenos Aires has *something* to do with this trip. However, I can't be bothered with this. I've got to hurry back to the hotel to await a call from our newfound friends.

It never comes. They don't show.

A few weeks later the Uruguayan manager drops in to my office in Rio and tells me how sorry he was to have missed us over the holidays.

"It's okay," I say. "Rosemary and I figured something came up with your family."

He gives me a funny look and closes the door.

"You were waiting for us?" he asks.

"Until eleven."

"Fascinating," he says. "We were there. We came to the

hotel. And Sergio Zyman was waiting in the lobby. He told me that you'd be tied up in a meeting all night and couldn't make it, so he and my wife and I had dinner."

I say nothing. But I wonder: Is this a misunderstanding, or is something else going on here?

A few months later, another incident occurs. This time the setting is Rio. Through the Zymans, Rosemary and I meet a Brazilian contractor and his wife. We hit it off and begin to see them on our own. And they invite us to their Rio apartment to watch the World Cup soccer matches one Sunday.

That Friday night, Rosemary tells me that Sergio's wife has called and left a message from the contractor—there's been a fire at his country house and he's had to cancel everything. No warning bells ring. Then, on Saturday morning, the contractor calls.

"How's your son feeling?" he asks.

"Fine."

"What?"

"He's fine," I repeat. "I'm just taking him to his Little League game."

"Zyman's wife told my wife he was sick."

"She told Rosemary you had a fire at your country house."

"Ah."

"Ah."

Naturally my sense of all this contributes to a rather rocky relationship between us. Perhaps there *is* a good explanation for these incidents—and perhaps there isn't. But before I can sit down with Sergio to sort things out, he manages to convince Ted Glover—by now in another new job running sales and marketing for Pepsi USA in Purchase—that he can't do his job without him. Off goes Zyman to weave his webs at Pepsi headquarters in Purchase.

It isn't long, though, before Zyman's colors show through. In less than two years, he demonstrates his loyalty to Pepsi USA by joining the Coca-Cola Company. But don't worry, he tells everyone, he's not going to work in Coke USA. He's going to Harvard for a while and then will work on some special corporate assignments.

He does. Zip . . . and he's a Harvard grad. Whoosh . . . and he's finished the special assignments. Zoom . . . he's vice president of marketing for Coke USA.

Bingo!

But I look on the bright side. Having Zyman at Coke made the Cola Wars a hell of a lot more fun for me.

One of the things that used to be true about Pepsi was that it churned executives; just when you'd begun to understand your job and figure out how to find your way around the strange city you'd been moved to, the company offered you a different job in a different business in another country. I outlasted Sergio Zyman in Brazil by only a few months. Then I, too, was offered a better job: vice president of marketing for Frito-Lay. Two years later, in 1980, I was offered an even better one: senior vice president of sales and marketing for the Pepsi-Cola Bottling Group. And then, in the fall of 1982, John Sculley asked me to be his executive vice president.

But of course there's a good side to all of this churn, too. For me it meant I had obviously been tabbed as one of the people who had a chance to make it big at PepsiCo. I didn't know it at the time, of course, but looking back, PepsiCo top management did. For them, it was a way to see me operate in a lot of different situations, under different pressures, handling different problems. If you're going to be one of the ten or so senior people who make the life-and-death decisions in a company, that's important. Because the situations, pressures, and problems you face every day in business often *are* different from one another.

And as I've come to learn in the Cola Wars, nothing stays the same for very long.

Winning a Cola War battle, for example, seemed very far away in December 1982, when Allen Rosenshine, the chairman of BBDO, our advertising agency, and Phil Dusenberry, BBDO's vice chairman and creative director, came up to our offices in Purchase to show us the new 1983 Pepsi commercials. That day, we were concerned about our own problems. And we weren't coming up with the kinds of solutions that would encourage us to see a big Coke mistake on the horizon.

What we needed was what every marketing executive in consumer products dreams of: a big win.

And great advertising is a very big win.

At BBDO we're a very important client—in the advertising business, soft drinks have a lot of glamour. So the "account manager" for Pepsi is really the chairman of the entire agency, and his vice chairman is our creative director, and every bright young person coming into the agency wants to work on our

account. That's one reason that BBDO has been hitting homers
for us for twenty years—they give us their best.

Another reason is: We *expect* great advertising from them.

So on that cold December day in 1982, Phil Dusenberry
stands at the head of the conference table and begins to speak in
that quiet voice of his, a bare whisper that makes you lean in a
bit. It's part of his technique—and charm. And as we all lean in, I
can feel everybody in the room hoping he's done it again.

We are *really* ready to see this stuff.

These aren't finished commercials. Those won't be ready until
shortly before our franchise bottlers' convention, three months
away. But it makes a lot of sense for us to see early cuts now—
to correct any errors the agency people might be overlooking, to
plan our media buys, and to plan our presentation to the bottlers.

The last reason is most important of all, because we don't
really sell *you* Pepsi. Our 208 independent franchise bottlers do
that. Our job is to sell Pepsi—Pepsi concentrate and Pepsi
marketing—to them. If the bottlers believe in what we're doing,
they do all the rest of the selling with great enthusiasm and,
usually, terrific results.

When you're about to see work-in-progress versions of
commercials, the agency folks usually say something like:
"These are only rough cuts. The color hasn't been corrected.
There are going to be arrows and dark patches and all kinds of
weird stuff where the special effects will go. The sound is wrong.
But . . ."

In the advertising business, this is sometimes called the
"preamble." At Pepsi we call it the "pre-mumble." It's clearly not
considered very important, so as Phil begins, his close friend
Alan Pottasch shouts: "Phil, skip the mumble. Show the film."

Because I've just joined this team, I have the least knowledge
of the forthcoming campaign. All I really know is that the theme
for 1983 is going to be "Oh, What a Time for Pepsi," that we're
going to use slower music for a change and try some new camera
techniques.

I personally don't feel any particular enthusiasm for this
campaign. But then, I haven't felt much enthusiasm from anyone
else at Pepsi. I figure that doesn't mean anything. All the other
men in this room have been in on the creation of the new
commercials. They were here when BBDO pitched the concepts. They've talked the ideas over together. They've seen the
storyboards. So they've probably used up their enthusiasm.
When they see the film, I think, they'll get it back.

The film rolls.

When it's over, nobody says anything. Not because the commercials are bad—they really aren't bad. But they aren't good, either. They just aren't there yet. All images, and constant cutting from one thing to another, and nice music. But there isn't any particular continuity or story line, and in commercial after commercial, you find yourself wondering: What does this mean?

I can feel John Sculley's disappointment. And his frustration.

"Oh, What a Time for Pepsi" isn't going to do anything for our image, much less cause Coke to panic—at least not in the shape it's in this day. But no one has any idea what to do about it.

I, for one, don't. Well, I do, but with 4 million dollars' worth of film on the table, does the newcomer take the first shot? Is it too late to change it? Is it really *that* bad?

So we sit there and look at Phil Dusenberry—and he looks at us.

It seems now that the echo of all those debates about Pepsi Generation image advertising versus Pepsi Challenge product-as-hero advertising are creating a big silence in our conference room.

The advertising agency has done its job—in a way. Perhaps even given us the only advertising we deserve, with all those contradictory voices swirling around. Very safe—nice pictures, nice music—and no point to it all.

I have the beginning of a thought about what's wrong. There isn't enough heart-throb. No goose bumps. As a theme line, "Oh, What a Time for Pepsi" just isn't a call to action.

We sit in the conference room and pick at the edges.

I probably put my two cents in. And they're probably taken as being worth exactly that.

A week later, we hosted one of the year's three MarCom meetings. MarCom is the marketing committee of the Pepsi-Cola Bottlers' Association. It's made up of a dozen or so Pepsi bottler representatives who meet with key people from Pepsi management to provide a real-world sanity check on our business plans, our marketing concepts—and our advertising.

What our bottlers feel about our commercials is important to us for very bottom-line reasons. Pepsi USA pays for television time only when commercials are shown on national TV. When the commercials are aired locally, we split the costs fifty-fifty with the local franchise bottler.

The rub is, we can't force a bottler to show the commercials on local TV. It's his choice as much as ours. He hates the spots—they don't run. So if there's anything we can do to involve our bottlers—or a representative handful of them, anyway—in the creative process, we do it.

Generally, we show the storyboards for the commercials we're about to make at one MarCom meeting. At the next meeting we show the almost-finished spots. This committee's reaction gives us an idea how other bottlers will react a few weeks down the line, when we bring them together for our annual convention and advertising preview.

If the MarCom committee likes the spots—and these bottlers, having been involved from the beginning, usually do—we sign off on them. But if the committee has some well-founded criticism, we'll definitely try to solve the problems posthaste.

This day our conference room is filled with people waiting to see the commercials. On top of the dozen members of the MarCom group, at least another dozen bottlers have showed up; they're just as anxious to see what BBDO had created as we were last week.

In the darkened room Alan Pottasch stands alone at the podium and shows the new commercials. One after another—all 4 million dollars' worth.

And, one after another, the same reaction. The worst possible reaction: stone-cold silence.

The MarCom screening is a dud.

The bottlers finally rouse themselves and begin to give their opinions. They're having a tough time putting their finger on what's wrong. I understand their problem. They want to be helpful, not just critical. And what they're feeling, mostly, is the same disappointment we all felt a week earlier.

John Sculley says nothing. As the new kid on the block, I say nothing. It looks like a very bad day for Alan as he tries, alone, to salvage his advertising—and flounders.

At this point I think: Someone's got to take charge here.

Now, even when you're an executive vice president of a major company, even when you've been brash and outspoken most of your life—even then, it's not easy to take charge. Especially in the middle of your first big meeting.

But I'm responsible for sales and marketing. So I say to myself: This is it. New kid on the block or not, taking charge here is what I'm being paid for.

I don't want my ideas to come across as undisciplined ranting, so I call for a "diplomatic" lunch break. It's funny how everyone suddenly decides he's hungry. Lunch sounds like a great idea.

I go up to my office, grab a pad, and start scribbling, trying to make a logical outline of all the random thoughts that have wandered in and out of my mind since the first screening of the commercials a week ago.

When I return to the conference room, the committee is still nibbling at their sandwiches—and at the problem.

"John," I say, "I'd like to take care of this."

John gives me a strange, what-the-hell-is-this-all-about look, and I go up to the podium. The bottlers see me up there—and go back to munching on their sandwiches.

"Look, let's be honest," I say. "None of us likes the film we saw today. There are lots of things wrong with it. The photography is beautiful, but it has no point. We need these commercials to tell a story. Now, we don't have time to reshoot these spots. And the good news is we don't have to.

"The agency has shot literally miles of film. We can re-edit. That's what we're going to do—create new commercials by editing the same film a different way. We're going to make these ads into clear, cohesive stories. And we're going to get rid of this song. We'll get harder, more *driving* music against the pictures—something more assertive. And we're going to shorten the slogan to make it more emphatic—say, 'Pepsi Now!'"

Everybody seemed to feel that was, more or less, worth trying. Not necessarily because they were enamored of my ideas. But because they saw a problem and were hoping for a solution. At least I had a point of view—I could describe a plan. It might or might not be the best plan, but at least it meant action.

In that conference room, I relearned something I'd observed many times before—at General Mills, in the navy, at Frito-Lay, in Japan, in Brazil. People, even the best professionals in the business, look for leadership. And the essence of all leadership is a point of view.

The new advertising campaign that came from the re-editing and new music was called "Pepsi Now." In all honesty, it never became a blockbuster. But it had liveliness and excitement, and both bottlers and consumers liked it. Not loved it—but liked it. More important to me personally, it demonstrated that I could have a positive impact on this part of the business: an important lesson, as the next two years unfolded.

* * *

But how, you may ask, did a guy who was, for all practical purposes, wet behind the ears when it came to Pepsi advertising get the nerve to hijack the podium, without apology abandon the "company line" on how great the commercials were, and usurp everyone's prerogatives by offering solutions to a problem that the ad agency and the president of the company hadn't yet agreed was a problem?

Well, one answer is that somebody had to do it. And another, more honest one is I didn't always have that kind of nerve. But along the way, I had a lot of encouragement to stand up and speak my mind. And, along the way, I discovered that being in business is all about being a leader, whether your title says you are or not.

That's why it always annoys me to see businessmen characterized as tight-lipped politicos who write memos that never express an opinion. Who never say anything in meetings that deviates from the company line. And who rise to the top by lodging stilettos in the backs of their associates as they sip martinis with the corporate bigwigs long after their co-workers have gone home.

And it annoys me even more to think there are young people entering the corporate world who believe that's the way to get ahead. There may be places where that kind of behavior is rewarded. I've never worked at one of them.

But I understand where that characterization comes from. Because I've seen that attitude toward business expressed, time and again, in the media and by people who have never seen the inside of a good corporation. Or who are in one, but are so removed from the real business of the company they have no idea what people who succeed really do.

In really good companies, you get paid to lead. In fact you *have* to lead. And in a marketing-driven business like Pepsi, the only way to move ahead is to come up with big ideas. And to express them forcefully.

As a youngster, at school, in the navy, and most of all at PepsiCo, I was encouraged—or, sometimes, forced—to confront the very natural fear of being wrong. I was constantly pushed to find out what I really thought, and then to speak up. And, over time, I came to see that waiting in the wings to discover which way the wind is blowing is an excellent way to learn how to be a follower.

* * *

In retrospect, I might have guessed that something was up with John Sculley. At our bottlers' convention in Honolulu in March—where we unveiled, quite successfully, the reworked "Pepsi Now" advertising campaign—John's presentation wasn't about the Pepsi business. It was a thirty-minute speech about computers and icons. The point he was trying to make was, if Pepsi bottlers wanted to be the industry leaders in a computer-run future, they'd have to get comfortable with this technology. At the end of his speech, as he stood in the spotlight, smoke rolled across the stage and lasers flashed everywhere.

The general reaction—and mine—was: What was that all about?

A few weeks later, we knew. It was about John trading colas for computers. Lured by a compensation package rumored to be worth about $4 million, John was, at forty-three, leaving Pepsi to become president and CEO of Apple Computer.

Let me tell you, as his assistant for just six months, I didn't spend a lot of time wondering if I was going to move into his office. And so I was as surprised to learn that he recommended me to succeed him as I had been to hear that he was leaving.

Why me? Well, John often said, "Having a point of view is worth fifty IQ points." And his belief was that a bold point of view would be crucial to Pepsi in this decade. In his opinion, we had, in the 1970s, come out of Coke's shadow and into the center ring. We'd become big and successful. But success had, he felt, made us cautious. If an executive with a strong sense of mission could reignite the fire of big ideas and intelligent risk-taking—change the rules of the game again and again—Pepsi might well replace Coke as the world's premier soft drink company.

That hasn't happened yet. But in the last three years, we've made terrific progress. Not easily. As you'll see, soon after I stepped into John Sculley's very big shoes, trouble started.

Did I say trouble? The first six months of my tenure were pretty much a *disaster*. And all the know-how and confidence I'd acquired from my mentors didn't seem to make any difference at all.

CHAPTER 4

The 180 Days War

Moving into John Sculley's office, I felt very much as I did my first term at college. Glad to be there. Eager. Anxious to make my mark, terrified of making a mistake. The good news was that at a pretty young age, I had become president of Pepsi USA. That was also the bad news. The first 180 days were among the worst of my life.

At the start of that tense season I consoled myself with one thought: In Washington, there's a honeymoon period when a new Chief Executive takes office. Friends and critics alike hang back for a bit to let the President and his staff settle in. Then, when he has a feel for the place, they start the wheedling and carping.

Pepsi's different from Washington in a lot of ways, but in the spring of 1983 one in particular stood out—at Pepsi, presidents don't get honeymoons.

Every Pepsi president has his own crisis list. All the lists, I'm sure, have Coke somewhere around the top. In my case, it was the annoying reversal of Coke's fortunes. After a lot of listless years, Coke was suddenly on a roll.

But the pressures weren't only external. In my eagerness to get the company going, I instituted a price increase that made Pepsi bottlers forget all about a grace period. And my other ideas—regardless of their worth—didn't immediately become programs or products. As everyone who gets to run an enterprise after years in the executive maze soon finds out, I was discovering that presidents sometimes have no more magic ability to turn ideas into deeds than do staffers down the line.

I don't want to make it sound as if every morning I had to walk a gauntlet to get to my office. On the contrary. PepsiCo brass gave me considerable encouragement to undertake great things. It was just that even the encouragement seemed, in those tense months, about as subtle as a cattle prod.

As soon as I was named president and CEO of Pepsi USA, for example, PepsiCo President Andy Pearson called me. "I know you report to Vic Bonomo," he said, "but Vic and I have this very comfortable relationship. So don't stand on formality. I want to see you a lot."

Andy didn't make this call because he didn't trust Bonomo, who, as head of PepsiCo Worldwide Beverages, was my boss, but because he wanted to coach me. He felt John Sculley hadn't taken enough risks. He wanted to exhort me to take more.

Those who have worked with Andy Pearson are well aware that *exhort* can be a tricky verb. Andy was, after all, once listed by *Fortune* magazine as one of America's ten toughest bosses. I knew I was his friend. He knew he was one of my mentors. But in business, that didn't make him hold anything back. I knew he would demand a lot. But I thought I knew exactly how to deal with him: I'd sandbag my plan!

At the start of each year, you see, a division president has to present a financial plan to the parent corporation. In that plan he predicts sales volume, capital expenditures, and profit. At the end of the year, the division is judged not only by the results it produces but how those results stack up against the plan.

At Frito-Lay, years earlier, I learned from Harold Lilley not to come on too ambitious with the numbers. This attitude had become a Frito-Lay maxim: "Don't be a hero at plan time." Much better, it was felt, to sell your bosses on a goal you can't miss, and then beat the hell out of it at the end of the year. It worked for Harold there. Perhaps it could work for me at Pepsi too.

About three days after his "Welcome Wagon" call, Andy called again and asked me to lunch. Fine. I don't eat lunch—I can do without the calories and I always need the time—but we'll have lunch.

At lunch Andy doesn't waste a minute.

"Roger, I don't know how close you were to Harold Lilley," he says. "You probably didn't notice it, but although he was one of the best executives this company ever saw, he did one thing that was wrong—he sandbagged his plan. Each year, he deliberately set minimum goals for the business, then beat them by a mile. Sure, they surpassed the plan, but it was wrong."

I begin to lose my appetite—this guy can read my mind!

"Now I know, Roger, that you're not that kind of guy," Andy continues. "That's why I want you in this job—you're aggressive. I know you'll build an ambitious plan, then stretch to meet it. And I know how you'll do it, too—with big ideas."

Big ideas? What big ideas? My only big idea is to sandbag the plan.

"Now, Roger, what's your first idea?"

I look off into space, appearing to muse. This excites Andy.

"I'm really looking forward to your ideas, Roger. We've *got* to accelerate this business."

Silence. I reach for a sandwich.

Andy looks expectantly at me.

More silence. I reach for a Diet Pepsi.

"Well?"

"Andy, I don't want to hit you with a whole lot of big ideas at once," I say. "Let me sort through them for a few days and get back to you."

"Sure. Call me—no later than tomorrow."

That was when I started to understand why presidents of companies don't feel overpaid.

A day or so later, Alan Pottasch, our senior VP of advertising, says he wants to have dinner. Great. I need help. If anybody has big ideas, it's Alan: Mr. Big Ideas himself.

Over dinner, Alan's big idea boils down to this: He wants to quit—retire.

"Alan, how can you do this to me? You *can't* retire."

"Roger, I want out. I want to go to the Cayman Islands and teach scuba diving."

"Teach scuba diving?"

"It's a very good business, Roger."

"You want to teach scuba diving—as a business?"

I think: The best advertising executive I know of—my one big hope for the future—and he can't wait to get two thousand miles away from me.

"Alan, would you like a raise?"

"Sure—but money's not the problem."

Before he deserts me, though, I've got to have at least one heart-to-heart talk about our advertising. Alan will certainly give me that much. And as he talks, I see that what Alan fears, with this former brand manager as president, is the unholy marriage of a whole *lot* of Pepsi USA brand managers and his advertising.

He's seen this happen before. It's fine for brand managers to provide the strategic direction for the commercials—but when they start massaging the copy and translating strategy to film, it's damn tough for the creative people to make good advertising. Besides, we'll have this incredibly cumbersome approval process: the agency presenting in turn to the brand manager, marketing director, marketing VP, *ad nauseam*. By the time the stuff gets to me for final approval, it'll be trash.

"No, no—you don't understand me," I say. "I have no intention of allowing the brand managers to run the advertising. I know what you're talking about—I've been there before. When I was vice-president of marketing at Frito-Lay, we had just the problem you're worrying about. And I saw what happens: Too many people all in a row can, and will, kill a good idea. Even when they're good people, somehow they cancel each other out and make the advertising worse, rather than better. What I want to do here is make you even more important—completely in charge of advertising."

Alan's look makes me feel I'm making some progress with him. But I figure it's not likely I've won him over yet. What do I say now? After all, competing with Coke is one thing, but how in God's name do you compete with scuba diving?

Maybe Alan is challenged by a chance for greatness. Most superstars are. And they respond to personal appeal. Business isn't cut and dried. People, especially talented people, work best for people they believe in—and who, they believe, respect them.

"Alan, twenty years ago you created the Pepsi Generation," I say. "It's a legend. And that's fine. Most people in their lives never do anything of the magnitude you accomplished with the Pepsi Generation. But wouldn't it be exciting to do that *twice*? That's what I want you to do. And nobody else can do it but you. So don't talk to me about retiring, Alan, because I can't run this business without you. You are the most important resource for what it is I think we've got to do with Pepsi-Cola."

"Well, I just wanted to know you wanted me," he says. "Okay, I won't retire."

As I drove home that night, I was still in shock. It had worked.

What worked, you ask? All you did was con an experienced old pro.

Well, I didn't see it that way. What I did was tell the truth. I genuinely liked Alan, respected his abilities, and I honestly believed Alan Pottasch could make my presidency of Pepsi-Cola great.

Without him, God only knew where I'd end up . . . and I wasn't entirely confident He had great things in store for me.

To give you an example, it was my good fortune to take over Pepsi just as Coke was unleashing Diet Coke.

For twenty years the world had been patiently waiting for a diet soft drink that Coke would deign to put its name on. Just my luck, they do it at the start of my watch. It's a real savior for the boys at Coke headquarters.

In the past when Pepsi made a diet drink, we used to measure its taste against the taste of the original sugar-added product. We knew Diet Pepsi could never really taste just like Pepsi, but we tried. Coke's big idea was not to worry whether Diet Coke tasted like Coke. They attacked the problem from a whole other direction.

What Coke did is develop a product with "an absence of negatives." That is, they eliminated everything from the formula that people had even the smallest objection to. At the time, you see, diet colas didn't taste as good as they do now. People who drank them did it mostly for the benefit of one calorie per twelve ounces—but they really didn't like the taste.

Diet Coke is a drink with very little flavoring in it relative to other diet sodas. Its taste comes mainly from a good-sized dose of vanilla. The result is something that resembles a cream soda more than a cola. But as Diet Coke sold and sold, the only unanswered question about it became why they waited so damn long to introduce it.

You say, "What's the big deal? It's just a diet drink, not the flagship brand." Ten years ago, you'd have had a point. Even as late as 1979 diet colas accounted for only around 6 percent of all soft drink sales. But by 1983, they had grown to over 12 percent of the market—a $4 billion business. Either everybody was on a diet all of a sudden, or diet colas had become respectable.

Diet Coke wouldn't have haunted me so much if I'd been happier with our Diet Pepsi commercials. They were "new wave European" in tone. High-contrast colors, amazing angles, everybody posed and moving slowly—if it weren't for the product shots, you'd swear it was advertising for cosmetics.

Like any advertising that relies on visual tricks, this campaign wore out very quickly. In its first year, as I saw it. And this was the second year.

So I didn't quite see the point of having some super-skinny beauty arch off a diving board, drift slowly toward the water, and have the pool become an ice-filled glass that miraculously fills with Diet Pepsi.

Conceptually, this might sound like great advertising. But the execution was weak. And at the bottlers' convention, I hadn't seen anyone rushing out to the phones to book local TV time for these spots.

So I call Allen Rosenshine, the chairman of BBDO, and express my concerns.

Rosenshine calls Phil Dusenberry, who oversees all Pepsi commercials.

Dusenberry, who started working on our account in 1963, calls Alan Pottasch.

Pottasch, whose office is two doors down from mine, calls me.

"Roger, it's not just that you bypassed the chain of command," he says. "It's that you've ignored the way I manage the creative flow. BBDO talks to us through one person—Phil. Pepsi talks to BBDO through one person—me. Anything else takes away my authority. I won't stand for you going directly to the agency. You're going to screw everything up. I don't need this and don't have to put up with it."

Alan Pottasch is, as I've said, so valuable to Pepsi that if he leaves, there's no obvious candidate—inside the company or out—to replace him. I get mad anyway.

"Alan," I say, "there is no goddamn way you are going to tell me who I can talk to and when."

"Roger, I can't work your way."

Lovely. Alan's one beat from quitting again.

"Listen to me, Alan. One, there's no goddamn way you're going to tell me who I can talk to and when. Point two, you and I get on well, but you are *not* going to talk to me that way. Point three—you are absolutely right."

I can feel Alan raising an eyebrow at that.

"You're absolutely right," I repeat. "But I wasn't saying I don't trust you to get the advertising right. We haven't worked together long enough for you to know, but this is just my style—I try to make sure from four different angles that every base is covered."

"Are you going to call Rosenshine again?"

"I don't know. But I'll promise you one thing. I'm going to be a lot more sensitive about this."

On that note, we end the call. Alan doesn't quit. But restoring the status quo when you're staring at a big defeat is not what you'd call my first victory.

Andy Pearson wants big ideas. Fine. I've got one. It later turned out to be a huge success called Slice. But trying to develop that product during my first months at Pepsi USA was enormously difficult.

In the fall of 1982, when I became Sculley's assistant, the company had been working on the development of a lemon-lime soft drink called Surf. We'd done the R&D work. We'd done some taste-testing against 7-Up and Sprite. And it looked as if we'd test-market this very respectable product some time in 1983.

The thing is, as I saw it, the world wasn't waiting for a third lemon-lime soft drink. Yes, we could get a piece of the business, simply because of the marketing and distribution power of our bottlers. But to what end? Coke had been pushing Sprite since the 1940s. And they've gotten what? A 3-share—which means, with each share point representing about $250 million in retail sales, a $750 million business. The sales leader, 7-Up, is an 8-share, or a $2 billion business.

The best we could do, I figured, was about as well as Sprite. Maybe we could get there quicker than Coke did, but it was going to be muscle marketing. Because the consumers, as we say in this business, vote every day. And although they'd give our lemon-lime a try, they were eventually going to find out that our product was Tweedledum to 7-Up's Tweedledee. In the consumer's mind, our product wouldn't have a real reason for being.

No sustainable competitive advantage. No hook—we were looking at a very hard-to-win 40- to 50-million-case business. And I was dreaming of a new brand that would sell 100 million cases in its first year. A $500 million first-year business that had the potential to grow much, much bigger.

There aren't a lot of those in the consumer-products field.

The way you get one is to have a point of difference. A point of difference that quickly translates into a competitive advantage—an angle that so distinguishes your product from all others that people just have to try it. And once they do, they're hooked.

If the difference is one they care about, that is.

I didn't have to think long about this before I remembered Japan. About the time I first visited Japan, Coke introduced their fruit-based Hi-C there. I'm told Coke didn't think it was such a hot idea. Their bottlers did. The Japanese Coke bottlers were right—Hi-C developed a huge business literally overnight.

By the time I moved to Japan, the vending machines in the street were filled with soft drinks that were enriched with fruit juice. There would be five selections. You could have orange soda with 10 percent juice or you could have it with 20 percent, 30 percent, 40 percent, or 50 percent juice. The 50 percent drink cost more, but it didn't exactly discourage the customers— every time you turned around, there were more vending machines with juice-added soft drinks.

Then I remembered my year in South America.

In South America, we put 10 percent fruit juice in Teem, our lemon-lime product, and in Mirinda, our orange soda. The reason we did that had nothing to do with marketing. In Brazil and Argentina, the government wanted to protect their fruit juice industries from the multinational soft drink companies. So they put a value-added tax on carbonated soft drinks—but if you put 10 percent or more fruit juice in your product, you were exempt from the tax. Because juice cost less than the tax, it made sense to add juice wherever possible.

And—funny thing—the juice made Teem and Mirinda taste better.

I arranged to have dinner with our head of R&D. Long before the Sambuca arrived, I made my pitch for a juice-added soda.

"Can't do it," he says.

"Why not?"

"Costs too much."

"You let me worry about the economics and the marketing appeal. What I want to know from you is whether it can be done."

"It can't."

"Why not?"

"Can't control the quality."

"Wait a minute," I say. "If we can do it in our antiquated plants in South America, we can sure as hell do it in our plants here."

"Well, we have a lot of trouble in South America."

"Look, I was there for a year. We had occasional problems— we worried about the juice fermenting in the bottle; we had some concerns about the clarity of the drinks—but I never saw one recall of the product."

"Does it have to be all-natural?"

"Yes."

"Not possible."

"You could be right. But we don't know that yet."

There was a little silence. He was thinking hard, to figure what other negative argument he could find. I was thinking hard, to figure how to tell him he damned well better start looking for ways to do this. I got there first.

"I know what we'll do," I say. "You guys take a shot at it. If you fail, we'll hire consultants, say, Arthur D. Little, to do it." This was tantamount to telling the R&D director that he's about to be the *former* R&D director. He got the idea, and, a few weeks later, brought some samples to my office. The regular lemon-lime was excellent. The diet was sensational.

I ran the samples into John Sculley's office. John tasted one.

"Fabulous," he said. "What is it?"

"Surf—*Diet* Surf!"

"This," Sculley said, "is our next big idea."

I went back to my office and stored the precious samples in my refrigerator. Then I spent the rest of the morning trying to think up a code name for this project. By noon I had chosen "Overlord," because if this worked, 7-Up and Sprite would feel as if they were on the receiving end of the Normandy invasion.

Then I called the R&D folks and told them we wanted more batches of these wonderful products. And while they were off in the lab whipping some up, Sculley left and I became president.

It's now April 1983, and I am *really* primed to taste juice-added Overlord. Some of the new batch is sent over. I compare the new concoction with the samples in my refrigerator. It's nothing like the product Sculley got excited about.

Back to the drawing board.

Another reason I had no honeymoon when I took over Pepsi USA was a confrontation with our bottlers that took place just two weeks into my presidency. The confrontation was over a price increase, and it had the makings of big trouble for me. To understand why the bottlers challenged me right away, you've got to understand something about the franchise soft drink business and about Pepsi. There are no more Pepsi franchises in the United States. They were all granted years ago. And, over the years, Pepsi bottlers have made huge investments of time, energy, and money in their business. As they see it, they didn't make those kinds of investments just for the profit the business can provide each year. Rather, they were building equity—permanent value—that would continue to grow into the future.

By 1986, the value of a Pepsi franchise was increasing by more than 23 percent a year. Sales were way up; in the past two years we'd added as much new volume to the business as we did in the previous five. And the new products we rolled out were among the largest-selling grocery products ever introduced in this country.

But Pepsi hasn't always been so prosperous. As you've seen, we went bankrupt twice. And because a good number of the bottling franchises are passed from father to son, there are many people in our organization who grew up hearing just how tough times once were for Pepsi.

So when prosperity finally arrived, it did not make our bottlers fat, dumb, and happy. They were Depression kids who'd made it. While they were now driving Cadillacs, as Al Steele had promised, it would have taken fortunes beyond fortunes to blur their memories of the many years when they worried about losing their Fords.

The suddenness of our bottlers' prosperity and the sacrifices they'd made along the way have given them a strong proprietary attitude about this business. They resent any increase in the price of concentrate, the ingredient they buy from us to make the final beverage. In their view, it already costs a great deal. And they are not afraid to express themselves forcefully on the subject.

"We want to talk to you about this untimely price advance," says Mario Pastega, then president of the Pepsi-Cola Bottlers' Association, calling from his bottling plant in Corvallis, Oregon. "Could you join a few of us in St. Louis for a little chitchat?"

Untimely? It's May 1983, and I've raised the price of Pepsi concentrate by about 10 percent, just a few weeks after the price has gone up by 5 percent.

I have a perfectly good rationale.

Pepsi is made of sugar, concentrate, and carbonated water. We sell only the concentrate; the bottlers buy sugar themselves. And because of a very effective sugar lobby which manages, through government import quotas, to keep the price of sugar in this country far above the rest of the world, they pay more for this sweetener than they'd like to. But in 1983 we approved the use of high fructose corn syrup to substitute for half the sugar the bottlers buy to use in making Pepsi. Fructose is a lot cheaper than sugar, and the bottlers' costs will go down by more than the amount I had raised the concentrate price. And even with the price increase, they'll still enjoy a cost advantage compared to their competitors in the Coke system. But they don't see it that way.

What they're seeing, as I enter the meeting room at the hotel in St. Louis, is red.

A brief flashback.

In March of 1980, while John Sculley was addressing two thousand bottler personnel at a convention in Las Vegas, the Coca-Cola Company made an announcement that was like a little Pearl Harbor. No longer was Coke going to be sweetened just with sugar; now the game was 50 percent sugar, 50 percent high fructose corn syrup.

It's not that Pepsi wasn't aware of fructose. When the world price of unrefined sugar is, say, 6 cents a pound, and a very skilled political lobby keeps United States sugar prices around 18 cents, you're going to look at any sweetener that can save you money. But fructose didn't seem like the answer.

If Pepsi had been a different product—if Pepsi had been Coke, say—we'd have jumped on the fructose bandwagon right away. But Pepsi has a more complex and delicate flavor than Coke. It's more aromatic; it tastes a bit subtler. In a harsher cola like Coke, you didn't notice the difference between fructose and sugar. In tests of Pepsi sweetened with the fructose that was available in 1980, you did.

Coke's 50 percent fructose decision was probably the first that Roberto Goizueta, Don Keough, and Brian Dyson—the management team that was about to take charge of the Coca-Cola Company—made using their new ready-fire-aim philosophy. Given that new philosophy, they probably didn't do much testing. More likely they just looked at the cost savings, bet that it wouldn't hurt sales, and blasted away.

Don Kendall could never be that flip. Not with the Pepsi formula, which he considers the crown jewels. Kendall believed that the fructose difference was something you really had to test thoroughly. Maybe most people wouldn't notice it, but the heavy consumers of Pepsi would, and whether they told you of their intentions or not, they'd start to find other things to drink instead of Pepsi.

Besides, Kendall could taste the difference. And he didn't like it.

He was right, of course. Forget what Coke does. We've got Pepsi. Twenty million people around the world have taken the

Pepsi Challenge and given us consistent victories. So we've got to be extra careful tampering with a winning formula.

So as not to tinker wantonly with our crown jewels, Pepsi spent 1980 to 1983 pressuring the fructose manufacturers to improve the quality of their sweetener. Late in 1982, when I joined John Sculley's team, I made this issue my first priority.

I was right to do this. Coke wasn't kicking us down the steps thanks to fructose, but they had blunted our momentum by pouring all the money they saved into wheeling and dealing with their product in the supermarkets. I had a young fellow named Chris McGurk, a very bright guy who became our director of planning, work up the numbers. His calculations showed that it was costing the Pepsi system—the company and its bottlers— $120 million a year not to use 50 percent fructose.

We did some more in-home consumer testing with a 50 percent fructose Pepsi. We opened more test markets. We tore the business apart on this issue—analyzed every number we could get our hands on.

Numbers alone, I knew, weren't going to be enough to convince Kendall. I brought all this in to John Sculley.

"I don't want to hold you back," he said, "but we've been trying to get Don to move on this for three years."

"I know, but we've *got* to do it."

"Good luck," John said. "Take the lead if you want."

In December of 1982, John and I went in to make our case to Don Kendall, Andy Pearson, and Vic Bonomo. I explained that we were giving Coke a $120 million-a-year advantage. An enormous pot. It gave them strategic options we didn't have. They could add it to their bottom line; they could put it into advertising; they could use it to cut prices. Hell, over three years, with a $360 million strategic kitty, they could introduce *two* Diet Cokes and have enough left over for a nice celebration party.

But more important, the consumer research and test marketing said that fructose quality was now good enough that people— including our heavy users—actually preferred Pepsi with the new sweetener.

Fifteen minutes into the presentation, I knew we had Kendall. Nobody had ever explained it to him quite this way before. Kendall, of course, did not telegraph his agreement. Just the reverse. He likes to test commitment, to see if you've got round heels, or if you believe enough in what you're doing to put your reputation on the line. I could tell he was going to be very, very tough.

"I think we should have done this years ago," Vic Bonomo said. "I'm absolutely for it."

"Me too," Sculley said.

"Yeah," Pearson added. "Let's get on with it."

Kendall turned to me.

"So, Roger, you're prepared to be the guy who screws up Pepsi-Cola?"

A when-did-you-stop-beating-your-wife question, if I ever heard one.

"No," I said. "I'm as concerned as you are about small product changes that might cause us to lose our consumer franchise. But I think our risk is very small—if there's any risk at all—and over here on the other side, there's a clear and present danger: A one-hundred-and-twenty-million-dollar-a-year competitive disadvantage. With that kind of money, we all know there are a lot of things we can do to get this business moving again. So I don't think there's a choice. We've *got* to go ahead."

"I'll think about it," Kendall said.

While he waited to tell me a decision I knew he'd already made, we went off to meet with the fructose suppliers. We weren't trying to negotiate price—that's for our bottlers to do—but we did want assurances that there would be enough fructose available to supply our needs without driving the price through the roof.

Kendall gave us the authorization to go to 50 percent fructose. We went out to Hawaii in March for our 1983 convention. And while we were there, Coke announced that it was going to 75 percent fructose in fountain syrup.

A year later—also around the time of our bottler convention—they announced an increase to 75 percent in bottles and cans and 100 percent in fountain syrup. Three bottler conventions, three fructose announcements.

Coincidental? Not on your life.

Would I, if I worked for Coke, have voted to make those announcements just then? No. And I doubt anyone else in our organization would have. I once heard Harold Lilley say, when someone jokingly proposed a bit of good-humored trickery, "Dammit, we'll do business as gentlemen or we won't do business at all." The way he said it, you wouldn't want to hear him repeat it.

But sometimes the Cola Wars take a turn like that—you can't always stay on the high road. So I filed the "gentlemanly" timing of the Coke announcements. And, as you'll see, a time came when I decided to return the favor.

* * *

"You've been running Pepsi USA for less than a month," says a bottler, beginning our "chitchat" in St. Louis about the concentrate price advance. "Maybe you don't know what happened to the last president who tried to take an unjustified and untimely price increase."

I do, but don't want to think about it.

"I have one piece of advice for you," says another.

"Yes?"

"Rent—don't buy."

Mario Pastega reads the resolution supposedly drafted by the committee—but ghost-written, I could swear, by the Ayatollah Khomeini. The punch line is poster-simple: Rescind the price increase.

Despite the obvious anger of the bottlers in this room, I conclude this is not the time to be irresolute. Nervously, I review the competitive situation. I point out that bottlers' costs will still be lower. I discuss the need for Pepsi USA to generate more marketing funds. And I explain that I took this job to do what's right for the business, not to enhance my résumé.

I'm determined to do what's right. The price advance stays—and if it costs me my job, so be it.

This scores some points. Now it's the bottlers' turn.

If I won't rescind the price increase, they demand that I at least delay it so that bottlers can adjust their businesses and contractual agreements—and make sure all of them get the benefit of using the lower-cost fructose.

I decide we need a break. This chitchat is not how I've imagined I'd begin my relationship with our bottlers. I like them. I believe I can create a new spirit of cooperative partnership with them. Working together, we could take the business to new heights. But now it's beginning to look as if the only height I'd get to is the cliff I'm standing on the edge of.

I'm depressed—and a little scared—as we leave the room. Clearly they are mad as hell at me. Just then one of the bottlers pulls me aside.

"I'm sure you think they're mad at you," he says. "But they're not so much mad as worried. They don't *know* if you're the kind of guy who'll do what's right. You have a lot of power over the future of their businesses. They need to know you can listen—and that you can respond to their legitimate concerns."

They're worried? Now what do I do? I've announced the price rise. We've completed our planning and know exactly the new marketing programs we'll invest in. I've sold this whole game plan hard to Kendall and Pearson, and they've agreed.

I go off to a quiet corner to huddle with my VP for bottler relations, Chuck Mangold, and our legal counsel, Gerry Casey.

"The bottlers raised a lot of good points," Gerry says. "They're upset, but I think they're sincere. This isn't just a bargaining session."

"Yes, the bottlers made some legitimate points," I reply. "But they don't add up to a whole hell of a lot in terms of the magnitude of this thing. We can—and maybe we should—go ahead as planned."

Then I think about what that insightful bottler just told me in our private conversation.

"But we won't. We'll agree to delay the price advance for six months. The marketing programs can wait. It's far more important that the bottlers have confidence in us. They've got to know that we care as much about their half of this partnership as we do about ours."

"Shouldn't you call Purchase and see what the top brass thinks?" Chuck asks. "Can you really do this on your own? After all, this is a forty-million-dollar decision."

"We're not calling Purchase," I say. "The bottlers need to know we'll make a decision—and that we'll make it on the spot when it's right to do so."

We delay the price advance by six months. The right thing to do, but again, not exactly a great battle victory.

Aspartame. Today it is one of the greatest things that ever happened to me. During my first 180 days, it was one of the worst. Aspartame taught me how *not* to lead.

Today you see aspartame—or its brand-name equivalent, NutraSweet—on every can of diet soda you buy. In 1983, you didn't. Then you saw only saccharin. All aspartame was, at that time, was a pain in the neck to people like me.

It may have been giving the same fits to the people at Coke, but from the way it tastes, I'd guess that Diet Coke was formulated with aspartame in mind. Pepsi USA, in 1983, is another story.

"What do we know about aspartame?" I ask.

"Oh, we know everything about it," one of our research people tells me. "Our regulatory staff worked out a special deal with Searle almost two years ago to help them with their approval petition to the Food and Drug Administration, and we've been testing it ever since."

"Okay, so we're ready to go?" I ask, somewhat relieved.

"What do you mean, ready to go? It hasn't been approved by the FDA yet."

"Yeah, I know," I say. "But we do have our formulas down pat and our consumer testing all finished so we can launch as soon as the FDA gives its approval, right?"

In response to that question, I get a blank stare.

Get the idea? We don't know *everything* we need to know about aspartame. Maybe we do know a hell of a lot more than Coke, but we've done virtually nothing to finalize our formulas— to mobilize our system so we'll be ready when the FDA does approve it.

So here we are, like a bunch of chickens with their heads cut off. For practical purposes, all I know as I become president is that the FDA is now likely to approve aspartame for diet soft drinks, and that it is one hell of a lot more expensive than saccharin, which is how Diet Pepsi is sweetened at the time.

Jim Stanley, our VP of regulatory affairs, jumps into the picture.

"How do we formulate our diet drinks with the stuff?" I ask him. "How much better than saccharin is it? How much do you use? Do you blend aspartame with saccharin?"

Jim tells me consumers rate aspartame a whole lot better than saccharin. He also tells me that saccharin and aspartame are synergistic—a little of both, blended properly, gives more sweetness than the same amount of each by itself.

"But this may be a moot point," he says, "because, though I've been pushing hard on Searle to see the benefit of using a blend of aspartame and saccharin in our products, they're holding firm to requiring their customers to drop saccharin and use only aspartame."

Well, I think, here's someone who's actually doing his job. But I have a sinking feeling that Coke is way out front of us on this one. That's no big deal if many companies are making aspartame. Unfortunately, Searle holds the American use patent—you want aspartame, you've got to get it from them.

Searle is a pharmaceutical company. They've invested time and R&D money in aspartame. Once the patent expires and aspartame becomes a generic product, they're going to have competition. So as soon as they're allowed to market it, you know they're going to want a return on their investment in about four days. Their game is to make immense profits before the clock runs out.

Saccharin is then around $3 a pound. Aspartame is going to $80, maybe $100—we don't know how high Searle is going to set the hoop. All we hope is that there's some reasonable relationship between the price of aspartame and the amount we'll need to make a good-tasting product.

And we hope that we're not going to have too rugged a time with Searle's management and sales representatives. They're all lawyers! They don't know anything about customer management or the soft drink business; without this patent, they couldn't sell their way out of a paper bag. I think they know this. If they don't, they certainly know there's not a damn thing we can do to slide around them.

Even as we're warming up to dealing with Searle, we have this nagging fear. Remember cyclamates, once the much-beloved diet sweetener? In late 1969, a test—since found to be faulty—showed that if you feed a rat something like the equivalent of four hundred cans of diet soft drinks a day, it might develop a tumor. Boom! The FDA bans cyclamates. Tens of millions of dollars spent recalling and dumping product, and quickly getting something else out there to sell.

Later, the same thing almost happened with saccharin—out of the blue. A Canadian study was supposed to demonstrate that "clean" saccharin is okay. Results came in. You guessed it—more tumors in rats. What did they expect to get when they fed the rats enough saccharin every day to sweeten a thousand cans of diet soft drinks? Hell, if you feed them that much Perrier, they'll *drown*.

Needless to say, that's not how our regulators saw things in 1977.

The upshot was that the FDA wanted to ban saccharin. But with saccharin gone, there wouldn't be any artificial sweeteners left. What about the diabetics? What about the people who would gain five pounds the first week without saccharin? Would there be enough cotton in the world to clothe all the fat people this country was going to grow? Or would we just gain so much weight that we'd sink the continent and none of this would matter?

And all this because of a well-intentioned but archaic regulation called the Delaney Amendment, which basically says that anything—in whatever quantities—that can be made to cause tumors in laboratory animals must be taken off the market. Never mind how you got the tumor to grow. Never mind the quality of the science. Ban it.

Unlike our experience with cyclamates, this time the soft drink industry decided not to roll over and just let the FDA ban saccharin. We felt like the guy in the movie *Network: "We're not going to take this anymore."* Consumers joined the cry; they wanted saccharin on the market, too. We petitioned Congress. And in 1978, Congress passed a law—which it later extended—declaring a moratorium on the saccharin ban.

So when 1983 comes around and the FDA seems to be ready to approve aspartame for use in soft drinks, we think: We've been burned twice. We know that if aspartame is approved for soft drink use, the crazies are going to come out of the woodwork. No one's going to care that aspartame is already approved for dry use, and it's already sweetening coffee and tea and Kool-Aid and Jell-O. Carbonated soft drinks are such a visible, high-consumption product, we're going to have every two-bit researcher in the country pumping *tons* of aspartame into innocent rats in the hope they can give them some kind of ailment and—in the process—get famous overnight.

If that happens, we want the FDA to stand tall. Anything less than "We've done all the tests; we've considered every damn thing; the product is safe" just won't do.

So the president of the Coca-Cola Company, Don Keough, suggests that the National Soft Drink Association send a letter to the FDA on behalf of all the soft drink companies, asking them to be absolutely sure this time. Check and recheck everything. Please.

The letter goes out. Searle sees it. And goes wild. Searle figures we're trying to influence the FDA not to approve this stuff because it will make our costs go up.

Absolutely not so, but they're paranoid from all the delays.

Now things really get interesting. Bob Shapiro, the president of Searle's aspartame division, calls me. He wants to know what the hell this is all about. I tell him the truth. He wants to have dinner.

We meet at Auberge Argenteuil restaurant in Hartsdale, New York. If this pace keeps up, I could moonlight as a restaurant critic. Over dinner, it becomes clear that Shapiro's game plan is to get either Coke or Pepsi to sign a purchase order. I suppose with that in hand, the industry petition to the FDA looks pretty foolish—no way would I sign a contract with Searle if I had doubts about the product, right?

"I need friends now," he says.

I can relate to that. And to encourage me, he says he's willing to be more flexible about price than he's inclined to be later on. But there's a catch. Two, actually.

One is supply. "I can't guarantee that the supply of aspartame is sufficient to satisfy all the potential buyers," Shapiro says.

"Well, how long would the losers have to wait—a year?"

"Oh, no. A matter of months. If that."

I can, I think, live with that. But I can't endure the second catch: Searle does not want to give us the right to formulate our diet cola to our taste. Shapiro wants us to use a certain minimum amount of aspartame in the formula. If that's more sweetness—and more aspartame—than we'd like, tough.

I resist.

"This damn formulation minimum doesn't make any sense," I say. "If you dictate to us on this, you're telling the whole soft drink industry how its products should taste. You're eliminating the possibility that one company or another can create a superior product. That's going to come back and bite you. If consumers don't like one drink, under your rules they're going to hate them all."

"I'm not prepared," he says, "to change it right now."

"Then I don't see how we can make a deal right now."

A few weeks later, Shapiro calls again. He has news for me.

"I've just signed a deal with Coke."

"What?"

"Coke is going to buy aspartame for their diet products. As a matter of fact, they're buying just about all I have available."

"No, Bob, they wouldn't do that."

Or would they? What about Don Keough? We've met just a couple of times, but I have a very clear sense of him as a nice guy and an ethical businessman. But would he have encouraged all of us to write to the FDA about aspartame knowing he was going to strike a deal with Searle before the FDA even responds? Was all of that a ruse by Coca-Cola? To make us drop our guard while they cut their deal?

Whatever the answer to that question, I figure my first mistake was not to say yes when Shapiro offered me the deal at Auberge Argenteuil. I should have signed that damn contract and taken possession of as much aspartame as they'd sell us. Then, like every other clever businessman in the world, I should have renegotiated the deal to get the freedom to formulate our product the way we wanted.

But remember, this is my first 180 days, I'm not satisfied with one mistake. I'm determined to make another. And so, while trying to close a better-late-than-never deal with Searle, I allow our lawyers to negotiate every last detail with their lawyers— and there are pages and pages of these subclauses.

Consider what's important: getting the damn aspartame. Nothing else. But I'm listening to lawyers telling me what I can and can't do, and every day is one more day that Coke will be first in the marketplace with aspartame-sweetened Diet Coke. I let these negotiations drag on like this for two months.

Much, much later, I learn that Coke had the same problems with Searle—only they wised up. As I hear it, they brought all the Searle negotiators to Atlanta, shut them in a conference room, and announced that no one was leaving until they had an agreement. I don't know how long it took—it could have been days—but in the end they did hammer out an agreement.

But however it happened, I doubt the agreement required reams of paper. And probably, the day after the contract was signed, Coke told Searle it wanted to renegotiate. And Searle, well aware of how big a customer Coke is, probably went along.

One star for some smart person at Coke. He saw the forest instead of the trees. This was a perfect execution of their ready-fire-aim operating philosophy.

Andy Pearson knew I'd made a major, major error. "Being first in something like this is important," he said. "But if you're not going to be first, being a very close second is *critical.* You let the lawyers and the staff people take control of something that was significant to the company—something that required you to step in, cut through it all, and make it happen."

Three months later, with aspartame-sweetened Diet Coke already in the stores, we finally completed our contract with Searle. It would take two or three months to get the refor-mulated Diet Pepsi into the stores. By then, Diet Coke had a 4.0 market share—and remember, when one point means $250 million at retail, that's about a *billion* in sales.

But I learned. I vowed then that I'd never hang back like that again. And now, whenever I find myself losing aggressiveness, I remember my dinner with Shapiro at Auberge Argenteuil.

Small wonder, as I complete my first 180 days as president, that I feel I've been through a war. Nothing that started right stayed right. Everything that started wrong stayed wrong.

The "big idea" memo I finally gave Andy Pearson? A brilliant, straight-ahead program, to be sure. Inspirational, without question—far from sandbagging my plan, I came on like a Ferrari Testarossa. Watch out, Coke! The Pepsi army was, in my plan, being commanded by a neo-Patton whose strategic philosophy was, in Cola War terms, the equivalent of Patton's "L'avance, l'avance, l'avance." Only one problem with it: It's a little hard to keep your troops advancing when you're desperately trying to avoid an ignominious retreat.

Scratch a businessman, find a philosopher. The philosopher may not be a deep thinker, but at the very least he develops some way of seeing the bad times in a context that allows him to go on. For a lot of men and women I know, the trick is to focus on something completely outside the business—to remind yourself that the business isn't everything.

Unfortunately for me, I'm not one of those executives who can pop a cassette in the tape deck for the drive to work, learn another language or listen to Dylan Thomas, and arrive at the office spiritually enriched and ready to tear into a day. It's a short trip from my home in New Canaan, Connecticut, to Purchase, and because I'm not a morning person I usually require silence. But one morning during that 180-day siege, when I was at my lowest and I could really appreciate the structural beauty of Mozart, I switched on the radio.

Unless my wife had suddenly developed a liking for Led Zeppelin, my son had set the dial—some group I didn't know was shouting about something I couldn't care less about. Then a John Lennon song came on. And I heard—as you're wont to hear in popular music when you're looking for an anchor, any anchor—a line that I could relate to. "Life," Lennon sang, "is what happens while you're busy making other plans."

That line inspired no epiphany. I was still trapped: big job, big salary, big failure looming on the horizon. But it was nice to feel—it was necessary for me to feel—that someone, somewhere, had some sense of the torture I was going through.

What changed the way I felt? Other people, really. For with the invaluable help of Mike Feiner, our vice president of personnel, I'd assembled a management team that was actually starting to mesh.

Most of the choices had been pretty obvious. It wouldn't have required a Mike Feiner to know, for example, that Dan Clark should run brand marketing, John Swanhaus should head up marketing operations, and Ron Tidmore should be vice president of sales. It was equally obvious that Ann Hailey, who can hold more meaningful data in her head than the hard disk of my computer, should be vice president of finance, and that Tom Williams, a superb manager, should head up technical services. Richard Blossom's ability to administer a business and savor Eastern European fiction showed that he was versatile and imaginative enough to run a new product development department. Getting Alan Pottasch to want to become an advertising legend in his own time—for the second time—was another sensible decision. And anyone who wanted to support these people with the best public relations department in the country would have called on Joe McCann, whom I'd come to know and admire at Frito-Lay.

Other choices required more persuasion or inspiration. Chuck Mangold, our vice president of bottler relations, was so set on retiring that the right thing to have done would have been to wish him good fishing. But Chuck is invaluable—in a people-intensive business, he had encyclopedic knowledge of more than two hundred bottlers. When he agreed to stay on, I knew I had an in-house mentor. And to give a new sense of mission to our all-important research and development unit, we picked Bennett Nussbaum. Bennett was the furthest thing from a bench chemist. He started out as a financial analyst, then switched into quality control; when I came on board he was vice president of manufacturing for our own company-owned bottling plants. But if he could manage scientists as well as he could deal with people on our executive floor, we knew we'd soon be taking some amazing products to test-market.

Individually, these people were strong and competent and remarkably bright. Mike Feiner's genius was to recognize that they could not only work well, but work well together. It took time—you don't endorse people, give them some direction, and then give them their head and get results right away—but by the end of 180 days, I felt that second best wasn't going to be our fate forever.

Having gotten ten years of CEO training in six months, I was pretty humbled by then. I still had big dreams, but they didn't blind me to reality. And so, in the late summer of 1983, I prayed for a single victory—something to prove that the Pepsi team *could* hit one out of the park.

CHAPTER 5

Seeking the High Ground

It's all in the point of view, isn't it? In the summer of 1983, I was convinced that Pepsi was in trouble—but then, Rosencrantz and Guildenstern thought Hamlet was a minor player in the drama. The facts were otherwise. Pepsi's condition, to my surprise, delight, puzzlement, and, ultimately, edification, wasn't really the same as mine.

Pepsi was, thank you very much, doing considerably better than I was.

Burger King had given us a huge shot in the arm by switching from Coke to Pepsi. And over at our R&D lab, the first thing Bennett Nussbaum had done was to have the building unlocked on weekends; until then, if a chemist had a brainstorm after office hours on Friday, he couldn't do anything about it until Monday. Now the building was buzzing on weekends and Project Overlord was moving back on track.

Most of all, we were on our way to a huge success with Pepsi Free, the caffeine-free cola we introduced while Coca-Cola was putting all its efforts into Diet Coke. This was a real coup. We knew there was nothing we could do to keep Diet Coke from getting great trial. But rather than run out and defend Diet Pepsi, we felt it would be better to roll out a product that stood alone in its category.

Now, we had no idea how big the caffeine-free market would be. But Phillip Morris's 7-Up division had just introduced a no-caffeine cola called Like—their long-awaited move into the soft drink big time. We weren't about to let them have the market to themselves.

I'm sure they thought we'd be boxed in, with no way to respond—because to put out a caffeine-free Pepsi is to admit there's something wrong with regular Pepsi, right? But even great marketing organizations like Phillip Morris can occasionally forget one of the great consumer-products truths: Companies are in business to fulfill the desires of consumers. We're *not* in business to dictate those desires. Consumers have the right to a choice. If people want a caffeine-free drink and we know they like the taste of Pepsi, then if we just make a Pepsi without caffeine, how the hell can it fail? It's impossible.

So we didn't spend a lot of time agonizing over the subtleties. And we didn't spend a lot of time test-marketing. We just rolled Pepsi Free across the country with 33 million dollars' worth of advertising behind it. And while I was getting whipsawed by other problems during the first months of my presidency, Pepsi Free was on its way to a 150-million-case, $600-million first year.

Which translates thus: With Diet Coke, Pepsi Free was among the most successful new brands in the history of American consumer products.

But not even Pepsi Free was big enough to guarantee that our momentum would accelerate for long. We still needed what John Sculley used to call "prime mover events" and I call "leadership marketing": calculated risks so massive, so attention-getting, and so well executed that the consumer's imagination is completely captivated—and business responds like gangbusters.

Bringing out new products is just one element of leadership marketing. To be a leading company in the marketing field, you need to search for big ideas in support of most everything you do: package design, promotion, advertising—even in the ways you build motivation among your employees.

Admittedly, big ideas require creativity. And in large companies the most difficult job for a president is getting employees to consistently think and act creatively. The fact is, *every* individual has immense creative potential. The hard part is finding the courage to use it.

Helping your people find the courage: opening the windows, challenging them, encouraging them to dare and to dream—that's the responsibility of the man in charge.

At Pepsi, we don't stand on form. We make phone calls instead of write memos. We talk business in the halls and in the men's rooms. On rare events when we need to send something to a co-worker, we don't wait for mail boys—we bring the thing up ourselves.

So I'm "Roger," not "Mr. Enrico." If my secretary's away from her desk, I'm likely to answer my own phone; whether she's there or not, I tend to place my own calls. I've got a Macintosh computer on my desk, courtesy of John Sculley, and if I have a letter to write, I'm much more likely to bang it out there than to dictate it.

We're not all-the-way-casual—as in most big companies, you can tell our executives, male and female, by their conservative suits and starched white shirts. But when you're working as a team, you spend a lot of time together. And in that kind of culture, with that kind of commitment, your energies get directed to results, not to observing rank. We also tend to talk business at events that other, saner people would call parties.

Which is why, in retrospect, I'd say the seed for our first "leadership marketing event" of the 1980s was sown at John Sculley's 1982 Christmas party.

It was a beautiful evening at the home John designed himself in Greenwich, Connecticut. Just enough of a dusting of snow on the ground to get everyone in the Christmas spirit. Between greeting old friends and making some new ones, I talked a lot with Alan Pottasch. And, because I was working up a hypothesis, I was kind of pushing him.

"We can take some liberties now," I said. "Maybe we don't have to keep batting people over the head with 'In nationwide taste tests more people prefer the taste of Pepsi over Coke.' Now that we've got the Challenge pretty much everywhere, why don't we move to advertising that's more imagery-oriented and yet retains a competitive, product-superiority theme without all of the legalese?"

"I think that would be just puffery," Alan replied. "Like saying, 'We're the Best,' without any substantiation—consumers don't pay much attention to those kinds of ads."

"Think about it, Alan. If we never had done the Pepsi Challenge it would be puffery. But the Challenge gives us the credibility to take some liberties—we can afford to be less direct and more entertaining."

"Maybe," Alan mused. "I never thought of it that way."

I couldn't be more specific—and it *was* Christmas—so we let it go at that. But I left the party with the feeling we had a glimmer of something.

Alan and I didn't have a chance to follow up on that

conversation. We were, you recall, too busy retooling the "Pepsi Now" campaign. Then, when we came back from the convention, we set to work fixing the Diet Pepsi commercials.

Only I wasn't interested in just fixing the commercials. I wanted a totally new campaign. And a curious thing happened. I got one instantly out of the back pocket of the agency. No more European filmmaking. Now the theme was "Sip into Something Irresistible."

The idea of this campaign was to do for women what the Miller Lite spots had done for men: focus on relaxation and comradeship. In one spot, three women were going into a boutique on their lunch hour; in another, as their dates cooled their heels downstairs, the women were getting ready to go out. It was all very real, very natural. And BBDO had a great piece of music by Peter Cofield behind it.

We loved the whole package. So did our bottlers. So did the public. And thanks in large part to those ads, Diet Pepsi was once again a mainstream soft drink. Feminine, perhaps, but definitely not Tab.

In fact, we were pleased to have a good lineup of ads for the year ahead. And considering what we'd put BBDO through, we decided we owed the agency and all the other people who worked on these commercials a party. So we threw a bash at the Olympic Tower. And afterward, Allen Rosenshine, Phil Dusenberry, John Sculley, Alan Pottasch, and I went out to dinner at Le Perigord on Manhattan's East Side.

This was my first time at Le Perigord and I must admit I was dazzled. It's a beautiful place, elegant in an understated sort of way. Allen Rosenshine was obviously well known here. He huddled with the maître d'—no menus for this group—and the chef proceeded to create one of the best meals I've ever had. Course after course arrived at our table, each one more interesting and more beautifully presented than the last.

Inevitably, we got around to one of my favorite topics: What is great advertising? Lord knows, this was a conversation we'd had often at Purchase. But because we rarely got a chance to sit down with Dusenberry and Rosenshine and kick it around, our questions were pretty basic. Like, how much does it cost to get a song written? Phil explained that it cost $50,000 for this guy, $10,000 for another—he wasn't tossing off astronomical figures.

At this point, John said, "We're not saying we don't have wonderful music. We do. But think what it would be worth to us to have a song like 'New York, New York'—*before* it became

'New York, New York.' What would it cost to hire that songwriter?"

Phil shrugged. "Fifty thousand? Three hundred thousand? Half a million?"

"Okay," John said. "Say it's half a million—would it be worth it? If you got something so extraordinary it then became a popular song?"

"I don't think it would make a lot of difference," Phil said. "The guy who writes a hit has usually written a thousand other songs. 'New York, New York' came out of a Martin Scorsese movie that was only a cult favorite. In the movie, the song was Liza Minnelli's. But I'll bet no one really paid much attention to it until Frank Sinatra recorded it. So you see, there are no guarantees."

This seemed very sensible. If what we wanted was to put better music behind the images we were already using, we were already working with the best. The idea of changing the visuals—of hiring a songwriter who was also a singer who was also a star—didn't occur to any of us. And why should it? We were selling soft drinks, not records.

So we moved on.

"How about Steven Spielberg," I asked. "Could we get him to direct a commercial?"

"Never," Phil said.

"How about other big directors—Lucas, Coppola?"

"They don't do commercials. Only English directors do."

Another conversation that didn't lead to a breakthrough. But it was simmering.

All during the exceptionally hot and dry summer of 1983, I watched our commercials. "More people prefer the taste of Pepsi to Coke," they said. And as you'd see people taking the Challenge, you'd hear, "They pick Pepsi, time after time after time." Then the music would come in, reminding you once again that now *is* the time for Pepsi.

The hot weather was great for our business; sales surged throughout June and July. But despite the glowing reports I received from our sales team every week, I had an uneasy feeling about the effectiveness of our advertising.

They were about as well done as semi-Challenge, semi-imagery commercials ever could be. But they weren't exciting—and by trying to sell with both product superiority and imagery, they didn't do much of a job with either. It was clear we weren't going to find the answer here. Nobody could make truly wonderful advertising pulling this heavy a ball-and-chain around.

I asked Dan Clark, our vice president of brand marketing, and John Almash, our director of marketing research, to do some imagery research—to find out what consumers thought about us and Coke, so we could build on our strengths and Coke's weaknesses.

Dan Clark is one of our most talented executives. He's worked for PepsiCo ever since he graduated from Dartmouth's Tuck School of Business Administration in 1973. He lives with his wife and children in the home he grew up in and appears to be the very embodiment of the button-down look—but there's nothing traditional about Dan's imagination, or his zest for taking piles of numbers and data and reducing them to their comprehensible essence.

John Almash was the ideal marketing-research whiz to do this work with Dan. We lured John away from General Foods in 1981 with the promise that he could build—from scratch—a total research and analysis team here. That was so tantalizing an offer that John was, in turn, able to lure a lot of very good people with him.

Now Dan and John were going to have a chance to do some truly important work: researching our consumers, then using that research as a significant basis for changing our business.

This is not simple work. When consumers make choices among soft drinks, they're really making three choices. First they decide on a soft drink instead of juice, water, or milk. Then they choose cola versus non-cola. Only then are they at the choice between Pepsi and Coke and the other available brands.

What Dan and John did was assemble seventeen groups composed of people who identified themselves as loyal Pepsi or loyal Coke users. Some were in Cincinnati, which is heartland Pepsi territory. The rest were in Dallas, where Coke rules. In both cities the questions were the same: What do you like about Pepsi/Coke? What sort of company do you think Pepsi/Coke is? What sort of values does Pepsi/Coke suggest? What don't you like about Pepsi/Coke? The results confirmed everything we suspected.

There was a clear perception that Pepsi was a young company, with new ideas. We were exciting, innovative. We were perceived as growing faster, with a good shot at becoming the number one soft drink company. Our negatives were that we were brash and maybe a little pushy.

The positives on Coke were all about Americana. Coke was

"the real thing." They owned what I call the "warm fuzzies"—the Norman Rockwell imagery of family and flag. On the minus side, Coke was old, stodgy, arrogant, and a bit corporate.

Now, the idea is to build on your positives and your competitor's negatives in such a way that they can't respond. Our advertising wasn't doing that.

But could we really walk away from Pepsi Challenge? From the most famous taste test in history? Would PepsiCo top management buy it? Could the advertising agency come up with something better?

I weighed these questions and decided we'd never know the answers unless we tried. So, at our midyear operating review with Kendall and Pearson, I ran the idea up the flagpole. No one saluted, but no one pulled it down, either.

With that—as far as I was concerned—the Pepsi Challenge was dead. Then, for good measure, I killed the use of jingles.

I didn't want just a new advertising campaign. I wanted one great new commercial after another. Jingles force you into formats. Formats are umbrellas. They protect you from uncertain weather, but they also block the view. The idea was that our advertising people should get wet, if necessary, in the pursuit of ads that were, without exception, breakthrough. The only through-line permitted would be our strategy—a triumphant return to the Pepsi Generation.

"You want to be 'leading edge,'" Allen Rosenshine said.

I did. Wanted to go there so badly, in fact, that I asked him to do a "white paper" on the idea.

Twenty years earlier, not long after BBDO got the Pepsi account, the agency did a white paper for us. It was called "The Necktie Memo," and it's a classic.

The memo never mentions soft drinks. It's all about neckties. Paragraph after paragraph, it asks why men spend so much time and agony buying ties. Are ties essential? Not at all. The only purpose they serve is to express the personality of the buyer.

Which leads to the point of the memo: The necktie doesn't make the buyer feel good about the manufacturer of the tie; it makes him feel good about *himself*. So don't extol the virtues of your product. Extol the virtues of the consumer who selects your product. Find out who he is; then praise him for being himself.

Allen Rosenshine's 1983 "white paper" said pretty much the same thing. It also said we'd put Pepsi on the leading edge of what was happening. And we'd show that leading edge through the eyes of youth. Not just for teenagers—we'd appeal to everyone, using young people as the vehicle. They're fun; they're exciting; they're innovative. We'll stake out territory that Coke can't or isn't willing to own.

It's all well and good to know where you want to go. The trick is actually to get there. Though I feel I have given Alan Pottasch and BBDO clear direction, and Allen Rosenshine has, from the beginning of our discussions, been clear that the advertising should take us to the leading edge, we can't know until we see the storyboards for our 1984 commercials if the dozens of people who work on our advertising have gotten the message.

In October, as I anxiously wait for Phil Dusenberry to arrive to show us the results of their creative work, I begin to realize that our meeting may well be the most important of my presidency. For in the minds of our employees and bottlers alike, it has become commonplace to say that "Enrico will either make his mark—or miss it—on what he does with Pepsi advertising."

As Phil and Alan Pottasch stroll into the conference room, I sense that their confidence is only skin-deep today. They're nervous too. And they're wondering: "Did Enrico really know what he was doing when he killed the Pepsi Challenge? Will he really like commercials without jingles? Is the view from the cutting edge perhaps a bit too rich for his blood?"

Today, there are no pre-mumbles. The questions are too urgent, the desire for each of us to find out if he's communicated effectively too strong. Phil just opens his folder, takes a deep breath, and, in a whisper that makes his everyday conversation seem like a shout, presents the storyboards. And those boards knock us off our chairs.

There is "Shark," an animated fin moving through a beach jammed with umbrellas while music from *Jaws* plays. Only at the end do you see that Pepsi's customer isn't a shark but a kid carrying a surfboard.

There is "Basement Visitor," which shows a young girl's mother chastising her for drinking so much Pepsi. The young girl goes to her closet and tells her extraterrestrial friend to cool the cola intake.

There is "Soundtruck," in which an entrepreneurial kid in a van broadcasts the sound of a Pepsi fizzing in a glass to thousands of sweltering beach-goers.

There is "Reflections," a hymn to a motorcycle's shiny gas tank, its rearview mirror, and the reflection of a can of Pepsi.

Then there is "Spaceship," which shows an alien craft hovering over two soft drink machines, testing the two products—and beaming the Pepsi machine up.

"'Spaceship' doesn't say a word about Pepsi tasting better than Coke," I say, "and it's the best damn Pepsi Challenge commercial ever dreamed up. But all those special effects—a spaceship, a floating vending machine—how in God's name will you do it?"

"Oh, it can be done," Phil Dusenberry says, in his whisper of a voice.

And that's that. Except for one thing I'm still not sure of. The theme line.

I mean, would you leap out of your seat at "Pepsi. The Choice of a New Generation"? I didn't.

"We can't have that," I say. "It's too damn long."

"What's wrong with you, Roger?" Alan says. "Don't you remember 'You've Got a Lot to Live and Pepsi's Got a Lot to Give'?"

"Yeah—but this one's not as catchy."

A great many sighs around the room.

"All right, let's keep thinking about this," I say, in the interest of corporate peace. "Let's see if we can't come up with a better line."

And we break up the meeting. We're all on a high.

The BBDO people are even higher than we are, because despite all my pushing for breakthrough advertising, they've really been expecting me to chicken out. But I'm with them, beat for beat.

A few days later, Alan Pottasch, Dan Clark, Joe McCann, and I are sitting in my office, scratching our heads. Now we've got a new problem, a nice one to have but a problem nonetheless. It's that these commercials are so good we've got to find some *big* way to make people aware that we've changed. A prime mover event. A bit of leadership marketing.

"How can we make it like the original Pepsi Generation?" we ask ourselves. "Like when Kendall got Khrushchev to drink Pepsi in Moscow? And across the whole world, there were pictures of Khrushchev drinking that cup of Pepsi, with the 'Pepski Break' headline."

"We'll get all kinds of awards with these commercials," someone says.

"Great."

"Who cares?"

So we sit and ponder, trying to think of some way we can make news. Nothing comes.

And then, because the gods drink Pepsi, the phone rings.

CHAPTER 6

Hand in Glove

Years spent trying to get through to elusive people have taught Jay Coleman to save his important phone calls until five-thirty P.M. At that hour, he believes, secretaries have gone home, leaving their bosses unprotected. When phones ring in executive suites, CEOs answer them themselves. And before they know what's hit them, Coleman's pitching a blue streak.

Patti Giordano is an exceptional secretary. She gets me to all the meetings I've forgotten about, knows who to wave into my office even when the door's closed, and is shrewd enough to avoid me on Monday mornings, when I'm feeling the ravages of a weekend without coffee. And another thing—she doesn't cut out early.

This disappoints Jay Coleman. But he recovers quickly and introduces himself. He is, he says, the founder and president of something called Rockbill, which brings rock groups and corporations together. Does Patti happen to like rock music?

Like it? *Loves* it.

"Well," Jay says, "maybe you've seen some shows we set up."

"What shows?"

"Oh, the tour the Rolling Stones did in '81 that Jovan sponsored. Earth, Wind and Fire. The Charlie Daniels TV special. Rod Stewart. Hall and Oates."

"Not bad."

"Really."

"Why are you calling Roger?"

"I'd like to come in," Jay says, "and talk to him about sponsoring Michael Jackson."

"What's your number?"

A few minutes later, Patti brings my phone messages in. Among them is Jay Coleman's. Though I've never heard of him before, I call him right back—after all, I had heard of Michael Jackson.

"Jay. Roger Enrico."

There's a little silence on the other end. Unknowingly, I've just trumped Jay at his own game.

"Roger, thanks for getting back to me."

"What's this about Michael Jackson?"

"You've listened to 'Thriller,' his new record?"

"Yes," I lie.

"Well, it's taking off. And he's doing another with his brothers that'll come out next summer. And Don King's convinced him to do a tour with them. I thought this could be good for Pepsi."

"We're interested," I say. "When can you come up here?"

"Whenever."

"How's eight forty-five tomorrow morning?"

"Uh . . . fine."

The next morning, Jay Coleman shows up. I'm in a great mood. It's a beautiful fall day in New England, the foliage beyond the PepsiCo sculpture gardens outside my window is at its most spectacular, and maybe—just maybe—we're going to get the big event we need to launch our new advertising campaign.

Jay's got an M.B.A. type along with him. The B-school guy will, it turns out, depart without uttering the first word of the jargon-filled presentation Jay hired him for.

On the couch in my office, Alan Pottasch fidgets impatiently. He's not here under protest, but he's hardly thrilled at the prospect of spending the morning with this curly-haired guy with the thick moustache.

"You know, Roger, I've been trying to work with Pepsi for seven years," Jay begins. "It's sort of funny. One call to you, and here I am."

"Yes," I say. "And we are very interested to hear all about Michael Jackson."

Now seven years of suppressed pitch start pouring out of Jay. He tells us how he developed *Rockbill* as a fold-up poster-magazine in the late 70s, with four pages of editorial on one side and a big picture of a group like Pure Prairie League on the other. In the center of the picture, on the table, is a big bottle of tequila—the sponsor. This worked well, and soon he was convincing Jovan Fragrances that the Rolling Stones have 100 percent awareness with Jovan's target group, and that if Jovan wanted to glom on to that, $500,000 would buy sole tour sponsorship. He goes through a number of other stories. Then, as we move into the second hour, he starts on Michael Jackson.

The previous summer, Jay says, Michael's managers approached him—for the second time in as many years—about arranging tour sponsorship for Michael. This time, they said, it's for real. They showed him the record cover of "Thriller," which wasn't out yet, and played him a couple of songs. Jay remembered how "Off the Wall," Michael's last album, sold 6 million copies and yielded four hit singles. This album is just as good and should do just as well—which is a solid basis for soliciting corporate support.

So, Jay approached some folks in Pepsi-Cola's promotion department, figuring that going through the chain of command was the way you got things done in a big company.

"We're not sponsoring music tours," our people said.

Then Jay went down to Atlanta—to the Coca-Cola chain of command. With twenty-five people listening, he pitched the Jacksons.

"An interesting ethnic opportunity," the Coke people concluded.

Then they passed.

Comes the spring of 1983, and Jay got a new client, Simon and Garfunkel. The duo was reuniting after a decade apart. Jay thought: Baby Boomers, Yuppies. Then he thought: Pepsi Free. Good thinking—Yuppies like Pepsi's no-caffeine cola a lot.

Jay took this idea to the Pepsi Free brand manager. He thought it was great and passed it on to Dan Clark. Dan Clark brought it to me. I shot it down.

I mean—$500,000 for a bunch of Yuppies in Central Park? Where's the value? It's not for a series of commercials, just for one concert. And $500,000, in the spring of 1983, sounded like a fortune to me.

The Pepsi Free brand manager told Jay I'd killed the deal. What the hell, Jay thought: I've never sold anything to Pepsi anyway. He took the Simon and Garfunkel idea to Volkswagen. Volkswagen went for it. All they wanted was for Simon and Garfunkel to pose for pictures with a VW Rabbit. But no way was Paul Simon going to pose with *anything* made in Germany. Bye-bye, Volkswagen.

Now Don King called Jay. If ever two people are not likely to know each other, it is the wild-haired, stop-me-if-you-can-get-a-word-in boxing promoter and this bridge between rock and Madison Avenue. But a year earlier, through a concert promoter who dabbles in boxing, King had indeed met Coleman. And Coleman had helped set up a five-year, $32 million television deal for King's fight program. This had fallen apart, but left King feeling very good about Coleman.

"Jay," he said, "you are the second-greatest man on the face of the earth."

From Don King, there is no higher praise. And now Don King was in the music business. Sort of.

What's happened, he said, is that Michael Jackson and his manager have parted. Which is right on, because the greatest musician on the planet deserves the attention of the most excellent promoter in the galaxy. Don has, therefore, rushed out to Los Angeles, invested $500,000 of his own money in the Jacksons, and gotten every last one of them to sign a contract with him. Joe Jackson, Michael's father, will continue to be the Jacksons' nominal manager. But Don King will set up the tour.

"I've been hearing about this tour for two years," Jay said.

"This is a *happening* thing," exclaimed Don. "And you, my dear main man, are just the white boy who can walk into a corporation and tap them for the change."

"How much?"

"Five big ones."

"God damn!"

"Five mill, Jay."

"Where'd you get this figure? Did Michael tell you he wants five million, or did you make it up?"

"Five mill, Jay," Don said, confirming the latter.

"Don, the *Rolling Stones* only got half a million."

"This is *Michael Jackson*," Don intoned. "He is bigger than God."

"Don, the biggest deal in Madison Avenue history—Alan Alda for Atari—is only a million."

"Five mill, or no deal."

Jay sighed.

"The obvious place to take Michael is to a soft drink company," Jay said. "Cars, liquor—for a dreamy, clean-living kid like Michael, these make no sense. He needs a product that's soft, cuddly, harmless, and fun. And that's soda."

"Gotcha."

"Little problem here, Don."

"Tell me."

"I've already been to Coke and Pepsi about the Jacksons."

"Yeah?"

"They said no."

"Jay, you are looking at a ten percent commission on five million dollars. You'll do fine."

Don hung up. And Jay, deciding that the only way *this* deal could be done was to ignore the chain of command, called me.

Jay doesn't tell me how much Don wants for the Jacksons. He shows the tape of the Motown special and Michael's videos for "Beat It" and "Billie Jean." Mostly, he's just pitching like crazy—music marketing, the way the Jacksons can kick off a long-term thing, target-group identification, like that. I can see that Jay and I are on different tracks. And the only way to get him totally on mine is to tell him yes, we're interested in all that good stuff—here's a little money and come back in a few weeks with some recommendations on a music marketing strategy. So I do that.

"Now," I say, "let's get back to Michael Jackson. You haven't told me how much."

"Five million," Jay finally blurts out.

It doesn't bother me. Mostly because I don't believe it. I'm thinking $2 million—maximum.

Jay pitches some more.

"Look, we're ready to go," I say.

"You're interested in Michael?"

"Jay, for God's sake, I told you that hours ago! Yes, we're interested in Michael. We want to start on it right away."

Jay's a little surprised. He can't believe he's *that* great a pitchman. He doesn't yet realize that I'm thinking about Michael Jackson as a way to draw attention to our new campaign.

And I'm thinking about how good Michael would be as an attention-getter for Coke's campaign—a thought that makes me want to close this deal yesterday.

"How soon can you set up a meeting with Don?" I ask.

"Right away."

"Good. Leave the videos here."

Jay leaves. Alan and I watch the videos again. And again.

" 'Beat It' is a little . . . violent," I say.

"Compared to what?"

Good question. What, after all, do I know? I'm not the world's most with-it rock fan. Put the best album of the year on, and it's possible I'll think it's no big deal. And these are the first music videos I've ever seen.

But you don't have to be an expert to know what you're looking at here. Because this kid is not only about music. The music is fine, the beat is flawless, and the orchestration Quincy Jones has surrounded it all with couldn't be improved on. With Michael Jackson, though, it's all in the visuals. Turn the sound off, and you're still going to jump out of your chair.

Alan and I watch the Motown special again. Everything we feel about the videos, we feel double about this. It's live—no retakes, no cutting every two seconds, no Bob Giraldi filling the frame with fabulous sets and perfectly choreographed dancers. This is pure Michael. And he just comes through the screen. The world has never seen anything like this guy dancing.

He's magic. We've got to sign him.

Many important personages have come to PepsiCo headquarters in Purchase. None of them made the entrance Don King did.

A land yacht of a limo pulls up, and out steps this man in a white fur coat that has to cost as much as the car. King's pearly-gray hair has been freshly electrocuted and is now reaching the sky. Around King's neck is a blindingly shiny necklace, on which hangs his logo, a crown with DON on top, just in case you might forget he is *the* king.

Such a man does not come quickly through the halls. "Hi, everybody, I'm Don King," he tells one and all.

Some of them already know this. A few go, "You've got to be kidding."

Patti finally gets Don upstairs. She stashes him in the conference room and hurries into my office.

"Roger," she says, "you're not going to believe this."

I go into the conference room, unsure if I'm supposed to be intimidated, amused or what. One thing is certain. In a Paul Stuart suit, white shirt, and striped tie, I'm definitely underdressed.

I'm not alone with Don. Jay Coleman's there, as are Dan Clark and Alan Pottasch. And Pam McGuire, one of our attorneys. She's seen some conference rooms before and a good many tough negotiations. But she's never seen anybody like Don King in one.

To no one's surprise, Don opens the meeting. Michael Jackson is not mentioned. Don King's method, we soon learn, is to promote Don King first and whatever he's selling second. So we get Don and Ali and the "rumble in the jungle" and the "thriller in

Manila" for a good twenty minutes. The whole globe tuned in! And in the jungle, where the natives don't have TV, round-by-round accounts of fights Don has promoted go from village to village by *drum*! Can we appreciate this? Do we get the significance? Don King isn't a promoter—he's a *communicator*!

"Great," I say. "What about Michael Jackson?"

Don now turns his attention to Pepsi-Cola. Naturally, it's his favorite soft drink. More, it is the soft drink of light and truth, the elixir of life. With his help, the world will know that. He will—yes, he *will*—get Pepsi-Cola to the Great Wall of China! Yea, even to the heart of the jungle. Remember those drums? Well, they're going to be pounding out Pepsi's message soon.

"Sounds good," I say. "Which brings us to Michael Jackson."

Wrong! It brings us back to Don King. Now we hear the back-story about Don. The rough-and-tumble childhood. The man-slaughter conviction. The subsequent pardon. How he fought the fight promoters to bring boxing into the twenty-first century. How they fought back. And how, despite adversity to make Jesus weep, he triumphed.

"Now I look around me," Don says. "And I am proud that I struggled and toughed it out. Because now, I'm here. You don't see many blacks who made it like I have. And you sure don't see many blacks in rooms like this."

Don clearly doesn't know the first damn thing about our company, which was sponsoring minority scholarship programs and had black executives long before he promoted his first fight. But I decide to let it go.

"Then you and I ought to get along pretty well, Don," I say. "Because I'm an Italian who made good. You don't see many Italians running the show in rooms like this, either."

On the far side of the table, Jay Coleman's moaning. He's sure the deal's dead. No way would the president of a major company see eye to eye with a fellow like King.

But Jay is wrong. I appreciate people who do big things. Despite his lengthy monologue, King *is* a mover and a shaker. And besides, he's got something I want—Michael Jackson.

"Here's the deal," I say. "We want Michael, but we're not going to pay five million dollars. Nobody's ever gotten that much for a commercial. It's outrageous."

"Yes, it is," Don says cheerfully. "But that's what it's going to take. Because that's what it's *worth*. This is, you know, the biggest tour in the history of the world. Four hundred million people will see it."

"Fine. We love that. Love it all. Just help us get to a more reasonable figure."

At this point, Don decides to share a little problem he's got.

"Ah, Roger, if we can only move quickly and agree on this five million, we would both be *so* happy," he says. "You see, Michael's got a whole bunch of people around him. Lawyers all over the place, you know? Believe me, there are a lot of different groups fighting for this and that. Now, I am with his mother and father. I do what they want me to do. But these lawyers—well, I think they've gone to Coke. And the thing is, we've all agreed to have a press conference next month. We're going to announce the tour, and we're going to announce the tour sponsorship. I'm being straight with you—if the lawyers pull a Coke deal together because you and I are arguing about a couple million dollars, I'll have to go along with that. So we must come to an agreement very, very quickly."

Something inside tells me to believe him. "Okay," I say. "Pam and Alan will negotiate for us. You guys get together and get it done ASAP."

The meeting ends. I go back to my office and immediately look up every five-syllable word Don has used. To my amazement, these are real words. And he's used them all correctly. But that doesn't change my mind about the deal. I'm still convinced that when the ink dries, Michael Jackson and his family will get no more than . . . well, maybe $3 million.

Negotiations begin. Alan, who thinks I'm crazy, has very little trouble telling Don we're not paying $5 million. Don and his attorney hold firm. Pam twiddles her thumbs—there's nothing to negotiate. Slowly, very slowly, I'm starting to wrap my mind around the idea of $5 million.

I move closer to agreeing to this price one afternoon as I walk out with Dan Clark. Dan's very levelheaded and a clear thinker. At this point, I know, his take on the Jackson deal is mild amusement.

"How much did Coke pay for the Olympics?" I ask.

"Oh God, that was fifteen, maybe sixteen million dollars."

"And they were just the official soft drink, not the sole sponsor. Everybody was an official something-or-other. So on top of that, Coke has to spend a fortune to make their presence felt."

"For a third of the money," Dan says, finishing my thought, "we own the Jacksons."

All of a sudden, $5 million seems outrageous, but not ludicrous.

Joe McCann, our terminally sane vice president of public affairs, also saw the Jackson deal as a good one.

"Long after this contract with Jackson is over," Joe said, "people will remember Michael Jackson and Pepsi. It'll be just like Kendall and Khrushchev and Nixon drinking Pepsi in Moscow."

Great! Just what we were looking for! Visions of a big leadership marketing event danced through my head.

"Another thing," Joe continued. "It's not just a question of advertising. The Jackson deal would do a lot for morale here. We blew fructose for a while. We certainly blew aspartame. Nothing exciting is happening. People are beginning to feel like we're the gang that can't shoot straight. And whether you do this or not, you've got to do something that gets us over the hump."

Okay, okay, I'm convinced. The hook has been set. All King has to do now is reel me in.

Days pass. We make good progress—for our $5 million, we're getting the Jacksons for two commercials, the tour, and personal appearances at press conferences—but the closer Pam gets to the final strokes, the slower King's lawyer seems to work. By the morning of November 11, Pam is beginning to despair that this deal will ever be done.

November 11 is my birthday—a good reason to call Don King.

"I'm thirty-nine today," I tell Don. "I would really like to sign this contract before midnight."

"Roger, I'm going to give you the present of your life."

That morning, Alan Pottasch comes into my office.

"We're going to sign this deal today?" he asks.

"Looks like it."

"Have you told Don Kendall about this?"

"No."

"Don't you think you ought to?"

"Yes! Thanks, Alan—it completely slipped my mind."

"I think he's leaving for Russia tonight. You'd better call him now or you'll miss him."

Having saved my life, Alan leaves my office. I call Kendall. He's not in. I call him at home. In the background, I think I can hear the sounds of suitcases closing.

"Uh, Don, I'm doing something new, and I wanted you to know about it before you go off."

"Yeah?"

"We want to kick off this 'Choice of a New Generation' campaign in a big way, with a news event, that kind of thing. And there's this young fellow Michael Jackson. He's a singer, and he's very, very hot. And we think we can get him—and his brothers; he's going to do a reunion tour with his brothers—to be in our advertising."

"Sounds good."

"I've had them checked out. The reports came back *sterling*. These people haven't been near alcohol, much less drugs. They're very religious. Very family-oriented. They're not political. I see very little chance of embarrassment for us here."

"Great, Roger. Thanks for calling."

"Uh, one more thing, Don."

I take a breath.

"We're going to pay them five million dollars."

The pause that follows is like one of those nightmares in which you're falling, and you fall and fall and fall—you're never going to hit bottom.

"Will this get a lot of publicity?" Kendall finally asks.

"Yeah. I think so. I think it will get a fair amount."

Kendall pauses again. I tumble downward some more. This time, I think I can see the bottom. And I think: Gee, I've really liked working for this company.

"Well," Kendall says, "you know how I feel about these things."

I quickly review everything the chairman has ever said to me about wantonly spending millions of dollars. I can't think of one thing.

"No, Don, I'm not sure I do."

"You've got to do big things to keep the image of the product out there. Big news is what it's all about."

"Right," I say. "Right."

"If this helps our imagery, if it's going to do that sort of thing, I'm all for it."

"Don . . ."

"Yeah?"

"Have a good trip."

I also haven't yet told Vic Bonomo, head of PepsiCo's Worldwide Beverage Group and my immediate boss. But no sooner have I said *bon voyage* to Kendall than Vic calls me.

"What's this Michael Jackson stuff?"

"Uh, hi, Vic. How'd you find out about this?"

"The lawyers."

"We've been keeping it kind of secret," I say.

I take him through the idea. Of course, I leave the $5 million to the end.

"Goddammit! *Five* million!"

"Well, Vic, we think it's worth it."

"I don't know about that."

There's a little pause.

"I understand you're going to sign the contract today," Vic says.

"Hope to."

"Let me ask you a question, Roger: Just when was it that you were going to tell me about this?"

I didn't exactly have the answer to that. "Uh, today. Before we signed the contract."

Another pause.

"Look, do you have a record or *something* this guy has done? I'd like to listen to it over the weekend and see what we're buying for five million dollars."

"Sure thing, Vic," I say. "I'll send one up. But we've got to sign the contract today."

We send a copy of "Thriller" to Vic's office. I don't imagine he's going to be very impressed. And he's not.

The day passes without a word from Don King. I go home to New Canaan, pass the time with Rosemary and Aaron, pretending I'm really interested in my birthday cake. Around eight the bell rings. My heart jumps. But it's only a delivery man. He's got a big silver tray from Don King (you can tell—it has his not-so-subdued logo on it) and a birthday telegram. Nice. Where's the contract?

At ten I get a call from Pam. She's completely exhausted. But she's got something for me from Don. At eleven forty-five Don's limo swallows my driveway. Pam reels out. In her hand is the contract.

I'd like to say I read it over carefully, lawyer-style, one hundred words a minute. But I'm much, much too excited. On a Connecticut night so clear I can *see* Michael Jackson dancing his way into history, I sign the contract with a flourish.

My signing of the contract, of course, means nothing until the Jacksons sign. Don King flies out to California with the contracts on a Saturday. I fully expect he'll be back on Monday. Monday comes. Monday goes. I start to worry.

Don finally comes back. And there are the signatures. Joe and Katherine Jackson, the parents and managers. Tito, Jermaine, Jackie, Marlon, and Randy, Michael's brothers. And, in a huge script that fills almost a page, Michael Jackson's. You would think that Michael's the most enthusiastic of them all.

Just the opposite. Don filters the story of what went on in California through Jay Coleman. But I get enough to know that everybody signed right away—except Michael. Michael felt pressured. He really wasn't wild to do this tour. Given his own way, he would have stayed in his house with his animals, watched the royalties from "Thriller" roll in, dreamed his dreams, and maybe written some new songs. So it took King several days, with a lot of help from Michael's family, to get that last name on the contract.

When Michael finally signed, it was four A.M.

Don Kendall comes back from Russia. Alan goes over to fill him in on our advertising plans. And, to show him what $5 million buys, he brings along the Michael Jackson videotape. By the time Alan's finished explaining the advertising, Don's late for a meeting.

"Let me just show you a few seconds of this," Alan says.

He punches up the Motown special and there's Michael leaping through the screen again. Thirty seconds into the tape, Alan leans over to turn it off.

"Leave it on," Don says. "I want to watch this."

Outside, the people waiting for Kendall are getting restless. But Kendall watches all of Michael's act.

"Alan," Don says when it's over, "that is the most remarkable performer I've ever seen."

We felt pretty damn good about that.

All during this time, we're meeting with BBDO to work up the ideas for the Jackson commercials. They come up with a pleasant, behind-the-scenes feeling—all the Jacksons hanging out before a concert, then coming onstage. We approve it, and Phil Dusenberry and Alan Pottasch go out to L.A. to talk about it with Michael and his brothers.

The Jacksons couldn't be nicer. Michael takes Alan and Phil on a tour of his house and introduces them to his animals. Alan and Michael get to know each other a bit. And Phil and Alan break out the storyboards and show everybody what we'd like to shoot.

The Jacksons are fascinated to see themselves in the storyboards. Those little figures—that's *us*! Lots of enthusiasm. Everybody's psyched.

Alan and Phil return to New York just as pumped up. Now it doesn't matter that there are a slew of Pepsi, Pepsi Free, Diet Pepsi, and Mountain Dew commercials being shot and edited by the agency. This is the big one. And it's the one with the tightest schedule.

The earliest we can record the music track is early January. Okay, then, we'll have Bob Giraldi, who directed Michael's "Beat It" video, shoot it a week or so later. After that, though, it's an all-out crash. These commercials *must* premiere on the Grammy Awards telecast in late February. If they don't, we're all going to feel terribly stupid.

We are ready for the Jacksons' press conference at Tavern on the Green. It's just off Central Park West at Sixty-seventh Street, so it's easy for media people to get to. Because it's in the park, the area can be closed off from Michael's fans. And if it gets really crazy, it shouldn't be too difficult to move Michael out of there.

With "Thriller" starting to make the most monumental Christmas sales drive in the history of the record business, the New York police are thinking along the same lines; mustered outside the Tavern is the largest assemblage of blue uniforms I've ever seen. But the fans have stayed away. All the madness is inside.

It starts with the cameras. They're everywhere. One crew, in particular, seems to have total access, for it follows Don King as he comes backstage. At first, I'm impressed that Don is so newsworthy. About the third time he swings by with this crew at his heels, it finally dawns on me—Don owns this crew.

I'm anxious to meet Michael, but I know, because he's the star, he'll be the last to arrive. The rest of the Jacksons are here, so I go over to them and say hi. I've never met Michael's sister, Janet, who'd been featured on some of our Mountain Dew radio spots. This breaks a lot of ice, the whole family is terrific, and soon I'm chatting with them as if we've all known each other a while.

Still no sign of Michael, but Don says it's time to start. I go closer to the stage to watch Don do his stuff. Don doesn't do this right away. Instead, he starts things rolling with a videotape about the eighth wonder of the world, Don King Productions. Visible moans from the press. I think: Well, it'll only be three or four minutes. I think this four or five more times before the tape mercifully ends.

Now Don takes center stage. We're here, he says, to mark a great day in history: Don King's debut in the music business. No more Mr. Boxing. From this day forth, he's Mr. Entertainment. And how nice it is that so many of his friends are here to bear witness! Muhammad Ali! Larry Holmes!

As Don reels off these glittering names, I can see heads turning. And an undercurrent of voices: "Where? Where?" The laundry list of glitterati continues, minute after punishing minute of celebrity name-dropping. And very few of these people are anywhere to be seen! Maybe Don's going right over the heads of everyone present for the benefit of all the television cameras— as long as they don't pan the room, everything he says is History!

All this time, the Jacksons are right behind the stage. The doors are supposed to open; then the platform they're sitting on will move forward and they'll be on. While they're waiting, though, they get to hear what we hear: Don's hymn to himself. Not, it seems to me, the shrewdest way to handle your star.

Don finally tires of all this and turns the microphone over to me. Me, I'm quick. I welcome the Jacksons to the Pepsi family. I quote something Michael's told Alan and Phil about wanting to "make magic" with these commercials. And I'm off.

Michael and his brothers come onstage. Jermaine acts as spokesperson, and then Michael introduces his family. He's not comfortable answering questions, but he likes doing this—and he does it well. He's very appealing. Soon it's all over and we go backstage to take some pictures.

What do you say when you meet Michael Jackson? He's so shy he makes you shy. So we stand next to each other and don't say much of anything. After a bit, I make some small talk. And then Michael leans over and whispers in my ear.

And what he says is: "Roger, I'm going to make Coke wish they were Pepsi."

"Michael," I reply, "that is music to my ears."

CHAPTER 7

"When You Wish Upon a Star"

Then there's reality.

Some hours after the press conference, I find myself back at my room at the Palace Hotel, eyeballing the television set. Yes, there are Don and Michael. Flick. There they are again. Flick. And again. All these reports have one thing in common: None mentions Pepsi. It's just Michael Jackson and Don King, over and over.

I'm ready to kick the set in.

Next day in the papers—zip again. A few days later, in the trade publications, a mention. A little mention. This is what the biggest celebrity endorsement contract in history buys? Clearly, we've got to do something.

Joe McCann is more upset than I am. Joe's as energetic and intense as they come—"It can't be done" is not in his vocabulary. So it doesn't take him long to figure it out. There *is* one easy way to get some attention: Throw caution to the winds—let's tell everyone we're paying the Jacksons more money than anyone's ever been paid to do commercials.

We do. And the headlines roll in. So do letters from lots of little old ladies who think we're nuts. And on WNBC radio in New York, Don Imus, the morning deejay, calls me a clown. From him, that's almost praise.

But the press is having fun with all of this—*they* love what we've done and that's what counts. We are now *big* news. And they spell our name correctly: P-E-P-S-I. We love every minute of it.

The excitement among our employees builds daily. And all the disappointments and confusion of my first 180 days are rapidly becoming ancient history. Morale is visibly on an upswing.

Our bottlers—whose first reaction to our announcement of the Jackson deal was Michael who?—become quickly educated in the world of the here-and-now and rock and pop by their kids and their employees. Their enthusiasm and anticipation explodes.

I decide this is bigger than a new advertising campaign. Michael Jackson can be used to breathe a new aggressiveness into the entire Pepsi organization. A new spirit. A new attitude. Because we're not scheduled to have another bottlers' convention until 1986, I invent a mini-convention in New York to be held the week before we premiere our new commercials on the Grammy Awards telecast.

I call in our vice president of graphic arts, Frank Rupp. In addition to creating the Pepsi "look"—package designs, signs, truck designs, and the like—Frank produces our conventions and shows. Nobody does it better—and nobody's less flappable than Frank.

"I've decided not to wait until '86 to hold our next convention," I tell him. "I think this new advertising Pottasch is doing can energize the entire company. I want to have a premiere. A Hollywood-type premiere to showcase it."

"Sure, sounds great," Frank replies. "Where and when?"

"New York in the third week of February," I say.

This is mid-November. Frank flaps a bit.

Pepsi bottler conventions are not your normal run-of-the-mill, pump-them-up-with-dull-speeches affairs. These are big events with professional casts, original story lines, original music, and original choreography. Everything that goes into a major Broadway musical extravaganza goes into a Pepsi convention—and then some. Of course, as far as I'm concerned, I'm just having a little get-together with two thousand of my closest friends.

"I'd like to take over the Waldorf—where Don Kendall announced the birth of the original Pepsi Generation twenty years ago," I continue. "But just for our home base. I don't want to have our show there. I want a theater instead of a ballroom. And not just any theater. It's got to be a legendary place, because we're going to make history.

"Make it Lincoln Center or Carnegie Hall, and make it black-tie. I want this to be a night to remember."

Frank Rupp catches the spirit of the occasion and cheerfully ignores the impossibility of this request. "Roger, it'll be a killer," he says. And off he goes to lock in the New York State Theater at Lincoln Center for February 25.

Early in December, I go to Houston for a meeting of the Pepsi-Cola Bottlers' Association. Considering the rocky start of my presidency, I feel I've got to show our bottlers I really do intend to lead this company. And by that, I don't mean only by spending a fortune on the Jacksons.

"When you return home, you should have an invitation on your desks," I tell the bottlers. "It's not just for the unveiling of a new advertising campaign. It will be the premiere of a new Pepsi-Cola Company. My friends, we're going to take this business on a roll."

I can't stick my neck out farther. No. Strike that. I can.

I'm so up to my tail in alligators that I take less than thirty seconds to tell Kendall what we're doing: the New York convention, the Grammy advertising premiere, and, oh, by the way, a little party for a few hundred bottlers, employees, and important retail customers in Los Angeles before and after the Grammy telecast. Does Kendall even hear me? If he does, I'm too rushed to notice.

Now Don Kendall goes to a dinner in New York. Tom Wyman, the chairman of CBS, which telecasts the Grammy Awards, comes over to him and says something about the premiere we're having at Lincoln Center and our little event in L.A. on Grammy night. And Don's a bit embarrassed because he doesn't know what the hell Wyman's talking about.

Now there is one cardinal rule I'd like all you future company presidents out there to remember forever: Never, I repeat never, embarrass the chairman of the board.

Kendall, to put it mildly, is upset. He calls while I'm on the road, in the middle of one of the thousands of details necessary to run a business like Pepsi.

From our conversation, I sense that basically he's trying to determine what's going on—not with our advertising plans but with me. Is it ego? Do I have to be king so badly I can't let anyone play in my game? Can this just be written off to inexperience, or am I too green to run this show at all?

As soon as the phone cools, I call Alan Pottasch. He's worked with Kendall for more than twenty years. Kendall trusts him to tell the truth. I ask Alan to go over to Kendall's office and bail me out. And explain in detail everything we're doing. Alan goes right in to see Kendall.

"Don, don't worry about this," Alan says. "We've all been so busy, we're like a Chihuahua trying to bury a bone on a marble floor."

Then Alan tells Kendall that if he wants to stay closer to the details of what's going on, he ought to get closer to me. Give me direct access to him, because the chain of command doesn't work so well when it comes to communicating the fine points of what we're doing.

Kendall calls me back.

"Roger, I don't see enough of you," he says. "From now on, I'd like you to be in my office at least once every two weeks, if not more frequently. No one has to know about this, although it doesn't have to be a secret. I'll leave it up to you to make the appointments."

The crisis ends. But I dread the first visit. Should I make a presentation? Before I can decide, it's time to go to his office. And as soon as the door opens, all the tension disappears.

I start by mentioning a few things I'm doing. Don doesn't comment directly. Instead, he tells a story from his experiences running the Pepsi-Cola Company, or makes the most modest suggestions.

As the weeks and the sessions with Kendall go by, something remarkable happens. I learn what being a mentor—a coach—is all about. Kendall's the best damn mentor ever invented. He takes an interest in you as a person, not just as an employee. He expands your horizons not only on business issues but on what's going on in the world, what's happening in the arts.

My sessions with Kendall were as much about U.S.-Soviet relations as about relations with our Pepsi bottlers. As much about opera as about Michael Jackson. As much about the need for employees to have a sense of community involvement as about our profit-and-loss statement.

About a second ago, I caused this man to have an embarrassing moment in front of one of his few peers. Now he's treating me like a son.

I'm hooked. And even more determined to make this advertising premiere the most memorable night since Don Kendall himself introduced the Pepsi Generation at the Waldorf twenty years earlier.

Like everywhere else, it's very hard to get anything done at Pepsi around the holidays, so it's early January before Alan Pottasch and Phil Dusenberry tell me that Michael Jackson is having a change of heart. What kind of change? Well, it's hard to know exactly.

Don King, for one, seems to have fallen from the Jacksons' Christmas card list. We hear rumblings that the Jacksons are no longer sure that Don has what it takes to run a full-fledged concert tour.

We, of course, are the other targets of this purported change of heart. Michael's buddies—Paul McCartney, Jane Fonda— have been calling him. "Why are you doing *commercials*?" they ask. "People do commercials when they're looking at the downhill slope of their careers, not when they're shooting up like a rocket. You do these commercials, you'll get overexposed."

Are they right? By all the then-known laws of show business, of course they are. And Michael is freaked. Overexposure? This is a new one. All along, *he* thought the problem was the idea of endorsing a product!

Alan and Phil fly out to Los Angeles with revised storyboards. They also have a cassette of a song the agency has had written. The song's been recorded by a Michael Jackson sound-alike so Michael can get a sense of the whole package. Michael looks over the storyboards. He hears the song.

"Everything's fine," Michael says.

Alan and Phil grin like fools.

"There's just one problem," Michael says. "I don't like the music and I don't like these commercials."

"We can change the music," Phil says. "What's wrong with the commercials?"

"My face. I'm on camera the whole time. I don't want you to show me for more than a few seconds."

A brilliant solution to the question of overexposure—but not one you expect to pay millions of dollars for. Alan and Phil try to change Michael's mind. But Michael knows what he wants. And what he wants is a world-class commercial in which, as they read it, he does a cameo.

Alan and Phil come home and give me the bad news. I react appropriately: I panic. But why get upset about a little thing like Michael's on-camera time when John Branca, Michael's lawyer, is starting to emit the kinds of noises lawyers make when they are looking for a way to get their client out of a contract?

With this much on the line, I get personally involved.

Ever try to call a star? Even when you have the phone number, it's not easy. First, you've got to get past the answering service. Then there's the secretary. Somewhere, hidden behind moats and walls and guards, is the star, happily living in a world without phones and phone messages.

When I don't get through to Michael, we enlist Don King. One cheery thing about King's effort—I discover he's no more successful than I am.

Finally, I talk to John Branca. Yes, Branca says, there are problems. But he hints at a solution. Money. Another $5 million, to be exact. Because he has another endorsement offer, from Quaker Oats, on his desk for—don't faint—ten big ones.

"John, you've got to forget about that," I tell Branca. "We have a *contract* with you!"

Branca is too good a lawyer to deny this. On the other hand, his job is to do the best thing for his client. When I hang up, I don't feel he's about to pound a stake into the heart of this Quaker Oats offer.

Then I hear a rumor that the son of a Quaker Oats executive adores Michael Jackson. And he's had a vision: Michael endorsing Granola Bars. He's shared this vision with his dad, Dad's handed it over to his marketing folks, and Michael has supposedly decided that Granola Bars are somehow healthier than Pepsi. Then, too, there is that $10 million.

This is like *The Twilight Zone*. I call our lawyers.

"Call the people at Quaker Oats and tell them we're going to sue for interference in a contractual relationship or whatever. Tell them that you just don't go around interfering with somebody else's contract by offering more money. And be very, very clear that if this thing falls apart, we *will* have damages from them."

I have the feeling Quaker Oats didn't know that the Jacksons had actually signed a contract with us, because once they are so informed, that's the end of the $10 million offer. It's not, however, the beginning of our second honeymoon with Michael.

The date of the first filming approaches. We talk to Michael's lawyers and aides, but never to Michael. Slowly it becomes clear that nobody with the name Jackson is going to show up on the set.

We cancel the shoot and make noises—lawyer to lawyer—about the Jacksons' having to pay the $200,000 we've blown preparing to shoot the commercial that never was. Their lawyers don't seem to notice.

The best meeting we can arrange is between Alan Pottasch, Don King, and Joe Jackson, Michael's father. Alan packs a big

suitcase—who knows how long it will take to crack this code?—
and flies out to L.A. He pitches camp at the Beverly Hills Hotel
and soon enough is sitting around with Joe and Don.

"I think I know how to resolve this," Joe says.

"Do it . . . please."

Joe calls his wife and gets Alan invited to lunch.

Katherine Jackson doesn't ask if Alan comes with any culinary
preferences, so she makes fried smelts. As it happens, Alan is
not exactly partial to smelts. But you'd better believe he cleans
his plate this day.

And, over lunch, Alan and the Jacksons talk about their kids.
How tough it is to bring them up right. How wonderful you feel,
though, when you work and work to build ethics and integrity
into them, and then, one day, those aren't just words anymore.

For another advertising man, this might be a con job. But one
of the great things about Alan Pottasch is that he's a well-
rounded human being. His family *is* more important to him than
anything else in his life—and there's nothing he's more justifiably
proud of than his accomplishments as a father. The Jacksons, it
turns out, feel the same way about their kids.

Alan and the Jacksons conclude that Michael has a moral
responsibility to go through with this deal. We've announced it,
spent money, put our integrity on the line.

Katherine Jackson says she'll talk to Michael. She does. In a
day or so, Michael agrees to a meeting.

Phil Dusenberry flies out to join Alan at the meeting, which is
to be held at the Jacksons' home. Michael brings along John
Branca. Everybody lines up like chessmen.

"It isn't that I don't want to do this commercial," Michael says.
"I just think there are better ways to do it."

Alan and Phil say they are very open to Michael's ideas.

"I don't want to be on-camera very long—one close-up of no
more than four seconds. But there are other ways to show me
than push a camera in my face. Use my symbols. Shoot my
shoes, my spats, my glove, my look—and then, at the end,
reveal me."

A brilliant use of imagery. But now it's *four* seconds? And only
one close-up?

They kick this around for a while, not resolving anything but
not arguing either.

"What do you want to do about the music?" Alan asks.

"Well, I don't like the song you had written," Michael says.
"It's not big enough. Why don't you just use 'Billie Jean'?"

"Billie Jean"! Alan exclaims silently to himself: My God, he's just offered us "Billie Jean"! Well, why not use it? It's only the song of the year! And Michael's offering it like a free hors d'oeuvre!

"That seems like a good alternative," Alan says quietly.

Now all the other stuff—a few seconds or four, two close-ups of Michael or one—seems unimportant. We've got Michael and his best song, and he hasn't even asked us to pay for it. (Later, his lawyers requested a very reasonable fee. We were happy to oblige.)

Looks like we're back on track again. We may pull this one off after all.

The filming is rescheduled. Alan and Phil show me the revised storyboard.

The commercial starts with the Jacksons—but not Michael—drinking Pepsi and relaxing in their dressing room before a concert. There's a flash of Michael in front of the makeup mirror, and then we move behind the stage, where Michael's about to make his entrance, and we're tantalized anew with glimpses of Michael's look—his symbols. Then the set opens, and with a flash of fireworks, Michael dances and spins into a full-fledged concert, singing the reworded "Billie Jean" to a mob of screaming kids in the audience.

And then . . . but what's this? Ah, the *second* commercial. I've never seen this one before. It features Alfonso Ribeiro, the eleven-year-old dancer from the Broadway show *The Tap Dance Kid*. Here, he plays a Michael Jackson fan who can do all of Michael's moves perfectly. Only as he's moonwalking, he bumps into . . . guess who? And there's this beautiful moment between them before Alfonso and his friends break into a dynamite dance number with Michael and his brothers.

"They're magic," I say, borrowing Michael's idiom.

Jay Coleman calls. "You know, Roger, there's something Coke can do to neutralize you."

"What's that?"

"They can sign Lionel Richie."

I reach deep into my memory. "The Commodores? Isn't he the lead singer for the Commodores?"

"He *was* with the Commodores. Now he's out on his own. He's a hell of a talent—the singles are just flying off his album. He'd be great for Pepsi."

"Jesus, Jay, you know what we're going through with Michael."

"Yeah, but this will set you up for '85. Face it, you're going to need *something*."

"It's gonna cost. And we're about tapped out in the star budget."

"I know," Jay says. "But I just have a feeling about Coke. Look, Lionel's opening in Vegas. Why don't we go out Sunday and see him? If you go out there, I know he'll never forget it. And you can be back on Monday."

I sigh. I'd thought signing the Jacksons was it. It is just occurring to me that now, for better or worse, I'm in the entertainment business. It also occurs to me that Coca-Cola owns Columbia Pictures. That's a very large star-catching apparatus. Lots of people with contacts and lots of deal-makers out there in Columbia's Hollywood.

What have I got? Two advisers: my son, Aaron, and Jay Coleman. Aaron may be up on all the new music, but he also goes to school and has his own life. Hardly an entertainment wheeler-dealer. All I can expect from him is an enthusiastic "Cool, Dad," or a derisive "Not cool, Dad."

And Jay Coleman is a guy who I don't know very well and who isn't even on my payroll. He's been impeccable so far, but I don't see how we can keep our early lead in the battle for the stars with this combination.

All I may have done by signing the Jacksons is start a war in which I'm hopelessly outgunned.

"Bring a cassette," I tell Jay.

Allen Rosenshine, Phil Dusenberry, Alan Pottasch, Jay Coleman, and I fly out to Vegas. Most of the way out, I listen to Lionel's tapes. And I really like his music.

We meet Ken Kragen, Lionel's manager, then go to see Lionel's show. Two songs in, Allen Rosenshine and I turn to one another. Lionel Richie is a *big* idea.

After the show, we go backstage. Despite the crowd in his dressing room, Lionel is open, warm, delighted to see us. We manage to find a quiet corner amid the flow of well-wishers, security people, and the like. We talk about the possibility of a long-term relationship. Exchange views on education, community involvement, role models. Lionel's with us, beat for beat. He's articulate, intelligent, sensitive. Then we discuss Pepsi advertising—how Lionel might get involved.

For a long time, I've had this idea of a commercial that's not a commercial. It's a three-minute, maybe even a five-minute story. I'm not sure of the story line, but say it takes us through a day. Lionel seems just right for this idea. He thinks so too.

Within minutes, we've got the notion of Lionel as a kind of Pied Piper. What then? Well, we don't know. The point is that the approach fits.

I feel we're making a handshake deal right there. Nothing is said about money, but we all sense this can be done. And we agree to get together in Los Angeles in a week or so to hammer out the deal.

Michael goes into the studio to record the new lyrics for "Billie Jean." His brothers are supposed to be there with him. They're nowhere to be found. Michael works his butt off anyway.

His brothers materialize. The song is terrific.

A few days later, Walter Yetnikoff, the president of CBS Records, throws a huge party for Michael at the American Museum of Natural History in New York. I don't see Michael— he pops in for just a few minutes—but Alan Pottasch introduces me to Les Garland, a vice president of MTV. Inevitably, we talk about Michael. And Les offers to premiere the Jacksons' commercials on MTV free of charge, if we give him an exclusive.

Premiere them free of charge? Has anyone ever done that before? Sounds good to Alan and me. Now all we have to do is get the film in the can.

The Jackson party ends early. We're not quite ready to call it a night, so we move on to a Manhattan hotspot, Regine's. We joke around with Regine about Michael Jackson and Lionel Richie. Where will this roller coaster take us next?

"Well, you know, Julio Iglesias is being wooed by Coke," Regine says.

No, I don't know. But I do know Julio's a huge recording star. The Frank Sinatra of the Latin world. And I know something else. Walter Yetnikoff has recently decided to make Julio a recording star in America. Walter's tried this before and failed, but now he's going to put the full power of CBS behind Julio and will team him up with such non-Latin blockbusters as Willie Nelson and Diana Ross. Nobody's going to think Julio's a Latin music type when Walter finishes with him.

"We'd be interested in Julio," I say. "That is, if he hasn't signed with Coke yet."

"I know Julio," Regine says. "And I can call his brother, Carlos, and find out."

I think: What the hell am I going to do with three music stars? Where will this end?

But I say, "Sounds good. Thanks."

A few days later Carlos Iglesias calls me.

"What sort of deals do you make?" he asks.

"There's no standard deal," I tell him, "but right now, we're working on commercials. And if there's a concert tour, we like to be involved."

"I see." He's thinking about something.

"I certainly have a great deal of admiration for Julio," I say, "and we'd like to be part of making him as big a star in this country as he is in the rest of the world."

Carlos is still thinking.

"Actually, I'm having dinner tonight with a fellow from Coca-Cola," he says. "I don't know if we're going to reach an agreement or not, but we have been talking for some time."

"Who are you having dinner with?"

"Let me look." He goes and checks his calendar. "Let's see. It's Sergio Zyman."

Zyman! Well, now's as good a time as any to return the favors from Brazil. My palms tingle.

"Yes, I know Mr. Zyman," I say, completely deadpan.

"I don't know what to do, Roger. I might make the agreement tonight."

"If you did, Carlos, that would be all right. But I would like to talk a bit more. You know we're tied up with Michael Jackson— and Julio *and* Michael for Pepsi would put your brother in very good company."

"Roger, let me ask you: How much are you paying Michael Jackson?"

"Five million."

There's a long silence.

"Dollars?"

That's when I knew my friend Sergio would get indigestion after his dinner with Carlos. Maybe he'd cut the deal with Julio, and maybe he wouldn't. But whatever the outcome, I figured I'd just cost Coke a lot of money.

In mid-January we go out to Los Angeles to negotiate the Lionel Richie deal with Ken Kragen. Everything's straightforward and pleasant. Kragen says the numbers have to get a lot bigger than we were thinking, but we should have no trouble seeing why: He can't make a deal for Lionel that puts him in Michael's shadow. It's a question of stature. No one denies that Michael's hotter right now. A year from now, when Lionel's going to be our main spokesperson, that may not be the case. And even if it is, you don't want to rub that in.

This is a new one on me. But Kragen's sincere enough and we figure what the hell, Lionel *is* a big idea. So we work out some ways to make it worth bringing Lionel's fee up. He's doing a tour next year. Perfect. We want that. But he's also doing a tour this summer. Well, we're not so eager to divide our promotional energies between the Jacksons and Lionel, but what can we do? We'll back it. Lionel wants to do a TV special. Fine. We'll buy the ad time on it. Maybe even co-produce. Lionel wants to do a movie. Okay, we'll commit to running some promotions behind it that could be considered "several million dollars" worth of support.

In this way, Ken gets the dollar amount of the deal up beyond the Jacksons, but because some of our commitment is for projects that may not happen, we're really getting Lionel for about the fee we were originally prepared to pay. And even if some of the projects come off, we'll get a lot of added spin from them. Everyone's happy.

All this takes one day. Now it's time for the lawyers to create reams of paper again. There's no further need for me to stick around, so I return to New York. A few days later Jay Coleman calls.

"Coke has called Kragen," Jay says. "They want Lionel."

"So what?"

"He feels he has to go down and listen to them."

"Dammit! We have a deal. Have Kragen call me."

Kragen calls. I know he's going to be the diplomat. And although I'm hugely teed off, I know I'm going to be one too.

"Roger, my first responsibility is to Lionel," Ken says. "I really feel I have to do this."

"Look, you do what you have to, but let me tell you something: This is not a good way to start a relationship."

"I've made my decision. I've got to go."

"Okay, but would you do me one favor?"

"What?"

"Put your arrogance-antenna up. I know I'm their competitor and that makes what I'm saying less credible, but you'll be able to see it for yourself—they're often arrogant, they promise things they don't deliver, and on top of that, they won't give you a quick decision."

"If that's the way it is, Roger, I'm not doing business with them. Either there's a deal on the table or that's the end of it."

I feel a little better. I just can't see Coke committing to Kragen on the spot.

Kragen went to Atlanta, where he was greeted by Sergio Zyman and a committee of middle-management folks. As I hear it, Sergio announced that he wanted to make a deal right then and there. It would be a better deal than Pepsi could offer. And with that, Zyman left. His subordinates would now handle the details. Arrogance, thank God, was alive and well in Atlanta.

Kragen now faced a committee. And a committee is, as a British scientist once said, a cul-de-sac down which ideas are lured and then quietly strangled. This one was a little better than that.

First, Zyman's aide apologized to Kragen. Kragen should know they couldn't finalize a deal on the spot. Coke USA President Brian Dyson would have to approve it. Kragen looked around. Nobody in the room looked like Brian Dyson.

But, Zyman's aide argued, Coke can do better for Lionel than Pepsi can.

Why?

"Because we need him so badly."

You've got to give that fellow points for telling the truth.

The meeting ended without an offer, and Kragen flew off to Detroit, where he and Jay Coleman were working on a Kenny Rogers deal with Chrysler. We have a conference call.

"We'll have to hold up finalizing our deal," Kragen informs me. "Coke wants another week to make an offer."

Apparently Kragen's seen enough of my diplomatic side. He wants to see the other one? Okay, here it comes.

"Wait a minute, Ken. Let's cut the happy horseshit," I say. "You told me if they didn't have an offer on the table, that was it. Now you're putting *us* on hold. You can't have it both ways, my friend."

I do not, however, tell him what he can do with our deal.

A few hours later Kragen calls back. "I just talked to Lionel," Kragen begins. "Know what he said?"

"No, what?"

"What are you doing, Ken? We've started a hell of a good relationship with the Pepsi folks and we're not treating them the way we ought to be treating people we're going to be friends with for a long time."

I'll second that.

"You're acting like the guy who's just asked his best girl to marry him and before she can say yes, he notices a good-looking girl across the street. So he says, 'Excuse me, dear, but before you answer I want to make it with her first and see if it's better.' That's not how I operate. Pepsi's offered us a good deal. Coke's offered us nothing. I think you should call Roger back and tell him we've got a deal."

Well, score another one for the good guys.

It seems like a lifetime since we made our deal with the Jacksons, but at long last the cameras start to roll. Everything costs a fortune and takes forever. I don't mind. The set is tranquil. Too tranquil. And so, naturally, disaster strikes on the day we have five-thousand kids in the audience for the concert sequence. I'm not on the set. Somehow Alan and Phil don't feel the need for my input when the cameras start rolling.

Instead, January 27 finds me in Phoenix, Arizona. The Pepsi-Cola Bottlers' Association Executive Committee always has its winter meetings in nice warm places. The meeting goes smoothly; I get on an afternoon plane. I arrive home late at night. All the lights are on.

Rosemary runs outside.

"Roger! Alan Pottasch is on the phone. There's been an accident!"

At the PepsiCo offices we have a terrific gym—not that I've ever been in it. My idea of exercise is pacing. But I break the house record getting to that phone.

"Alan!"

"Roger, there's been an accident on the set."

I brace myself.

"There's been a fire."

"Are a lot of people hurt? Is—?"

"Michael got burned, Roger. It was his hair."

I slump. "Oh, my God! How bad is it?"

"I don't know. His brothers jumped on him and put it out right away."

"Where's Michael?"

"They took him to a burn center. They think everything's okay."

"You sure?"

"I'm not positive."

"What can we do to help?"

"I don't think there's anything. We have a lot of security. The set's under control."

I'm one question away from normal breathing.

"Alan, I hate to ask this . . . but did you get everything on film? Or was this the beginning of the shoot?"

Okay. It was a crass question. But remember, we're less than four weeks away from the bottlers' convention.

"It was one take too many," Alan says. "Giraldi's such a professional, he shot over and over and over. This was like the fourth take of Michael coming past the fireworks. Apparently one of them landed on his head, and the next thing we knew, his hair was on fire. It was really *frightening*!"

"Have you been to the hospital?"

"No way. There are reporters all over the place. You can't get near it."

"Look, Alan, I want you and Phil over there. I don't care how you get in, but you've got to see if there's anything we can do. You have got to let Michael know we're concerned."

I'm beat. I decide to wait for Alan's next call in bed. No chance of sleeping. Rosemary's watching *Nightline*. And the lead story is Michael's accident. Now I see the ambulance zooming off, and quick interviews, and some old footage of Michael, and an interview with Michael from deep in the archives. The tone is very "the phenomenon of Michael Jackson." It's like he's dead.

And I'm sitting there saying, "Please, God, don't mention our name. Please don't mention Pepsi."

Ted Koppel says the accident occurred during the filming of "a soft drink commercial."

It's well after midnight, but I've got to call someone. I choose Joe McCann.

"It looks like a disaster, Roger," he says. "I've got to believe, unless God is nice to us, this is going to be devastating."

With just a little encouragement, I can play this game too. "Michael's fans will never touch another bottle of Pepsi," I say. "There will be lawsuits."

The other line blinks. I leave Joe to contemplate fresh disasters while I take Alan's call.

"I'm at the hospital," Alan says. "Michael's all right."

"How do you know?"

"I'm in the waiting room with the family. And they're joking and laughing. Phil and I are the only glum and mournful people here. When Joe Jackson walked by, he looked at us and said, 'Why the long faces? The burn's the size of a half-dollar.'"

"Thank you, Alan. Go home."

"Try and stop me."

The next morning confirms my worst fears. Michael says nothing, but a spokesperson issues a statement that indicates a lawsuit is likely. And, by the way, that Michael didn't want to do these commercials in the first place.

The press wants our response. We don't know what to say. No question Michael was hurt during the filming of our commercial. But it doesn't, thank God, appear to be too serious. We want to do what's right—but we don't know just what that is yet. Our responses to the press reflect our concerns.

I fly to San Francisco for another, previously scheduled meeting with Pepsi bottlers. Guess what? Michael's accident is news out here too. And about to become more so, from the panic in Joe McCann's voice on the phone.

"Michael has told his people to release the footage of him catching on fire," Joe says.

"What!"

"He wants the press to have it."

"Jesus! To what *possible* end?"

"God knows."

By this time, I can believe any number of things. But I can't believe Michael would want to do this. I'm convinced that *if* Michael said to release the film, he hadn't thought it through. Anyway, it's not his to release. We own the film.

"What have you told them?" I ask Joe.

"I had our lawyers talk to theirs."

"Good. It's on film and videotape?"

"Yeah. They were using the video to check the camera angles."

"Get me a cassette."

It's a sunny and warm winter day in San Francisco. I pace my hotel room for hours waiting for the cassette to arrive. Up to one window and the breathtaking view of the bay and the Golden Gate Bridge. Up to another and the equally impressive scene of San Francisco's unique skyline. I'm just starting to think that maybe we can make this publicity work for us when the cassette arrives. I activate the VCR.

The video camera is right behind Michael as he comes down some stairs. Did the press reports say his *hair* was on fire? To me, it looks like his whole *head*! Big flames! Like a human torch!

No way can *anyone* see this footage—it's grotesque. I'm stunned. How can I change Michael's mind?

With more anxiety than I've ever felt in my life, I pick up the phone and punch the number for the only person I think can help—Michael's father, Joe Jackson.

"Joe, what do *you* think we should do about this problem?"

"What problem?"

"Michael's people tell us he wants to release the film with his hair on fire."

"Why would he want to do a thing like that?" Joe says.

"Beats me. Look, I'm calling you because I can't get through to Michael. Would you tell him this: I think releasing the film would be a terrible mistake, but it's his decision to make. If he calls me directly and tells me to do it, I will."

"I'll tell him."

"I know you see it's wrong to let that film out, Joe—but to help you with Michael, let me tell you why I think it's a bad idea. When you think of John F. Kennedy, what do you think of? Well, for many people, it's his assassination on the streets of Dallas. A moment so horrifying it haunts you forever. And I'm afraid that's how Michael will be remembered, if that fire footage ever got out. People might forget what a great performer he is—their memories will be overwhelmed by the sight of his head on fire."

I never hear another word about releasing the film.

It's a freezing February day on Madison Avenue. But in the BBDO screening room, high above the street, everyone's sweating as though he's in the Sahara Desert at noon. And not because Allen Rosenshine and Phil Dusenberry like to work in rooms with the thermostat way up—it's time to show us the rough cuts of the most expensive and daring commercials in our history, and everyone's very, very tense. Today, there are no pre-mumbles, there are no jokes. Just the awareness that the results of months of labor and millions of dollars will be judged in a few minutes. The lights dim. The film rolls.

"Shark," "Basement Visitor," "Soundtruck," and "Reflections" all amuse and delight us. And "Spaceship"—the commercial that shows a UFO beaming up a Pepsi vending machine and taking it back to its thirsty planet—puts lumps in our throats and joy in our hearts. No difficulty judging this advertising: It's fabulous. The money we spent? It's all on the screen. We don't, this day, begrudge a nickel—the sun has shone on all our advertising efforts.

"What do you think?" Dusenberry asks.

"This is just your basic outstanding advertising," I say.

Phil smiles. "Now would you like to see the Jackson commercials?"

No. Of course not. We'll just get a new ad agency if you don't roll that film. Phil starts with a ninety-second version of "Street." There's Alfonso, stealing your heart. And then Michael and his brothers come in and take it to a whole other level. The music gives you goose bumps. The film is rich, exciting. Dynamite.

And Michael Jackson's face is *all over it*—there's a *lot* more of Michael than the four seconds we'd agreed to.

Now Phil shows "Concert." Everything Michael wanted—the snippets of clothing and image that build a character—works brilliantly. The white glove looks fine. The music's a killer. Once again, we're way over the four-second limit on Michael's face.

"They're mind-blowing," I say. "But we're way too long on Michael."

"If there's any less of him," Phil says, "these won't be Michael Jackson commercials. They'll be embarrassments."

"I don't know about this."

"I don't usually get involved," BBDO Chairman Allen Rosenshine says. "But I'm with Phil. We can't let Michael dictate to us on our commercials."

More voices chime in. I think: This team has just created the best advertising I've ever seen. They want it to be the best advertising *anyone's* ever seen. They want me to back them up. And I'll be damned if I'm going to let them down.

"Yeah, you guys are right," I say. "But what if Michael balks?"

"How can he? These commercials are so special, he'll be just as excited as we are."

"Yeah, maybe you're right. And if he's not, the hell with him," I say, mustering all the macho feelings I ever had.

"What does that mean, Roger?"

"We'll walk away from the whole damn deal."

CHAPTER 8

Take a Message to Michael

Was I really willing to kill the Jacksons deal?

Absolutely.

If you'd asked me why, I would have given you Sound Business Reasons. I'd have cited the strength of our other "Choice of a New Generation" commercials—which were so terrific the Jackson spots were almost a distraction.

I'd have said we'd still have a strategic advantage over Coke. We wouldn't have to worry about Coke rushing in to sign the Jacksons—there wasn't enough money in the world to make Michael put himself through this process again.

And if we absolutely had to have a celebrity commercial, we could always make one with Lionel and worry about 1985 later. Anyway, it seemed we'd already cost Coca-Cola a fortune; according to industry gossip, Coke had to pay Julio Iglesias *$10 million*.

How much had we spent so far on the Jacksons? At most, $2 million. There was nothing in the contract giving Michael final cut. Sure, it gave him approval rights over the spots, but those were not to be "unreasonably withheld." And wasn't he being unreasonable? If we wanted, we could probably run them anyway or go after him for our costs. But even if we had to write off the $2 million, we still had an $8 million gain on Coke—I mean, name ten people under the age of twenty who are wild for Julio. Kids just aren't Julio's audience.

Those reasons *might* have convinced you that I was a hard-assed, by-the-numbers guy who really knew what he was about. Those reasons are bull. The problem was that I'd ceased to think

like the president of Pepsi USA. Now I was a filmmaker. I wasn't
going to let anyone outside the company—even someone who
packaged himself as brilliantly as Michael—tell my team what to
do. I had final cut.

Was I certifiable? Not close. But I certainly wasn't your model
of sanity. And what's worse, I didn't know it.

To no one's surprise, Michael doesn't want to sit in a
screening room in L.A. with us and watch the commercials. He
prefers to have a cassette sent to his house, where he can watch
them alone. Then he'll make his decisions and get back to us.

We decide that Phil Dusenberry should bring the cassette out
and watch it with Michael. Now, during the filming of the commercials Michael's been pressured plenty by Phil Dusenberry.
Take off your sunglasses. Turn this way. Move this way. Just
one more close-up to be sure we've got it right. Don't worry, we
always shoot this many close-ups even when we're only going to
use just one.

Phil, of course, was just doing his job—he wanted Michael's
commercials to be brilliant. Michael was just doing his job, too—
he wanted his spots to be magic.

Two highly creative and strong-willed people on the same set
may well make magic. Almost certainly, though, they'll create
some conflict. So, can Phil Dusenberry bring the cassette out
and wait for Michael's reaction?

Michael, who by now sees Phil as kin to a Nazi SS officer,
says, "Mr. Dusenheimer? No way."

Okay, we'll send a cassette out. And it won't be hand-
delivered by one of us. In a few days we hear from one of
Michael's aides.

"Forget it. This isn't the commercial Michael agreed to. You
guys are trying to pull a fast one."

"Like, specifically, how?" Phil asks.

"There's much too much of Michael's face."

"Well, we can fix that. What else?"

The aide can't explain what Michael objects to.

"Time out," Phil says. "We can't edit unless we know *exactly*
what bothers Michael. Can I talk to him, please?"

"No."

"I see. Shall I *guess* what he doesn't like?"

"That's up to you."

Phil's apoplectic. He hasn't been jerked around like this in
twenty-five years. Alan's apoplectic. He's coming into my office

every day and announcing the temperature in the Cayman Islands, where he has his scuba tanks and his early retirement house. I'm apoplectic. Mess around with my team, you're messing around with me.

I call Michael's father. I get his father's secretary. Unlike Michael's aide, she passes messages on. And Joe Jackson calls back.

"It's hard to edit film when we're here and Michael's there," I say. "But it's impossible to edit when we can't communicate directly with Michael."

"I don't know where Michael is."

"What?"

"He's old enough to take care of himself," Joe says. "He doesn't check in and out with me. But I'll see what I can do."

A few hours later Joe calls me back.

"Roger, I have Michael here," he says, "and I'm sure you guys can work things out."

There's a pause.

"Talk to the man, will you," Joe whispers to Michael. "Get on the phone."

A very soft voice comes on.

"Hi."

"Hey, Michael. How are you?"

"Okay."

"Good. Michael, if you'll explain to me what's wrong with the commercials, we can fix them."

"Well, these just weren't what I agreed to do, I mean, even with the compromises I made. Mr. Dusenheimer made me take my glasses off. I didn't want to take them off, but he said there would be only one close-up. And now I see lots of close-ups of me with my glasses off, and there's too much of me in there anyway, and there are too many of my spins. And the film is too dark. I don't understand that. I had to fight with Giraldi about the same thing when he made my videos—he makes everything so dark. Your Pepsi commercials are always bright and light. That's why I like them. I want my spots to be that way too."

"They haven't been color-corrected yet, Michael. It's still a video transfer. Don't worry—it'll be much, much lighter. Let's go through your other problems one at a time."

"There's too much of me in the concert. Way over four seconds on my face."

"Okay."

"And in the street commercial, I want bells when Alfonso bumps into me—like the sound of a wind chime."

"Okay."

"The street commercial . . ."

"Yeah?"

"It's magic, Roger. It's just magic."

The way Michael says this gives me courage to continue. He's not just trying to kill the deal with all this talk of spins and cuts and seconds and close-ups. He's a perfectionist. To be sure, he's freaked about being overexposed, but creative geniuses are sticklers for details.

"I spin twice in the concert film," Michael says. "I should only spin once."

"But those two spins absolutely make the commercial," I plead.

"I only agreed to one close-up spin. And you can't show my face for more than four seconds."

"I'm sure it's only five now, Michael."

"It feels like ten to me."

"Okay," I say. "I'll tell Alan. We'll do what we can and send you another cut tomorrow."

"Thank you, Roger."

"Michael, we're a week from the convention—we have to move faster. Would you be willing to sit in a studio with someone tomorrow and show him exactly where you want to put the bells?"

"Okay."

"Thank you, Michael."

I give Alan my notes. He re-edits for the millionth time. We send the edits out to Michael. He watches them with our producer. The shots of him still seem too long.

"Let's watch it again," the producer says, "and you say 'Cut' where you want us to get away from you."

They play the film again.

"Cut," Michael says.

That's exactly where the editor has already cut to another shot.

"Cut," Michael says.

And again, the cut's right there.

Forget five seconds or four—Michael just *feels* his face is up there too much. He calls me to say so. The phone rings at my home. My teenage son, Aaron, answers.

"Hello, this is Michael Jackson. May I speak to Mr. Enrico, please?"

Silence from Aaron. His ear is frozen to the phone. His mouth is locked open. Could it really be? Seeing him in this state, I *know* who's on the other end of the line and peel his fingers from the handset.

"Hello," I say.

"Hello, Mr. Enrico," comes the soft reply. "This is Michael Jackson. You know, the person you spoke to the other day about the commercials."

Who? Oh, yes. Of course, now I remember—*that* Michael Jackson, the one I talked to about the commercials.

"They're better," Michael says. "But there's still too much of me. And you have me smiling in the scenes where I'm dancing."

"That's not okay?"

"I never smile when I dance."

I never smile when I dance? Is this really happening to me? Later, I pull out Michael's videos and watch them again. Guess what? Not a trace of a smile. But it's one damn thing after another. And this is Wednesday. The bottlers are coming in to see this stuff on Saturday night.

"What did he say?" Alan asks on Thursday morning.

"Forget what Michael says."

"Huh?"

"I don't give a damn what Michael wants," I say. "We're not giving up another frame."

"Did Michael indicate whether he's coming in on Saturday?"

"I didn't ask him."

"If he doesn't, are you going to show the commercials?"

"Alan, we've given this the college try. If we don't show the Jackson spots, we still have wonderful advertising."

"Yes," Alan says, somewhat vacantly. "We have wonderful advertising." He seems a little anxious to get out of my office.

I begin to doubt what I just said. Should I—could I—really pull the plug on the Jackson deal? When in doubt, call Rosemary. She always knows what's right. She listens in silence as I tell her I'm seriously considering dumping the Jacksons.

"What do you think the bottlers' reaction will be?" she asks.

"Well, there will be some disappointment. But I don't think there will be any really negative reaction."

"Roger, do you think you could get fired for this?"

"Fired? For Christ's sake! No way."

I mean, the thought had never crossed my mind. Impossible. But, then again, the bottlers *are* hyped up over this Jackson deal. I call Joe McCann to see what he thinks.

"I don't know what you guys are going through and I don't know what the issues are," Joe says, "but you are *nuts*, Roger. *Nothing* is worth canceling the Jackson commercials. Even if they only *sort of* look like Jackson commercials, they're worth it."

This isn't what I wanted to hear. I call Chuck Mangold, my vice president of bottler relations. He'll understand.

"Chuck, how disappointed do you think the bottlers will be if they don't see Michael Jackson commercials on Saturday night?"

"Why would that happen, Roger?"

I try to explain. Chuck keeps interrupting.

"What's that, Roger? . . . What's that? . . . I don't understand. . . ."

Finally he says, "Who *cares* about all that?"

"*I* care. A *lot*. Now what about the bottlers—will they be disappointed?"

"I think," my good friend Chuck says, with more menace than I have ever heard in his voice, "that they will be *very* disappointed. And if they ever find out that this is all about . . . what? A half-second? *One* spin?"

He just kind of trails off after that.

All of a sudden, just as the Buddhists promise, I have a revelation. I see I am absurd. I've gotten caught between our egos and Michael's, our idea of great film and his. A classic trap. The medium is famous for it. Untold careers have ended because of just this crap. I'll be damned if mine will.

I call Michael right away. I have forty-eight hours to save my career—forty-eight hours before two thousand bottlers show up at Lincoln Center expecting to see what a $5 million sponsorship deal buys. I get answering services and secretaries. And, finally, Joe Jackson, who agrees once again to hunt Michael down and get him to call me back.

Michael returns my call. At three A.M. Friday. Forty hours to oblivion.

"Michael, we don't have time to re-edit any more," I tell him. "But we *will* make the changes you want. Can we just show the commercials as they are to the bottlers on Saturday?"

You won't believe what Michael says. "Oh, Roger, that's fine. I don't care what you show to the bottlers. Show them anything you want. All I care about is what goes on the air."

Astounded, I say, "Thank you, Michael. I'll see you Saturday."

"Everybody's looking forward to it," he replies. "The whole family is coming."

God knows whether, after all we've been through, that includes him.

My shirt is strangling me. I'm convinced my tie is crooked. I have trouble remembering the bottlers' names.

I stand near the footlights of the Lincoln Center State Theater stage—the stage where I had often watched and listened as Beverly Sills's New York City Opera brought the excitement of the master composers to life. The stage where the late George Balanchine's New York City Ballet overwhelmed me with the beauty and power and grace of classic dance.

The house lights are up just enough for me to see the audience clearly—all the way to the uppermost balcony. It is a dazzling sight: bottlers and employees and their families elegantly dressed in black tie and formal gowns. I stand transfixed for just a moment, savoring the experience.

Then, out of the corner of my eye, I see reality. Off to the side, in the first balcony, banks of television cameras. In the orchestra section, Allen Rosenshine and Phil Dusenberry, their expressions filled with apprehension. Down in front, Don Kendall and Andy Pearson and Vic Bonomo ready to see—and assess—whether all this razzle-dazzle will have a positive impact on the business.

It's a good time to be brief. I welcome everyone to the "New Pepsi-Cola Company" and get off. This is Alan's night. Alan Pottasch can make good advertising sound great. When he's got great advertising to work with, he makes it sound so remarkable you want the projectionist to start the film before the introduction is over. Alan begins by showing "Spaceship."

The hall goes dark. On the screen, wind blows through the diner. Eerie lights flash. There's a rumble overhead. The UFO descends and hovers over the Pepsi and Coke machines. It elevates a can from each. Pauses. And, slowly, it begins to lift the Pepsi machine up.

As it does, a sound comes from the back rows of the New York State Theater. It's like a subway moving through the hall, a shuddering beast coming closer and closer, building speed, getting louder. You can't hear the blast-off of the UFO now—just this incredible noise.

It's the bottlers. They're cheering. And they don't stop. They just go on and on and on.

Rosemary and I are sitting with Don Kendall and his wife, Bim. I look over at them. Bim's face is all astonishment. Don is one big smile. Finally the cheering ends.

"I guess that means you like it," Alan says.

And the cheering starts all over again.

Alan shows the rest of the commercials, and the same thing happens every time.

"This is the best advertising I've ever seen," Bim says. "How many do you have?"

"Two more," I say, grinning like a fool.

And here it comes. One measure of drums, with the chunk-a-chunk beat that, no matter how often you've heard it, starts you moving. Then the bass. And then, way above the rhythm, the voice of Michael Jackson singing about a new generation.

"The Jacksons!" the voice-over announcer shouts.

The five thousand kids watching Michael and his brothers make this commercial go crazy. So, now, do two thousand Pepsi bottlers and their families.

So do I. Because this isn't Michael on cassette or on the screen at the advertising agency. This is Michael, thirty feet tall. This is "Billie Jean," blasting in perfect stereo through massive speakers.

The subway noise that filled the hall during "Spaceship" begins again. People can't possibly be more enthused than this.

Then Alan shows "Street."

In my wildest dreams I never imagined that anything I would ever be a part of could get this kind of approval. And when, at the end, there's a freeze-frame on Alfonso Ribeiro, his fist in the air and happiness tattooed on his face, that joy is mirrored on two thousand faces in Lincoln Center. It takes a while, but the hall finally settles.

Alan brings Alfonso out. "You know, I can do the moonwalk about as well as you can," Alan says. He takes a can of Pepsi and starts dancing backward. He's just awful.

Alfonso grabs the Pepsi. "Here, let me show you how it's done," he says. And as he's moonwalking across the stage, Michael comes on live, dancing backward from the other side of the stage. Just as they do in the commercial, they bump in the middle.

By now, the bottlers are on their feet, giving Michael a

standing ovation. It's hardly the first he's ever gotten, but he's never had two thousand middle-aged Middle Americans going wild for him.

Michael's wearing this great big hat. Now he stands at the center of the stage, sweeps it off, and takes a deep bow. And there, on top of his head, right where he got burned, is a little skullcap. With a big grin Michael points to it. A brilliant touch—and one we can appreciate better than any other audience.

"Michael," Alan says, "welcome to the Pepsi family."

Michael brings his brothers and sisters out and introduces his family to our family. And then, because even the greatest magic dissipates with familiarity, he's gone.

No longer does Becky Madeira, our director of press relations, have to sit on rainy streets in her darkened car at night and shanghai reporters as they trudge home. Now they come to us. The phones jump to life.

We're hot. Radio stations want live on-air interviews. We do them. Newspaper reporters want behind-the-scenes stories. We give them. Magazine editors want photos. We Federal Express them.

And in the days before they are to premiere on the Grammy telecast, television news programs are demanding—read this: *demanding*—copies of the Jackson commercials to run as hot news items.

We, however, have that commitment to premiere Michael's spots on MTV, so we don't, at first, pay much attention to the news shows. But as the demands keep coming in, we begin to cry a lot over the lost opportunity.

A deal is a deal. But we call Les Garland at MTV to see if he'd mind bending a bit. Can we release fifteen-second snippets of the commercials—or maybe one whole commercial—to the networks? MTV would still have the only true premiere of the whole ballgame.

MTV has already built a half-hour show around the premiere of the Jackson advertising. For days now, they've been promoting it as a major event. How's this for a first: "MTV presents a World Premiere—commercial?" Les Garland, however, is a real class act. He agrees that the networks are offering too big an opportunity for us to pass up—and besides, the more hype, the bigger the audience for MTV. Releasing one Jackson spot is fine by him.

With that, the dam breaks. Publicity floods our way. The

audience for this is so much wider than MTV's teenagers. Tom
Brokaw interviews Don Kendall. *The Wall Street Journal*
splashes us on page one. And, in New Hampshire, Gary Hart is
running for President as the candidate of something he calls the
"new generation."

You have to live right to be a good marketing guy. That is, God
has to smile on you a lot. It also helps to have professionals like
Joe McCann, Becky Madeira, and Ken Ross working the
phones.

We hold a press conference at the Carnegie Hall Cinema.
Every television cameraman not covering the New Hampshire
primary is there. And Michael Jackson isn't even scheduled to
appear. Just Alan Pottasch, Joe McCann, and me.

Joe and I open with the strategy behind the "New Generation"—Pepsi on the leading edge of American life-styles. Then
Alan shows the commercials. He starts with "Spaceship." The
hype-hardened, cynical members of the press applaud.

"Roger," Joe whispers, "this is amazing. These people never
applaud for anything!"

They seem to like the rest of the commercials just as much.
But the fat lady hasn't sung yet; we get to the question and
answer period.

"How much did these commercials *cost?*" a reporter asks.

Alan hems and haws.

"*How much?*" echos another reporter. "Why won't you tell
us?"

One thing Alan or any of us is never going to do is lie to the
press—but Alan doesn't really want to tell anyone he spent
$20,000 for each *second* of these spots.

I tell the reporters the truth. "The reason Alan doesn't want to
tell you how much he spent," I say, "is because he hasn't told me
yet and he doesn't want to ruin my day."

That breaks the chill. Now they want to know how in God's
name I could okay the expenditure of $5 million for Michael
Jackson to appear in two Pepsi commercials.

How in God's name, indeed. Have you got a couple of days? It
defies any simple explanation.

They don't have a couple of days, and long explanations don't
make good TV news clips. Instead I say, "Nobody's ever been
paid this much to do commercials. So at first I thought: No
way—it's outrageous. So I went home and asked my wife and

she thought it was outrageous too. And then I asked my twelve-year-old son and he said it was a good deal. So I did it."

A tongue-in-cheek story, to be sure. But a lot less bizarre than the facts.

From the press conference, we rush off to Newark Airport, where we've chartered a Regent Air 727 to take a jubilant group of bottlers, customers, and Pepsi managers out to Los Angeles to see the Grammy Awards. It's an unbelievable flight. Flying Regent Air is like going first class on the QE2. Caviar, the finest wines, individual seating compartments, food by Wolfgang Puck, a barbershop on board—just your basic grossly extravagant airplane. Not our usual style at Pepsi, but this *was* our coming-out party.

We arrive in Los Angeles and check into the hotel. We're all rushing to get ready for the celebration dinner we're throwing at L.A.'s hot spot, the Rex Restaurant. I'm just going out the door when the phone rings. Would you answer it? I always do. And, after all, nothing has gone wrong for what—twenty-four hours now?

It's John Branca, Michael's attorney. "Michael's looked at the edit you sent the morning after the bottlers' convention," John tells me. "He's very upset—the commercials are still not what you and he agreed to at all. There's no way he'll allow you to run them on the Grammys."

"John, the Grammys are *tomorrow* night, for God's sake. The commercials have already been sent to CBS to be integrated into the show. There's no way we can change them and still make the telecast. And besides, we've shipped out hundreds of prints to bottlers to be run on the time they've bought on their local television stations."

John insists I pull the commercials, mumbling something about getting an injunction.

"John, we have bought literally millions of dollars of TV time to start day after tomorrow in hundreds of cities," I say. "These commercials *have* to run. After the Grammys, I'll be happy to continue working on them, and when Michael's completely satisfied we'll send out the new versions to the bottlers and pull the old. But in the meantime," I continue in the firmest tone I can muster, "the commercials *will* run as they stand. On the Grammys and in the local markets. If that's not okay with you, go ahead and sue me."

Branca says he'll talk to Michael again—if he can find him.

I think: Jesus, will this never end? And slam the phone down in frustration. A few minutes later Branca calls back. He's gotten to Michael. My plan is fine with him.

You could have knocked me over with a feather.

Understandably, Rosemary and I are a little late getting to the Rex Restaurant. What I see when we arrive throws me for a loop.

The *Los Angeles Times* has listed our little affair as "one of the places to be seen during Grammy week." To the public and the press, that means Michael must be coming.

The crowd outside includes several television crews. And over to one side is Dan Clark, our brand marketing vice president, giving an interview.

Now Dan Clark is one of the brightest stars we have. He's usually very buttoned up—and buttoned down in the best New England prep tradition. I suppose he rightfully ought to be famous—for owning more pairs of boating shoes than any other man in America who doesn't own a boat. But giving television interviews?

"Australian TV," our press manager, Ken Ross, tells me.

"Oh, *right*," I say, as if this is old news. Clearly, we must all—even the most private of us—learn to be mini-celebrities in this Jackson era.

Our celebration party continues late into the night, which leaves Alan and me very little time for sleep. And, at the ungodly hour of four A.M., he and I take over Dan's job. While Alan goes over to the ABC studios for an appearance on *Good Morning America,* I zoom over to NBC in Burbank for a long-distance interview with Jane Pauley on the *Today* show in New York. Meanwhile, back in the Big Apple, Phil Dusenberry and Jay Coleman are doing the *CBS Morning News*.

Companies sometimes have their advertising agencies buy the same exact time on all three networks. That way, no matter how active the viewer's channel-switching finger, there's little likelihood he'll miss seeing your ad. In the advertising business, that's known as a "roadblock." But nobody's ever gotten to where we are about to go—a series of interviews and commercial previews so closely spaced that they may as well be roadblocks. Except that these are for free. And oh-so-painless.

"Good morning, Roger," Jane Pauley says. "Well, you've got the hottest thing in the country. The New York *Daily News* reviewed your commercials this morning—in the movie section. And you got three stars. That ought to make you feel good."

"Why, yes, Jane, it does. And thanks so much for sharing that with fifteen million Americans."

No, I didn't say that. But I surely didn't curse Jane Pauley for making me get up at four in the morning to do this interview.

And this party just won't quit. That night, when the Jacksons' commercials go on, it's like the old days of Elvis Presley and the Beatles on the Ed Sullivan show: Juvenile crime halts; water consumption drops markedly throughout the country, as no toilets are being flushed; parents suddenly regain access to their telephones but nobody's calling.

The next day, the Burke advertising research company discovers that the Jacksons' Pepsi commercials are the most-remembered commercials in history—by a factor more than double any commercial ever run before.

At last—at long last—we come home. Tired, very happy, and, because we want to understand what we've set in motion, ready to assess what it all means.

A star, magnified and superproduced, creates a pure Hollywood moment. Does it matter that, in our commercials, Michael Jackson doesn't do the "drink shot" that is the *sina qua non* of soft drink advertising? Does it bother us that he never even *touches* a can of Pepsi? Not at all.

It's better, in fact, that he doesn't. This way, the film is an event, not just a commercial. This way, we merge Pepsi imagery with Michael's imagery. *We* identify with *him*.

Just having him sing the name of our product is like playing baseball on the moon: A little tap sends the ball beyond Mars.

Moreover, nearly every television station in the country has run these commercials on its news programs—for free. Not to mention millions of dollars' worth of radio, newspaper, and magazine coverage.

And, if that weren't enough, there *is* the bottom line. Not thirty days after the Jackson commercials began airing, sales of Pepsi-Cola began to climb. They climbed high enough to make Pepsi by far the fastest-growing regular cola on the market in 1984—and it's been that way ever since.

Well, that's what happened during the last week of February 1984, at Lincoln Center, at the Carnegie Hall Cinema, at the Grammys in Los Angeles—and in the news media throughout the country. With two commercials, Michael Jackson transformed a company.

You see, when our most important customers—Pepsi bottlers—buy Pepsi concentrate from us, they're not really paying for concentrate. They're paying for leadership. For marketing acumen. For hustle.

That week, you could feel that after the rocky start of my first 180 days as president of Pepsi-Cola, our bottlers finally came to believe they were getting what they paid for. The rhetoric of catching up and surpassing Coke became much more than speechifying. After all the months of feeling stuck, of taking the wrong shots and missing, there was suddenly a sense that we could be—no, that we already were—winners. We were on a roll.

A few days earlier, if you'd asked me what the Jackson commercials were worth, I would have said, "Nothing." And I was prepared to send Michael that message. After Lincoln Center, I had a different opinion. And a very different message for Michael.

What did Michael Jackson's making Pepsi commercials mean for us?

It meant everything.

CHAPTER 9

The Voice of a New Generation

Eighty-three million people saw about five seconds of Michael Jackson's face and watched him spin—twice—on the Grammy telecast. Of course, that was just in the Pepsi commercial—they saw an awful lot more of him that night live, as he returned to the podium again and again to collect his record-breaking eight Grammy Awards.

A week later Michael and John Branca and I have a conference call to talk about those five seconds and that second spin for the umpteenth time. I'd like things to stay as they are. Michael would still like the changes made.

Can we compromise?

I think so. I'm thinking of Michael's concern about being overexposed. In the whole scheme of things, five seconds of close-ups or four, and two spins or one, aren't going to make a whole hell of a lot of difference to him. But how long and how often we run the commercials on TV are.

"Instead of changing the commercials yet again," I say, "and then running them on TV through the end of November as the contract allows, why don't we run them as they are, but for a shorter period of time? We would be willing to stop airing the commercials right after Labor Day."

I figure I'm extending a very large olive branch which will neatly settle Michael's anxiety about overexposure. Branca is interested. They put me on hold while they discuss my offer.

After a few minutes, they're back on the line. Michael, very politely but also very firmly, says, "No, I'd like you to make the changes we agreed to."

The man knows what he wants. I run both versions of the commercials on my VCR one more time—and call Alan Pottasch.

"This is ridiculous, Alan," I say. "Let's just do precisely what Michael wants. No one is going to know the difference—hell, I can't even tell anymore. In fact, if anything, I like Michael's version better than ours."

And that's that—right? Don't you believe it.

A few days later I'm in my office talking to my old friend Howard Davis, the president of Tracy-Locke Advertising, when the phone buzzes. Patti's at lunch. I ignore it and continue my conversation with Howard.

The young receptionist who sits two floors below my office and covers the phones when secretaries are away runs into my office. She's out of breath.

"Roger," she pants, "Michael Jackson's on the line!"

"Talk about trying to impress a guy!" Howard says.

I pick up the phone, expecting Michael's secretary. But it's Michael.

"Roger, that idea you had about stopping the commercials after Labor Day? I've been thinking about it, and it's okay with me."

"Well, I appreciate that, Michael, but the thing is, I've been looking at the commercials over and over and I've decided I like your version better."

"Oh, okay."

"And I want you to know, Michael, I'm really sorry we went through all this, because the commercials are wonderful—no one's *ever* done anything like them before. You really have made a little history here."

"Thank you, Roger."

"By the way, Michael, how are the plans for the Victory tour going?"

"It's going to be magic."

Michael hangs up happy. The commercials air. Sales go up. And I get a call from a fellow named Frank Russo. The first magic of the Victory tour, it seems, is going to be disappearing promoters.

Frank Russo introduces himself as a concert promoter from Rhode Island. He passes on some news that surprises me not at all: Don King is out, and whoever puts up enough front money will be the guy who gets to own and operate the biggest concert tour in history. Russo thinks the right number is $40 million, up-front and guaranteed, so that's what he's offering.

This is not my department. We're just the sponsor. Our name goes in the tour ads, on banners, on the tickets and the like. But we really have nothing to do with managing the tour. We're just along for the ride.

That, however, is not the way the public, the press, our bottlers, and the hundreds of opportunists who want to jump on this gravy train see it. None of them can get through to Michael's people, so they call us. And, like it or not, our caboose gets attached to the speeding locomotive.

Russo's reign as promoter-designate lasts a few short weeks. His $40 million, it turns out, is not the highest offer. That distinction belongs to a man who drops a bid of $42 million on the table: Chuck Sullivan.

"Where did this fellow come from?" I ask Jay Coleman, who knows absolutely everyone who's ever even seen the backstage of a rock tour.

"His family owns the New England Patriots," Jay says.

"How does that qualify him to run this tour?"

"Don't know that it does. But forty-two million dollars is qualification enough. And that's only what he's guaranteeing the Jacksons. They get it if they never fill a single seat. Michael and his brothers get a lot more than that if they fill the house."

"How in the hell is he going to avoid losing his shirt?"

"Beats me. King tells me Michael's people really have the hook set in this fish. They can't believe it themselves. When Chuck Sullivan comes in to negotiate, they just look at each other and whisper, 'Here comes Charlie Tuna.'"

Now, Don King, like him or not, can manage practically anything. He's the unqualified tops at managing and promoting championship prizefights, and you can at least see how that would qualify him to manage the Victory tour.

And Russo, during our short phone call, gives the impression of competence. Besides, he's done this sort of thing before, if not on a scale as grand as the Jacksons.

Sullivan, however, immediately starts showing he hasn't played in *this* league before. What he does, I gather, is compute the number of concert dates, the dollar value of the ticket prices, and the size of the various stadiums and halls where the Jacksons will appear. He arrives at an astronomical dollar amount—more than enough to pay the Jacksons $42 million and still make a pretty penny himself. Fine so far—except for one little catch he hasn't considered.

Michael.

Michael Jackson is not the kind of performer who does things in a small way. His music—the orchestration—is big and complex. His videos are like feature films. Michael Jackson is going to put on the biggest and most elaborate show in the *history* of rock concerts. And he's going to do it on the biggest stage ever built.

Sixty feet long, ninety feet deep, and five stories tall. Three hundred and seventy-five tons of stage that will need twenty-two huge tractor-trailer trucks to haul it from place to place. Three hundred and seventy-five tons of stage that will take dozens of people days to assemble before each concert.

And three hundred and seventy-five tons of stage that will block the view from about a quarter of the seats of every stadium and arena it is set up in. No one is going to pay $28 for a Victory tour ticket and not *see* Michael Jackson. All those seats blocked by the gigantic stage simply cannot be sold.

When Chuck Sullivan sees the stage, even he does not have to be a mathematician to figure his $42 million up-front guarantee has guaranteed just one thing—bankruptcy.

He goes to Michael's people. They feel sorry for him and get Michael to agree to do more concert dates, and to put on more of the concerts in big stadiums instead of the smaller arenas where Sullivan's odds of just breaking even are less than zero.

Still, it is a *very* skinny deal for Sullivan. The steam pressure in the locomotive builds, and the Victory tour goes on a wild, uncontrolled ride even before the first concert date is played.

The ticket-buying arrangement is announced. Send in your money order, it says—$28 plus a handling fee for each of a mandatory four tickets. The computer will decide if you're actually going to get tickets. You'll receive them in the mail if you win. If you lose, you'll get your money back as soon as we can get around to it.

The public thinks that's a ripoff. The press has a field day. Michael holds a press conference to disavow the ticket-buying scheme. And—oh, by the way—announces that any money *he* makes from this tour will be given to charity.

Amazing. Consider how this all began. Michael's pressured into a tour he doesn't want to do. Do it for the family, they say. For your mother and father, for your brothers. Just one little tour and they'll be set for life. It'll make millions.

Yes, it will. It's Michael's soaring popularity the tour is riding on. Michael's creativity that makes the show—his look, his music, his costume ideas, his staging concepts, his choreography. Now all of that will earn *him* zip. His share goes to charity; everyone else banks theirs.

Everyone, that is, except Chuck Sullivan. He goes bankrupt unless he can keep the costs down *and* sell every seat at every concert. Chuck thinks of pro football. Won't this tour be just like the Super Bowl and bring in a lot of money to the cities in which it's held? You know, tax revenue from all of those people coming from all over to see the show. They'll pay for hotel rooms, eat in restaurants, buy gasoline for their cars. Why, the city tax coffers will literally run over from all of this.

So why should he actually have to *pay* for anything—the stadium rentals, the lodging and meals for the Jacksons and their huge entourage. Let the city councils and stadium authorities *bid* for the concerts. He'll take the tour to the cities and the stadiums that offer him the best deal.

The cities and stadium authorities do not rush to airmail their bids, and the tour schedule goes out the window. No one, least of all us, knows when the Victory tour will begin or where it will go, if it ever does either. My phone rings constantly.

Local concert promoters wanting to get a piece of the action—among them, a black local concert promoter threatening to start a boycott of Pepsi if he doesn't.

Stadium managers wanting the tour to play in their facilities—among them, a manager of a stadium that sells Pepsi threatening to throw us out if it doesn't play in his.

Old friends I can't remember and bigshots of all descriptions wanting tickets—among them, a great many who don't believe me when I say I don't have any.

And Pepsi bottlers wondering how we can be so incompetent as *not* to know exactly when the tour will play their town.

I don't have a good answer to that one.

The Victory tour needs a dry run. An incognito dress rehearsal where all of the lighting and sound and stage setup people can get coordinated with each other—and where the Jacksons, who haven't performed as brothers for years, can get their voices and their moves back together again. They secretly pick Birmingham, Alabama. The secret doesn't remain secret for long.

In Birmingham resides one of our smartest, most colorful

bottlers. His name is Jimmy Lee, and he's a legend in the soft drink business. Not only because his shrewdness and determination have built Pepsi in Alabama from a distant also-ran to a head-to-head position with Coke. But because he tells it like it is. A few years ago, when he launched the Pepsi Challenge in Birmingham, Jimmy said he did it for two reasons: One, he was convinced it would build his Pepsi business, and two, because it "drives the bastards up the wall!"

Like many Pepsi bottlers, Jimmy Lee's is a family operation, and so his daughter is his vice president of marketing. And with the Jacksons in town, it's Peyton Lee who becomes the point-person for the local press—as if the Jacksons work for her.

The media assault is overwhelming. Everyone knows that the secret dress rehearsal of the Victory tour is in Birmingham—everyone, that is, except us and Peyton Lee.

The Jacksons' PR people hold on to the myth of secrecy and ignore the press. The press ignore the Jacksons' PR people and barrage Peyton. The Jacksons may not care about the Birmingham press, but this is her hometown—she's got to tell them something.

When is the dress rehearsal? Will it be open to the public? Which hotel are the Jacksons staying at? Will Michael appear at his hotel window if the crowd on the street is big enough?

Peyton has nothing to tell them. They run their stories, anyway—constantly. Not an hour goes by on radio, not a newspaper edition gets printed, not a television news program airs without the latest on the Jacksons in Birmingham. Peyton Lee—telling the press nothing—is quoted a lot.

Frank Dileo calls.

Frank is Michael's new manager, which is to say Michael now *has* a manager. He's not actually had a manager for several months now—just lawyers.

I met Frank just before he signed on with Michael. A straightforward, get-it-done sort of guy who had been with CBS's Epic Records, and who—more than anyone on the promotion side of things—was responsible for the unprecedented success of Michael's "Thriller" album. I'm relieved that he's now Michael's manager. Frank and I understand each other; we can do business together.

Our first official business transaction was Frank telling me to get Peyton Lee to butt out.

"Michael's here to rehearse in private," Frank says. "All these distractions—fans at the airport when we arrive, hundreds of people on the streets in front of the hotel, all this speculation from the press—have got to stop. This Peyton Lee is leaking everything we're doing to the press."

"Frank," I say, "we didn't even know you were *going* to Birmingham. The leaks aren't coming from us. Your PR staff won't even return phone calls from reporters, so they're pressuring Peyton. All she's trying to do is keep a bad situation from becoming a disaster."

"Maybe so," Frank replies, "but you've got to get her to stop talking to the press, because to Michael it *looks* like you're the ones leaking everything."

I tell Frank I'll do what I can. Meanwhile, into this vacuum Jimmy Lee throws a carload of Jacksons commercials. Buys time on every show with a spare minute. Just swamps the fine folks of Birmingham with Jacksons spots. And some of these commercials are the five-second-close-up, two-spin, pre-final-agreement-with-Michael ones.

Does Pepsi ever advertise on the *Tonight* show? Never. Too late in the evening for our target audience.

What, then, are the odds that Michael Jackson will see what may be the only unauthorized version of his commercial in the world being broadcast at midnight in Birmingham, Alabama? Why 100 percent, of course.

Frank Dileo calls again—first thing the next morning.

"You're not going to believe this," he says. "Michael and I were talking about Pepsi last night. Michael was saying that even though he had these problems with Dusenheimer, he really liked you. Michael decides to watch TV, so I go into the next room to talk to Jermaine. Jermaine has his set on, too—watching the *Tonight* show. Michael's Pepsi commercial comes on and it's the wrong version. I say to Jermaine, 'Oh, God, I hope Michael's not watching this show!' Two seconds later, the phone rings. 'They've done it to me again!' Michael yells. 'They're running the wrong commercial!' He's mad, Roger. Very mad. You've got to do something."

"Frank, we told the bottlers *not* to run that version," I say. "But there are hundreds of copies out there. We don't have absolute control over this just yet."

"Well, I suggest you get control in Birmingham right away," he replies.

I agree and call Jimmy Lee to ask him to yank the unauthorized version of the commercial. The next morning, Dileo calls again.

"Since I call you to complain when you're wrong," he says, "I have to call you when you do something right."

"What did I do?"

"Last night Michael and I were watching the local news. And the anchorman announces, 'The Jacksons' Pepsi commercial has been withdrawn because of an improper edit. There's another version coming, but we won't be able to show it to you tonight.' That was very impressive, Roger."

"Well, we try, Frank."

Somehow, I fail to mention that being president of Pepsi does not carry with it the power to write television news copy.

The wonderful thing about sponsoring a hot concert tour is how much good you can do.

You can do a lot for your business. You can buy up to, say, 10 percent of the tickets, and in addition to the ones you give away, you can run consumer promotions. In exchange for mention of your company's name, you can have radio stations give them away. Grocers and convenience stores can sponsor contests. And at the concert site, you can plaster the walls with so many signs that no one goes home unaware of your involvement.

And because a hot concert tour can make your coffers overflow, it gives a company a chance to do good for others too. You can give tickets away to orphanages. You can create a special section, right up front, for handicapped kids and arrange transportation for them. You can give tickets away to kids whose families could never afford tickets. We do all of these things, which makes us feel pretty damn good.

A tour that throws off as much heat and excitement as the Jacksons' gives a company truly endless opportunities for community good and corporate promotion—for the Jacksons attract not just kids, but three generations of families: the kids, the mothers and fathers, and the grandparents. It helps, however, if the tour is well managed.

This tour is not. Equipment trucks weave across the country like drunks. The tour crisscrosses east to west, north to south—nobody knows where it's going next. Concerts are scheduled on such short notice we have a tough job setting up much in the way of promotions. Bottlers' vacation schedules are shot.

I call Chuck Sullivan endless times to complain. It does no good. I tell him I'm going to send him to a geography class when this is all over. He just laughs.

And then there are my friends at Coke. Many of the stadiums where the Jacksons' concerts are held are Coke houses. That means they serve Coke, and nothing but. And there are Coke signs everywhere.

Now my naïveté enters the picture. In 1984 some of the events of the Los Angeles Olympic Games were actually held at the Stanford University Stadium in Palo Alto, California. Stanford Stadium is a Pepsi venue—it serves Pepsi and nothing else. This created a problem. Coke was the exclusive soft drink of the 1984 Olympics. And, clearly, Coke was going to be less than happy about a Pepsi presence there.

Stanford called our San Francisco bottler, Richie Campodonico, to ask if we'd consider leaving the stadium during the Olympics. Richie called me. And Richie and I both agreed that while we are among the most competitive gentlemen this business has ever seen, we are as committed to acting like gentlemen as we are to being fierce competitors. So we stopped selling Pepsi at Stanford Stadium during the Olympics.

Does Coke return the favor during the Jacksons' tour? Not once. Instead, waving contract clauses, they put the word out: no Pepsi cups, no Pepsi signs—or else.

In Chicago, Coke gets hold of a block of tickets. Next thing we know, we're hearing "*Coke* welcomes the Jacksons to Chicago." And *Coke*'s giving away free tickets.

And in Atlanta, Coke executives are telling the press: "This tour is terrific—it's selling a lot of Coke." I doubt that's true, but it sure makes for good Cola War copy.

A year later, when Coca-Cola gave the world New Coke and its executives were stumbling around, word was passed through Coke's PR agency that I was kicking the boys in Atlanta too hard—that I was, in my interviews, going beyond the boundaries of gentlemanly competition.

After what they tried to do to us during the Jacksons' tour? You decide.

We live and learn, and, after a while, the Jacksons' tour gets on track. Somehow, bottler promotions get run. Pepsi sales respond handsomely when the Jacksons come to town.

It is now sensible to invite Don Kendall to a concert. We choose Washington, D.C. Deliberately.

When Jimmy Carter was President, there were only Coke machines in the White House. The new administration has less Georgian tastes—now the machines dispense Pepsi too.

And, in this administration, we can invite White House people, congressmen and their families, and reasonably expect them to come.

The publisher of *The Washington Post*, Katharine Graham, calls Don Kendall to ask for tickets. We oblige.

We are on a roll again. Our only problem, I find out later, was a White House prankster.

It seems the day of the concert, someone—I'm told Mike Deaver, or maybe Jim Baker—sent a memo to all White House staff. It contained good news and bad news. "The good news," it said, "is that Michael Jackson is going to endorse President Reagan's re-election candidacy tomorrow. The bad news is that attending tonight's Jacksons' concert with the free tickets Pepsi-Cola has provided constitutes a conflict of interest. Therefore, no members of the White House staff or their families may go to the Jacksons' concert tonight."

There were, I hear, long faces on many White House staffers that morning—but only for the few minutes it took for them to figure out it was a practical joke.

Don Kendall's wife, Bim, is on the phone.

"Roger, what should I wear to this thing?" she asks.

"Oh, whatever you usually wear to rock concerts."

"Thanks a lot. No, really, what do I wear?"

"Just wear slacks and a top. I'll send over a black satin Jacksons' tour jacket for you. You'll look terrific."

"Okay. Don't tell Don, I'll surprise him."

I send over the jacket. And I arrange to go to the plane with Don. The plan is for Bim to meet us at the airport.

We're seated on the plane when Bim comes aboard. She's a knockout. Don looks at her in amazement. In his conservative black suit and her "with-it" outfit, they do not look like they belong together. "Where in God's name did you get *that*?" he says.

"Oh . . . Roger sent it over."

Don gives me a look that says: "Where's mine?"

We have a great reception for hundreds of Washington guests, and then are off to RFK Stadium. Before the madness starts, I—now the big rock expert—take the Kendalls backstage. Don looks around at all the Jacksons, their gang of stagehands, and the many, many hangers-on.

"My God, how many people do they bring with them?" he

says, after we've had pictures taken with the Jacksons. "No wonder these performers don't end up with much money."

Concert time. The lights dim and on the stage a drama unfolds. There are monsters and dragons and—with a sword pulled from a great rock—a gallant knight to slay them. Then the stage begins to move. And like a huge UFO, part of it swings up and around, lights flashing and lasers popping, to become the overhead lighting system. A new floor arises, and with it, from the smoke and din—on stage and on a gigantic television screen high above—Michael Jackson.

It's Michael's magic. The crowd is energized. Don Kendall is just fascinated. He looks around at the crowd. He looks at Michael. Then, as lasers blast again, he looks up at the huge video screen.

Don, who has been close to Presidents and Prime Ministers and Premiers and Party Chiefs—to Nixon and Khrushchev, to Reagan and Brezhnev—says, "Now, *this* is power!"

With that kind of imprimatur, I'm still in a pretty good mood a few weeks later when it's time to deal with what my calendar describes as the "Jackson litigation issue."

We never denied, from the minute that Michael had been hurt filming our commercial, that compensation of some sort was in order. Considering what Michael was paid, however, we were not of the opinion that he was entitled to massive amounts of money. At any rate, the real question was: Just who should pay?

And we're not going to get involved in a lawsuit over this if we can help it. We're not, after all, the producer of the Jackson commercials. Bob Giraldi and his company are. We have a "hold harmless" as a standard part of our commercial production contract. If there's a claim for negligence, we feel it ought to be against Giraldi or the outfit hired to handle the fireworks.

Giraldi and everyone else remotely involved look to their insurance companies' lawyers. Of course, insurance companies don't always care about reaching a quick resolution, and may not mind going to court—particularly when they consider just how long it takes a case to get before a judge. The more time goes by, the longer they get to keep their money. And, of course, the more willing the injured party is to settle.

The weeks drag on. We try using our "good offices" to bring the parties to a settlement. No one wants to settle. Michael's lawyers ask for an astonishingly large sum; the insurance companies' lawyers offer an astonishingly paltry amount. No one budges because they all figure Pepsi's going to bail them out. Besides, everybody's got great lawyers, and as I see it those great lawyers are probably not *too* unhappy at the prospect of gearing up for hundreds of hours of very expensive legal work. We're the only ones with anything to lose—our good name. We are, everyone figures, the ones with the deep pockets.

Michael, meanwhile, is getting impatient. Legal technicalities notwithstanding, he figures: It's a Pepsi commercial—Pepsi is responsible.

We talk about it a while and decide that we're more interested in preserving our relationship with Michael than in legal considerations. But we feel his lawyers want an outrageous amount of money.

We make an offer—a reasonable offer. We do this, we say, in the interest of continuing a very satisfactory relationship with Michael. We're happy to see Michael get more money, but it will have to come from the other folks on that commercial production set.

Michael's team rejects the offer.

I get the strong feeling, however, that both Frank Dileo and John Branca see that reason is on Pepsi's side here. So I send a lawyer out to inform Branca that we want to settle, but aren't willing to be screwed. If it comes to it, we'll go to court. And, obviously, our litigator will be the meanest bastard who ever wore a three-piece suit. It is pretty clear to Branca that if this matter goes all the way south, he will not be playing with children.

Some time later, Branca calls me. "We've got to find a resolution," he says. "Michael's pushing me. And he's just as adamant as you are."

"I'm very sorry to hear that."

"You ought to know," Branca says, "that Michael's planning to donate whatever he gets to the Burn Center at Brotman Memorial Hospital, where he was treated. Actually, he's going to do more than that—he's going to add a lot of his own money to whatever he gets from you. In the end, it will be a *substantial* contribution, and it can be donated jointly from Michael and Pepsi. He doesn't want to disclose the actual amount of the contribution, but I think Michael's willing to hold a joint press conference with you at the Burn Center. You should be able to get some good out of that."

"That is a very different position," I say. "Let me think about it."

We hang up. I talk about it with Joe McCann and Alan Pottasch. And we all agree: Once again, Michael's out not for himself but for others. Let's join him.

After the Victory tour zapped its last laser and blasted off its last skybomb, Joe McCann and I went out to Los Angeles for the press conference at the Burn Center. The small auditorium was jammed with cameras and microphones and reporters. I spoke first. Michael was standing backstage, behind me and off to the side. For the first time—and, I suppose, much to his surprise— he heard me say a lot of nice things about him. I meant every one of them.

After my introduction, Michael came onstage with a stunned look, spoke briefly, and received thanks and a plaque from the head doctor at the Burn Center. We stood together for some photographs. Then he leaned over close to my ear.

"Roger," he whispered, "do you get nervous at these things too?"

I thought: In the beginning, there was Michael softly telling me, "I'm going to make Coke wish they were Pepsi." And then there were all these people—Don King, Frank Russo, Chuck Sullivan, thousands of reporters, a zillion lawyers—and all those misunderstandings. And through it all, Michael was a pro. He worked his butt off. He did make magic. And at the end, here we are again, Michael Jackson and Pepsi making another, different kind of joint contribution. It all seemed so fitting.

"Yeah, Michael," I said. "I get nervous too."

CHAPTER 10

Leveling the Playing Field

If it sounds as though all we did at Pepsi for six months was debate esthetics with Michael Jackson and play patty-cake with the press, that's very far from the truth. In fact, there was more than enough for everyone to do at Pepsi without the excitement—and the crises—of the Jackson commercials and the Victory tour.

As soon as my executive team was pulled together, we began tearing the business apart, assessing every aspect of it. As a group we challenged everything and assumed nothing. And from this perspective, we arrived at the strategies we would employ to put Pepsi on a faster roll than it had ever been on before.

To the bottlers and company employees alike, I would say, "Don Kendall didn't ask me to become president of Pepsi to administer this business. Or to operate it. He asked me to take this job to *build* the business. And that's what we're going to do. We're going to build it by being as innovative and aggressive and competitive as we know how. And we're going to do it together, as a team, as partners."

Many, many bottlers and employees took the charge. They offered encouragement, expressed their personal commitment, and gave suggestions.

"We need big ideas," they'd tell me. "We need to take more risks. We need more exciting advertising, new packages to sell, a more aggressive program to expand the number of Pepsi vending machines we have in the market, a more aggressive program to increase the number of restaurants that serve Pepsi from their soda fountains. We should decentralize the development of our promotions, let our local field people and our local bottlers have more say in how promotion money is spent. We should have a product to compete in the lemon-lime flavor business. And, with Diet Coke's big success, we've got to do *something* to turn Diet Pepsi around."

The way they said all of this, I knew they were with me. They wanted me to succeed—they hoped I had the leadership ability to make it happen.

We did every one of the things they suggested—and we began work on all of them in the first few months after I took over. Every idea I ever had to build the business came from those early discussions with our bottlers and our employees. They resulted in my announcing one overall goal and two broad strategies for Pepsi USA.

The goal was to double our business in the decade of the 80s. I set that goal for one simple reason: We had done it every decade since 1950. I wasn't about to see that sterling record broken in my decade.

Never mind the fact that the soft drink market wasn't growing as fast anymore. That it was, in 1983, a monstrous $35 billion at retail. And never mind the fact that Pepsi's volume was now more than eight times greater than it was in 1950. I believed the market would grow as fast as there were new ideas and products to offer the consumer. If the companies in the soft drink industry had real insight into consumers' needs and wants, they'd reward us by increasing consumption. And if Pepsi USA was first with those new ideas and products, we'd get the lion's share of the reward.

"We are the masters of our own destiny," I told everyone who would listen. "We can make this business *anything* we want it to be. And what we want it to be is dynamic and exciting and vital. We want it to grow and grow rapidly, and we can do that by implementing just two broad strategies."

One strategy covered the consumer side of the soft drink business. We would be first in the market with the most innovative advertising, promotions, packages, and products. We'd do that by knowing more about our consumer than anyone in the business, and by being bold in what we did with that knowledge. We'd take big but well-conceived risks. And we would keep the competition one step behind, guessing what we'd do next.

The other strategy covered the nuts and bolts side of the business—becoming a stronger competitor in all the places where consumers have an opportunity to buy soft drinks. Grocery stores, convenience stores, drugstores, mass merchandisers, restaurants, on the streets—anywhere two or more people congregated would be considered a crowd of consumers as far as we were concerned. And Pepsi would be there with product displays and fountain dispensers and big, beautiful vending machines. Together with our bottlers, we would invest more money, time, and energy in improving our execution and visibility than ever before.

My first order was for every Pepsi USA department director to stop the uncontrolled headcount growth that had been ongoing for several years. My justification was, in part, a reflection of my origins. As a marketing guy, I knew every extra dollar we could lay our hands on could, if spent effectively, lead to several dollars in sales and profit. History does not record the name of a single marketing executive whose idea of achievement was staff growth. All glory rightfully follows a rising sales curve.

But the best reason for keeping the division's phone book thin is that a lean staff is a productive staff. The enemy of productivity isn't overwork—it's boredom. If you always have a little more to do than you've got time for, you discover the pleasure of rising to the occasion. Your heart may pump faster, you may sweat a little and have to rely on your instincts—but when you go home and someone asks about your day, at least you'll have more to talk about than the Nautilus circuit at the fitness center.

At Coke headquarters in Atlanta, they've got so many executives that, as you'll see in a few chapters, they even seem to have a vice president of Synonyms. But when you've got a twenty-six-story building and have been number one ever since the dinosaurs roamed the earth, that's understandable.

At Pepsi USA, we know that the way to become number one is always to think like number two. Do it today, and do it yourself. Call, don't write.

By the fall of 1983, we were well on our way to delivering on all those employee and bottler ideas to grow the business. Just then, of course, the Jacksons came into our lives and we delivered on the first one—exciting advertising. And, just then, our cups suddenly overflowed with new products and new package ideas that urgently needed our attention.

Remember "Overlord," the juice-added lemon-lime that was stalled at R&D because subsequent batches were never as good as at our first tasting? Well, it took us a while, but our new R&D

vice president, Bennett Nussbaum, found a way to make the product taste the way I remembered it when I first brought it into John Sculley's office. Suddenly we all liked Overlord again. So much that we started doing consumer in-home taste tests.

And in every comparative test against 7-Up, we got slaughtered. And each time consumers preferred 7-Up, we played around with the formula. Was it crisp? Was it juicy? Not for long. Pretty soon it was a Xerox copy of 7-Up.

Finally we decided to go back to the formula we all liked and examine our testing methods. It was the hardest thing to figure out.

If people see a clear soft drink, they assume it's 7-Up. Then they taste it. It's different. "No," they say, "I like the other one." Meaning the one they're familiar with: 7-Up.

At long last we came up with a radical idea. We told people what they were drinking.

"One of these drinks," we said, "is a lemon-lime soft drink. The other is a soft drink with ten percent juice added. Which one do you prefer?"

The pendulum quickly swung. And we learned a very simple truth about marketing. I am sure that almost everybody in the world of consumer-products research already knows this, but when you are working on a product that has a real point of difference, it's pretty damn tough to beat the product that people are used to.

You can't go by the old rules of measurement. You've got to say: "I have a concept. How many people are interested in it? Of the people who are, how many think this product delivers on the concept?" Only then can you ask: "How many people prefer this product against its closest premium competitor?"

When we did that, we found a lot of potential Overlord-aholics out there. But it took us six months to figure that out.

Now we were ready to launch Overlord. Only problem was, my 1984 budget had already been approved. There was no money for Overlord in it.

What Vic Bonomo, head of Worldwide Beverages for PepsiCo, is supposed to say is: "No money in the budget for Overlord? Don't worry about it. We'll adjust a few things and here you are."

He's supposed to say this but he doesn't.

I go in to see Vic. He's completely forgotten that he and Andy Pearson told me not to budget for Overlord. They doubted we'd pull it off. If it came to anything approaching reality, they said, they'd adjust our profit plan to accommodate it. Now it's time to pay the piper. We're ready to spend some real money on test marketing.

"Why don't you wait until next year?" Vic says.

"Because there's nothing more to learn from research. The product has to go live into a test market to know what we've got here."

"Let's look at the plan."

I break out the plan. Vic frowns.

"Why does it cost so much to do this?" he asks.

I tell him.

"And this, Roger—why does this have to cost so much?"

I tell him. But I get the point. He's running a convoy, with many profitable tankers moving steadily toward a distant shore. To him, Overlord isn't an invasion vehicle; it's a very little boat way off to the side. If it sinks, nobody's going to mourn for long.

"Roger, I just don't have any money right now."

At this, I start gathering my papers from Vic's desk.

"Thank you anyway," I say. "If I'd known you didn't have any money, I wouldn't have wasted your time or mine."

"What are you going to do?"

"Take Overlord to test market."

"Where are you going to get the money?"

"I don't know—but I'll get it."

This may sound odd, but that sort of interchange is not uncharacteristic at PepsiCo. I can't speak for Vic, who's now retired and bubbles with delight when the price of PepsiCo stock goes up (he has tens of thousands of shares). But I think he saw it more or less like this: In our system, division presidents are responsible for making things happen. That's why PepsiCo is one of a handful of corporations that calls its division presidents CEOs. If Enrico *really* believes in this, he'll find the money. In other words, benevolent neglect as a test of commitment.

If you look at the PepsiCo corporate staff, you don't see a lot of big titles. You don't see a lot of names, period. The corporate personnel department? Just a handful of managers. And corporate marketing? What the hell would they market—the corporation doesn't *make* anything. Pepsi-Cola and Fritos corn chips, Pizza Hut pizzas and Taco Bell tacos—they're all made and sold by the divisions. Sure, there's a financial department and they do their job well, but nobody looks over my shoulder to see how I'm spending money while I'm spending it. If I don't use funds wisely, we'll talk about it—later.

All that's not to say PepsiCo acts as some sort of financial conglomerate. Just the opposite: the chairman and president are closely in touch in the operations of the business. But on a direct line to the division presidents, not through layers of staff people—and more to be supportive of what the divisions are doing than to second-guess their every move.

So where did I find the rather large sum I needed to go to test market with Overlord? In my own budget. And if I couldn't have borrowed from this line and begged a bit from that, I could always have gone to plead the case farther up the line. PepsiCo's like that. I've never seen a good idea turned down for lack of money.

So now we've got the product. We've got the money. All we lack is a name. And finding the right name for a new product is like trying to find the right person to marry. There are millions of eligible people out there. But all the good ones are already taken.

Here's where the commitment of an individual made all the difference. At the time, Richard Blossom was vice president of new product development. His brand manager was Judy Fearing.

Richard Blossom had then been at Pepsi only two years, but he'd understood from the beginning that this was a business where a point of view counted. And Richard could, in all areas of his life, be depended on for a point of view. After graduating from Colgate, he got his M.B.A. the hard way—at night, after working at a Wall Street bank all day. Richard soon tired of banking. Fortunately, he stumbled into marketing at General Foods, where he discovered that you could indeed enjoy what you do for a living. At Pepsi, he'd taken the initiative in revising the company's charter; we are, as Richard correctly perceived, now a "refreshment beverage" company, not just a cola manufacturer.

His colleague Judy Fearing was also new to Pepsi—she'd come up from Frito-Lay so she could live in the same zip code as her then-fiancé-and-now-husband—but she was with Richard step for step on that score. Their staff? Infinitesimal.

Richard and Judy were the brand champions. They had to be—there was no one around to compete for the role. They not only believed in the product, they believed it should be called "Slice."

We knew that BBDO had about the fullest Pepsi plate the

agency could handle, so we took the Overlord account to J. Walter Thompson. Alan Pottasch knew the senior people there, thought they were terrifically inventive, and felt they were capable of devising a campaign for a product that had no name and no obvious theme line. The people at J. Walter Thompson also liked the name Slice.

As it happened, Slice was a trademark owned by PepsiCo's Frito-Lay division. It was a good idea—you do think of slices of potatoes—but Frito-Lay had never done anything with it. Still, to hold on to the trademark, they'd slap it on some product or other and ship it around their distribution network. Only, in the summer of 1983, somebody forgot to do that. The trademark could be lost.

We found this out when everyone on the Overlord project started beating drums for the name Slice. Fortunately, no one at any other consumer-products company was thinking about Slice that summer. Our people frantically shipped Overlord fountain syrup around the country in order to reestablish a legal claim on the Slice trademark. Which brings us one step closer to adopting the name for Project Overlord.

Now it's time to sit down with the agency and sign off on the advertising plans. But can anyone create great advertising for a product without a name? Not likely. The morning of the meeting, Richard Blossom calls me.

"We've decided, Roger, to recommend the name Slice."

"Richard, there is no way I am *ever* going to put out a product from this company with that name."

"Roger . . ."

"It's ridiculous!"

"What name do you want?"

"I'd rather have a name like Pepsi or Coke, only I can't find one," I say. "But I love Sierra."

"You see freshness . . ."

"And clean mountain air. It's perfect."

The wonderful thing about great marketing people is that they don't give a damn what you say. If they think you're wrong, they're going to keep coming. And if they think your decisions are not only wrong but arbitrary—watch out.

That afternoon, I go to the agency meeting. And I can feel, as I enter, that Richard and Judy have gotten to everyone here. Not that anyone's bristling for a fight. The thing is, they're too *nice*.

And too rational. They take me through all the good reasons for Slice. Then they break out the *pièce de résistance*—some samples of the package design. The letters *do* look . . . juicy. The angle of the word looks . . . right. On the package, Slice seems quite . . . inevitable. Reluctantly, I conclude that I've been an idiot. Slice is the obvious trademark.

"I was wrong," I say. "It's Slice."

The room lightens up. A lot. After all, company presidents don't admit they're wrong very often.

J. Walter Thompson gets the theme line right away: "We got the juice." Why not, therefore, hire O.J. Simpson—the "Juice" himself? Well, because he's running amok through airports for Hertz, for one thing. And for another, we've already got a plateful on the celebrity front.

We settle, happily, on an approach that will show slices of fruit shooting through crystal-clear liquid. Lots of refreshment and lots of wonderfully appealing young people just grooving over Slice's taste. As the Thompson folks say: "Hard-sell advertising you love to watch."

Only problem is, their creative folks don't want Alan Pottasch to watch *them* create. They seem to have a not-invented-here syndrome going, which doesn't make sense because nobody in the world is better at soft drink advertising than our own Alan Pottasch. I decide, however, to pass over Alan's misgivings about some parts of the commercials—to let the Thompson folks do it their way. After all, they do Burger King and Kodak and all kinds of great advertising. Surely they will deliver on these Slice commercials.

Not very many weeks later, we're in the conference room to see the rough edits of the new Slice advertising. We've never worked with Thompson before, so we get pre-mumbles galore: Everything's right on target. The strategy and the visuals are married for life. These are good commercials. No, they're wonderful. Twenty-minutes of pre-mumbles later, the tape rolls.

As the singers praise the product, the film shows a turning can. It would be nice to see—hell, it's more or less expected—the Slice name appear on screen just as the singers belt it out. In these commercials, that doesn't happen.

And that's just the start of what I don't like. There are also these young people drinking the product. They're supposed to be fun and attractive—and if you have a thing for Valley Girls, maybe these females are pleasing. But the males! Are there thousands of Valley Boys in real life? Or have we managed to hire every damn one of them for these Slice commercials?

Now, I will go very far to justify a failed effort that represents the best that could be done. But inferior execution? I'm the wrong guy to deal with, particularly a week and a half before a bottlers' convention.

"What do you think, Roger?"

What do I think? I think we've been drowned out during the creative discussions. I think we've been promised a pot of gold. And then, I think, we've been kicked off a cliff.

Would *you* be philosophical at that moment? Presidents are supposed to be. Not, to the eternal unhappiness of the people in that room, this president.

I can't quote myself—I was too upset to remember now what I said with any accuracy. But the general idea is: "Who the hell ever taught you to do new-product advertising?" And, building on that theme, I say something like: "We don't have much time to fix these damn things, so democracy is *over*, folks. Now you'll do it *our* way." And then, for good measure, I probably say something like: "And don't come back until you've got some *advertising* to show us!" And finally, just to make their day: "I expect to see the redone commercials on Friday"—which allows three whole days to do the impossible.

Much huddling now between J. Walter and Alan Pottasch. Amazingly enough, they incorporate some terrific high-speed product photography into the commercials. The Valley Boys, meanwhile, are shot into a black hole, from which there's no possibility they'll reemerge.

I come down for a screening on Saturday—a day off the schedule I demanded, but still faster than mere mortals can pull film apart and reassemble it—and find, to no one's surprise, a good deal of the Thompson brass waiting for me in the screening room along with Alan. No pre-mumbles, which is a good start. Today, the meeting moves right to showing the film. And today, the film works—Thompson's pulled it out.

And ever since, we have had the warmest, most productive working relationship possible. The J. Walter Thompson people have done excellent—no, terrific—advertising on Slice. And I'm happy to give them a lot of the credit for the brand's overwhelming success.

Which raises a question: Was I right to blow up at the first screening? I'm afraid I have to say no. Presidents are supposed to refrain from intimidation and personal attack; the power of their position makes that behavior unnecessary. Anyway, anger, like revenge, is a drink best served cold. A little displeasure, in a low voice, *should* do the trick. But I will also admit that it's much easier for me to tell you this than to remember to live by it.

A week before the bottlers' convention, Slice got announced. Not by me—by *The Wall Street Journal*. It was all there: juice-added soft drink, test markets, advertising slogans.

It was pretty obvious how the news leaked out. Once you've shot commercials, your film is seen by free-lance film people, editors, and a lot of others who have no deep reason to keep your secret. I got mad anyway.

In my experience, it's Coke that announces everything. If they want to tell us, months ahead, what they're going to do, I'm thrilled. But imitation here isn't flattery—it's foolishness.

As long as the secret was out, though, there was no point keeping the news of Slice from our bottlers. So big announcements went out. And, looking back, it was just as well it happened this way—in a convention dominated by the Jackson commercials, Slice might have gotten a little lost.

Soon after the convention, we put Slice into test market. And in the first week in Tulsa, Oklahoma, we couldn't keep the cans on the shelves. Who was buying this stuff? Had we found the kind of taste sensation that, as the cliché holds, would sweep the nation? Nope. It's just our competitors—Coke, RC, and 7-Up—swooping in and buying enough Slice to satisfy every curious executive.

I've heard that in the Coke board room, they sat around and had a Slice taste test. They drank it, talked about it, sipped some more. I'm not sure of this, but I understand it was Goizueta who first expressed the opinion that became pretty much the general reaction to Slice at Coke: "This is no big deal."

Know what? Most people at PepsiCo agreed. Andy Pearson expressed it best. If Slice is a big deal, he said, competitors will have their versions out immediately. In consumer products, no one gets a virgin market for long.

I didn't believe that. Neither did Richard and Judy. But we didn't spend a minute rebutting that point of view. We were too busy figuring out what to charge for Slice concentrate.

Remember, we'd never really been in the lemon-lime business. And nobody had ever done a 10 percent juice-added drink in America. Juice is more expensive than the flavor oils usually used in soft drinks. Who should pay for it?

Well, the equitable thing is for us to share the cost with our bottlers as we're not going to ask the consumers to pay a premium price. Both we and our bottlers will make less money per case on Slice than we do on Pepsi. So what? The Slice we'll sell won't take away from our Pepsi sales. Slice drinkers will be *new* customers—customers we're taking from the competition. And if we sell enough cases—say 100 million a year—we'll make plenty of money even at the lower profit per case.

Besides, the competition will have a tough time wrapping their minds around adding juice to their products. It'll take away from profits they already have on their income statement. We'll buy a little time for Slice to get itself established by absorbing the extra cost of juice and keeping our prices down.

In test market, we don't take sales away from Sprite or 7-Up all that much. Slice does well, but it seems to be expanding the lemon-lime category. Where do the new Slice drinkers come from? As far as we can tell, from beverages like iced tea and mineral water. As we roll Slice out nationally, though, we start to draw blood.

Coke announces that Minute Maid orange soda—already in test market in Canada—is moving south and adding . . . guess what? Ten percent juice. Now every time there's a story about Slice, there's also a story about Minute Maid. Only there isn't any Minute Maid orange soda to be found in America! And there won't be for months!

Here's where good public relations people really earn their salaries. For by announcing to the press that Minute Maid orange soda is about to be introduced, Coke blunts our advantage, at least on the PR side. Does it matter that nobody can find the stuff? Not to the press.

As you're about to see, this is a lesson that, once learned, Coke uses again and again. I call it "smoke and mirrors." If you've announced it, it must be real and true.

But their publicity effort is useless in the place that matters most—the bottom line. For, to our not-so-great surprise, Slice is selling like nothing we've ever introduced. It's not just a winner, it's a *big* winner.

We start our R&D department working on new flavors. We roll national much sooner than anyone expected. And by the end of 1985, Slice is selling at just the rate we dreamed of: a $500 million, 100-million-case business.

And all Coke has is a phantom.

Soon after I became president of Pepsi USA, Jimmy Lee, the Birmingham Pepsi bottler of the secret-Jackson-tour-dress-rehearsal fame, came up to see me with a big idea: the biggest soft drink bottle ever imagined. Three liters.

Jimmy and his people had it all figured out. How to get the bottles, how to fill them, and how to give the consumers a nice cost-per-ounce savings and still make a good profit. They wanted my blessing and our help in marketing, along with a little financial assistance. Could we join them in the project?

Hell, yes. And we'd keep it a secret. The three-liter plastic bottle became Project Olympian.

I had some misgivings. Not the least was, would anybody actually buy a three-liter bottle? Could a housewife even lift one? And how would she get it into her refrigerator?

Jimmy filled some bottles and our marketing people ran some in-home tests. They came back positive. Jimmy's three-liter bottle looked like a winner.

In May of 1984, Jimmy introduced it in Birmingham. It took the competition completely by surprise—and took the market by storm. I went to Birmingham and toured the market with Jimmy. The stores were loaded with three-liter bottles, and they were selling like crazy.

Nearly every shopping cart I saw had a three-liter bottle of Pepsi in it. I went up to a shopper to talk to her about the package. Then another, and another.

"What did they say?" Jimmy asked.

"Well, they like the three-liter package," I said, "but mostly when I asked questions like 'Is the bottle too heavy to lift?' they looked at me like 'If it's too heavy for me to lift, how does this idiot think I got it from the shelf into this cart?'"

"Well, what do you want to do now?" Jimmy asked.

"I want to get on the airplane, fly back to headquarters, and roll this baby national," I replied.

I did just that. And Coke followed, running as quickly as their lumbering legs would carry them. Which was pretty quickly, but we beat them to the markets that counted most. And when the dust settled, we had more volume with the three-liter bottle than they had.

Remember aspartame, the bane of my existence? When we last tuned in, Coke had a three-month jump on us. And Diet Coke was getting a big boost from its aspartame-and-saccharin combination.

The idea behind Diet Coke's ad campaign was to position it as a one-of-a-kind drink. What about Diet Pepsi? Oh, that was a subject too distressing to mention, a soft drink down in the basement of the industry with Tab—a product that consumers were rapidly consigning to ancient history.

Connecting our Diet Pepsi with their rapidly sinking Tab was a very shrewd strategy, considering how little affection diet cola drinkers had for Tab. Not a strategy, however, we intended to let work. So it was crucial for us to tell the world about aspartame-sweetened Diet Pepsi with commercials that were *really* distinctive.

I'll never forget the afternoon that Martha Holmes, then a creative director at BBDO, presented the "taste improved by Diet Pepsi" campaign to us. Because she brings along *no* storyboards. This is a dialogue, mini-drama campaign—the words are everything. And rather than read them, she's going to act them out for us.

Martha starts portraying one of the characters, but she doesn't stay with that. She goes for word pictures—"Now we hear the creaking floorboards; now the camera moves right in on the woman's face, up close and personal"—in a way that almost makes the commercials materialize in our conference room.

These commercials barely mention or show Diet Pepsi. The photography is very close up. In one, we watch a conversation between a husband and wife as they read the Sunday paper. Halfway through, she asks her husband if he'd like to finish her drink. She pours some more Diet Pepsi. He tastes it. "What is this I've been drinking?" he asks. "It's Diet Pepsi, with that new sweetener in it," she says. "Hmm, it's good," he says. And they go back to their conversation.

The commercials generated terrific response. But not, I don't believe, because the public really liked them. Actually, I think people felt guilty if they liked them; the commercials were *so* intimate that to watch them felt like eavesdropping.

The good news about these "taste improved" commercials is that they put Diet Pepsi on one hell of a growth curve.

The bad news is that Diet Coke still grew bigger and bigger.

If you were running a company and launching a new, improved product and a breakthrough ad campaign to support it, what would be the *last* thing you needed? A crisis, right? So, of course, I got a crisis.

The initiator was one Dr. Woodrow Monte, an Arizona scientist. In November of 1983 he petitioned the Arizona department of Health Services to ban aspartame in carbonated drinks in that state. His reason? Aspartame, he said, breaks down at high temperatures to form methanol in amounts he believes to be dangerous.

The FDA publicly stated that this was not a new issue. The FDA maintained that it had studied all the scientific data regarding aspartame and methanol, and had found nothing to support Dr. Monte's claim.

Did this give Dr. Monte pause? Not at all. With James Turner, a consumer advocate who'd participated in earlier fights to stop FDA approval of aspartame, he filed a suit in U.S. District Court in Washington to force the FDA to hold hearings on the safety of aspartame. We knew all about this. We weren't worried.

After all, there's more methanol in a serving of green beans than in a totally deteriorated can of Diet Pepsi. And we've never seen anyone keel over after his mother made him finish the green beans on his dinner plate.

But as we moved into January of 1984, we got a call from CBS News. There was going to be an investigative report on the aspartame issue on the *Nightly News*. It would run for three nights. Naturally, CBS would like to interview us.

We weren't too interested. We deal with the news media all the time, and it's our policy to cooperate fully, even when we don't like the story. But, in this case, the producers of the segment seemed to be unfair in their approach. Their questions reflected a negative point of view, and they didn't appear to be interested in interviewing scientists who believed in aspartame's safety.

We limited our participation in this, therefore, to taking phone surveys after the first night of Dan Rather's report. And, not to our surprise, the world didn't give a damn! People had had enough of all these self-appointed do-gooders crying wolf. Of those who saw it, most thought the report was inconclusive. The American public once again demonstrated its good judgment.

Over the next few days, newspapers picked up the story—but it was buried on page 20. And the FDA held a press conference. Aspartame, the regulators said, is safe for all approved products. The few negative reports they've gotten are, they think, incidental, and have nothing to do with aspartame, but they've asked the Center for Disease Control to monitor them. If there's anything to be concerned about, they'll let the public know.

In my view, a courageous stand. Not like the FDA of old.

* * *

The most interesting part of this mini-crisis has never been completely revealed, so let's do it here.

Before the CBS story airs, the president of Searle's aspartame division, Bob Shapiro, calls me. "I just want you to know that there's been some unusual trading in options of our stock," he says. "The SEC is investigating and they think it's coming out of Arizona."

"Monte?"

"Could be," Shapiro says. "Maybe Dr. Monte has a sudden financial interest in Searle. And you know what? Some unusual option trading in New York too. Looks like some other folks may be playing in the market."

"When will the SEC know for sure?"

"Oh, I think they know now."

"When will they announce it?"

"God knows."

"This might be a good time to discredit the CBS report," I say. "Why don't we go public with the SEC's suspicions."

"Well, the thing is, the SEC informed us of this in confidence— they wanted to see if any Searle employees were suddenly dabbling in the stock."

We decide to respect the confidentiality of the SEC investigation. We'll let events take their natural course.

Some weeks later, the SEC does announce that Dr. Monte had been trading in Searle stock options. Seems he sold Searle short before he launched his attack on aspartame. In a story in *The Wall Street Journal*, Monte's fellow consumerists are shocked. "It's the American way," says Monte. After all, isn't making a buck America's favorite pastime? Who cares how you do it?

Later, the story breaks about that unusual option trading in New York. The SEC indicates to CBS that some of its employees may have been involved in Searle option trading— before the CBS report on aspartame hit the airwaves. At first, CBS declines to launch its own investigation. Then it reconsiders and questions some of its employees. But does it run the results on page one? Are they featured night after night on the news broadcasts? No way, José.

"We don't choose to discuss the status or nature of any internal review," said a CBS news official who insisted on remaining anonymous.

* * *

The aspartame crisis abated. Diet Pepsi sales soared. And as we reached the eighteen-month point of my being president of Pepsi USA, my world was very different from what it was at the end of my first six months. Michael Jackson was rapidly making Coke wish it was Pepsi. Diet Pepsi sales were increasing at better than a 30 percent rate. Slice was blowing off the store shelves in its test market. The three-liter bottle was beginning to roll across the country from its huge success in Birmingham. Our bottlers were turned on, investing in the business as never before.

Sales of PBG, our company-owned bottling division, were on the verge of a major upswing, due in large measure to superb strategies devised by the division's president and its senior VP, Bob Dettmer and Craig Weatherup, strategies which were brilliantly executed by their entire management team.

And for the coming year, we had more up our sleeve. Lionel Richie would carry the baton for Year II of our "New Generation" advertising campaign. Slice would roll out from its test market to the real world of a national expansion. Our new product development and R&D folks were working on a whole carload of promising new soft drinks.

Around that time, we held a midyear operating review with Don Kendall and Andy Pearson. We told them about all these things. The meeting was terrific. We were really on a high.

The next day I got a memo from Andy. "Your list of big ideas is solid, but not spectacular," he wrote. "I really think you ought to be reaching higher."

Today, Andy—who's now retired from PepsiCo and is a professor at the Harvard Business School—says he never wrote that memo. I say there was someone in the company writing annoying memos and signing his name to them. But whenever I tease him about it—and I often do because, let's face it, there aren't many divisions in *any* company that generate the kind of growth and excitement Pepsi did in 1983–84, and was about to do in 1985—Andy challenges me to produce it.

Well, I can't—that was one memo that got torn up so quickly, it never made it to my out basket.

Reach higher? God, that got me mad. Hell, we had leveled the playing field. Now we were really ready to take on Coke. The boys in Atlanta had better have their armor on. We were ready to roll.

CHAPTER 11

Controlling the Agenda

At this propitious moment, just as we were ready to go full tilt, the aspartame issue returned. It's like the proverbial bad penny. We just can't shake it. And this time, the overtones were eerily reminiscent of the fructose issue. For, just as in the fructose versus sugar decision, I now found myself in a potential foot race with Coke.

Tim Healey, the new vice president of marketing at Searle, started the next round of my unending aspartame crisis by suggesting that Diet Pepsi be the first drink in the industry to go to 100 percent aspartame. Why Pepsi? Well, Tim was marketing director of Frito-Lay when I was there. He knew me. He knew my team. And he knew that, with Diet Coke sales booming, we were the most likely candidate to attack the market with a 100 percent aspartame diet drink.

And—just possibly—Searle wanted to make up to Pepsi for the screwing they'd given us the year before.

Tim argued that 100 percent aspartame was something that consumers really wanted. And he had the research to prove it. At that time, when we marketed Diet Pepsi, the cans and bottles and commercials said "now with NutraSweet Blend." If you read closer, you'd see that Diet Pepsi also had saccharin, blended with aspartame. We weren't concealing the fact because we were uneasy about the saccharin; there's just so much you can put on a package or in a commercial, and you tend to go with what's new.

Tim's research showed that consumers believed aspartame

had *already* replaced saccharin. When they found out it hadn't, they got angry. That got my attention.

Tim's research also showed that consumers couldn't taste the difference between 100 percent aspartame and the aspartame-and-saccharin blend. Even so, given a choice between an aspartame-and-saccharin blend and 100 percent aspartame, they vastly preferred pure aspartame. They preferred it so strongly, in fact, that they were willing to pay more for a diet cola that had it.

Strong research. But we told Tim we wanted three weeks to do some research on our own.

Tim said he had only enough supply on hand for one big brand to have 100 percent aspartame. If we couldn't decide quickly, he might have to make a deal with Coke.

Too bad if he did—we had to do our own tests. We did. The results confirmed Searle's research.

Now we were confident: This was a *big* idea. The guy who got there first was going to have a *big* advantage. He was also, we realized, going to have taken one very big risk. The risk was purely financial.

It would cost anywhere from $40 million to $60 million to convert from an aspartame-saccharin blend to 100 percent aspartame. And if consumer reaction turned out to be only mildly enthusiastic, that $40 million to $60 million was going to come right out of the bottom line.

But taking risks, as I'd learned by then, is the name of this game. And so I called Bob Shapiro at Searle to tell him we wanted Diet Pepsi to be the first 100 percent aspartame-sweetened soft drink on the market. Would it cost us tens of millions of dollars? Oh, yes. But I couldn't care about that. If consumers wanted 100 percent aspartame, that's what they'd get—and they'd get it first from Pepsi.

In the late summer of 1984, several of our key executives and I fly out to Chicago to meet with Searle's management. This time, I am determined not to make the same mistakes I made last year. This time, I'll stay very close; the deal will not get bogged down by reams of paper.

The 100 percent formulas will use four to five times the amount of aspartame that the aspartame-saccharin blends use, so there are three things we've got to get from Searle to make this only a merely risky—rather than stupid—decision. A price reduction. Assurance of adequate supply. And enough time as the only all-aspartame products on the market to get the competitive advantage we need to push up our sales—and pay back our increased costs.

The Searle conference room fills up with lawyers. Needless to say, nothing is going to get done.

We take a break and I ask that only the top executives participate in the next session. We're going to lay our cards on the table—well, some of them anyway.

I take out a yellow pad. On a single page, I write the following: "I, Roger Enrico, am willing to go to 100% aspartame in all our diet soft drinks. I pledge that Pepsi USA will buy X million pounds at Y dollars per pound over Z years."

I can't release the specifics. Let's just say that X times Y times Z equals one *billion* dollars. My idea is to sign this letter of intent, and let the lawyers work through the subclauses later. Searle has to think about it.

You'll remember we've been through this dance once, and it didn't work out so well for us. So this year, I inform them, we must be assured that Searle isn't negotiating on this with any other soft drink company. We must be assured that we will never be disadvantaged as to the price of aspartame. And we must be assured that no matter how many companies eventually sign these contracts, we will never have to worry about getting our orders delivered in full.

Searle's response is to go off and do economic models. Time passes. No, it *drags*.

It's clear Searle doesn't quite know what they want. For them, the tonnage is higher; the price—and the profit margin—is lower. If everyone in the soft drink business goes to 100 percent aspartame, Searle will have to build more plants. And with all those new factors to consider, Searle's having trouble arriving at a price.

The negotiations continue long after our return from Chicago. But as we negotiate, it becomes clear that the original terms I offered on that yellow pad aren't going to be accepted. The price will be higher, the time to gain a competitive advantage shorter. I become uncertain whether we really should do this.

Now begins an endless cycle of meetings in our conference room. Our vice president of concentrate manufacturing, Lou Imbrogno; head of Research and Development, Bennett Nussbaum; legal counsel, Pam McGuire; and vice president of brand marketing, Dan Clark, report on the negotiations—very few of the "deal-breakers" we had in our original negotiating plan are going our way. At each of these meetings, I decide to scrap the whole 100 percent aspartame idea. And at each of these meetings, I run straight into the immovable determination of Dan Clark.

"We've *got* to do this," he says.

"Come on, Dan."

"You're getting hung up on the fact we're not getting much of what we wanted in these negotiations," Dan says. "But the bigger fact is, the consumers want one hundred percent aspartame in our products. So what if people can't tell the difference between an aspartame-saccharin blend and an all-aspartame formula in a blind taste test? Consumers aren't blind when they buy a product—they have their eyes wide open, and they're telling us they want to see one hundred percent aspartame. This *is* a marketing business, and we've got to give the consumers what *they* want, not what's convenient for us."

Everything I used to say! But not now. Now, I'm just irritated with Dan. Meanwhile, I change my mind every day; for a month, I'm like a damned on-off switch.

And every day, Dan makes the same case he made the day before. He is not making my life easier. But he's so in touch with the market research, so certain this is a big chance for us, that he keeps pounding me back into submission.

While Dan is doing a terrific job for the company and I'm playing Hamlet, Searle and our team conclude negotiations. Perfect timing! For now even *I* start to see that this *is* the biggest opportunity we've had in a long time to begin controlling the agenda in the diet soft drink business. Going to 100 percent aspartame is not a tactical move; it's a major strategic offensive. A few dollars one way or another on the price of aspartame is a pimple on the rear of progress. Now I'm willing to bet a billion.

I go into Don Kendall's office. Andy Pearson and Vic Bonomo are there to participate in Don's decision. So is Wayne Calloway, then PepsiCo's chief financial officer, now our chairman.

The first thing I do is go through all the negatives. The money involved. The possibility that we won't have much lead-time. The need for secrecy and, consequently, our inability to test-market. And of course, the potentially permanent reduction in our margins.

But then there *are* the positives. Consumers want 100 percent aspartame. So much so that when they are asked to choose between all-aspartame Diet Pepsi and Diet Coke with almost twice as much saccharin as aspartame, they pick Diet Pepsi nearly two-to-one.

"How do your people feel?" Kendall asks me.

"I've been all over the map on this one, but everybody else has been pretty consistent. Dan Clark's totally for it. Most everyone else isn't sure it's worth the roll."

"Considering that, Roger, how can you come in and recommend it to me?"

"Because you pay *me* to make the decisions in Pepsi USA. And I've decided Dan Clark is right."

"I'll think about it over the weekend," Kendall says.

On Monday morning I call Kendall's office to find out when he wants to see me.

"No, you don't have to come over," his secretary says. "He'll send you a memo."

Which means he's decided. Against. Andy Pearson's on vacation in Florida. I call him.

"Is there anything new to show Don?" he asks.

"We got some more research over the weekend," I say. "It doesn't tell us anything new. It just confirms what we already know: This will put Diet Pepsi on one hell of a roll, and Diet Coke in one hell of a box."

"Let me call Don."

Andy does. Essentially, he tells Kendall that yes, this is a close call, but that he can't turn it down. It's the classic PepsiCo dilemma: When a division president *really* wants to do something, it's very hard to say no without discouraging him from championing ideas that, though reasonable, are risky.

An hour later Kendall calls me. "I understand you have some new information," he says.

A *very* gracious way of signaling that he's willing to change his mind. The new data is presented. Kendall gives the go-ahead.

Of course, we haven't told our bottlers *anything* about the possible move to 100 percent aspartame. We've *got* to keep this secret until we're ready to roll nationally. When we are ready, we intend to make a "hard" conversion. That is, to destroy all the old packaging material in the pipeline—in bottlers' warehouses and at hundreds of suppliers. It'll cost millions, but it will get us on the market everywhere instantly—and take the competition totally by surprise.

But we can't just spring this on our bottlers, who are, after all, going to share the additional cost of going to 100 percent aspartame. So we decide to seek the support of a representative group.

As it happens, I'm supposed to go off on a fishing trip with Chuck Mangold, my old friend and vice president of bottler relations—and, not least, the man who finally convinced me that the bottlers would skin me alive if I killed the Michael Jackson commercials. We decide to use the trip as a cover.

Our first stop is San Francisco, where Richie Campodonico has his boat ready. Richie is an extraordinary bottler. His family has been in the Pepsi business for fifty years and they have built their company from very modest beginnings to sales of more than one hundred million dollars a year. He's also a man I've become very close to; his marketing sense is uncanny and his personal integrity is uncompromising.

"Uh, Richie, we're really not going fishing," I say.

Instead, I take out the latest in my never-ending series of presentation decks. I hand him a can of Diet Pepsi with 100 percent aspartame. And I lead him through all the pros and cons. This takes until the end of dinner. We're well into the Sambuca when I ask the (literally) billion-dollar question.

"What do you think, Richie?"

"I don't know."

"If we're going to move on this, we've got to move fast."

"Why don't we have breakfast in the morning?"

In the morning we have breakfast. Sometimes we talk about aspartame; sometimes we don't.

"Richie," I say, "I need your decision."

"I'll drive you to the airport, Roger," he says. "I want to see the new Pepsi airplane."

Richie drives us to the airport. Sometimes we talk about aspartame; sometimes we don't. Now we're standing in the door of the plane. The engines are warming up.

"Well?"

"Hell, Roger," Richie says. "Let's do it."

We fly off to Worland, Wyoming, to see Forrest Clay, who's not only a hugely successful bottler but a key member of our Bottlers Association and a very thoughtful guy. Forrest drives us to his home for lunch, talking a blue streak about the business and the enchiladas his wife, Mary, has prepared for us.

"Forrest, before lunch I want to take you through this plan and have you taste the product," I say.

"What for?" he asks. "If you want to do this, do it."

We make the presentation anyway. And Forrest still wants us to do what we think is right.

Next stop: Denver, and Richard Gooding, one of several extraordinary young entrepreneurs who carry on the family tradition as Pepsi bottlers. Richard meets us at the airport.

"You know, it's not our style to deal with the parent company this way," he says. "Usually, we bargain and fight—but I'm not going to do that today. This is the right thing to do, and I'll support you on it."

We thank Richard and fly on to Tulsa, where we're meeting Phil Hughes and Cleber Massey, the men in charge of our third- and thirteenth-largest franchise bottling companies. We go to Phil's house and between Stolichnaya vodka and the terrific hospitality of Phil's wife, Marge, we manage to discuss the business at hand. Later, after dinner at a Tulsa restaurant, we get two more "go for it" votes along with our cognac and cigars.

Early the next morning, Chuck and I race on to Chicago to meet with Bob Selleck, president of Pepsi General Bottlers, our second largest franchisee, and George Wolf, our bottler from Wausau, Wisconsin, then president of the Pepsi-Cola Bottlers Association. We take them through the plan. Then we give them the new Diet Pepsi to taste.

"This is going to *kill* Pepsi," Bob says.

"What do you mean?"

"It tastes so damn good," he says. "I mean, it's as good as regular Pepsi-Cola."

We take this as a green light and go on to Columbus, Ohio, where Tom Gross of Gross-Jarson, our eighth largest franchisee—and another of the young entrepreneurs in our Pepsi family—joins us on board our parked airplane. He listens to our pitch and gives his okay. Then, getting a little ragged now, we fly to Albany, New York, to talk 100 percent aspartame to Pepsi bottler John Strachan.

John is known in the Pepsi business as "the Admiral." Partly because he's a U.S. Naval Academy grad and is still an ardent supporter of the old blue and gold. And partly because, like most admirals I met during my time in the navy, he's smart and tough. He knows that every other bottler we've seen has approved the plan—and that those bottlers are counting on him to ask every hard question, just to be sure they're getting a fair deal from the company.

We go to dinner together. John listens, but we don't get down to the nitty-gritty. John doesn't like to bargain when he's having dinner with friends. But breakfast is another matter. We eat on board our plane, parked on the tarmac at the Albany airport. Now John *would* like to negotiate a bit on how the company and bottlers split the extra cost of aspartame.

"John," I say, "the split we've got in the plan is a fair one. Both the bottlers and the company will need the same increase in sales to break even. Besides, there's not really time to bargain over nickels."

John gives me a poker face. But it's time for him and Chuck to catch a commercial flight all the way back to Worland, Wyoming. They're going deer-hunting with Forrest Clay—unlike my fishing trip, for real. Picking up his rifle, he stands and says, "Go ahead."

Last stop is Boston. Bert Einloth of General Cinema, our largest franchise bottler, is an astute marketing guy. Today, he astutely makes the vote unanimous.

Glazed, I fly home, call four more of our most important and most insightful bottlers—Jimmy Lee in Birmingham, Alabama; Jim Moore in Columbia, South Carolina; Harold Honickman in New York City; and Jim Lindsey in San Diego, California—and get, for good measure, four more *yes* votes. Rosemary asks me, tongue in cheek, how the fishing trip went.

Kendall calls. "How'd it go?"

"Every single bottler was supportive."

"Go to it."

Where I go to is to bed.

The next day, we immediately placed an order for 100 million dollars' worth of aspartame. We would launch in two weeks. And we began the process of changing our packaging graphics. To get a few more days of secrecy, we selected just one trusted company to make the hundreds of printing plates necessary to get the ball rolling.

Now we contacted our packaging suppliers. When they got packaging plates, we told them, they'd know what we were up to. And we asked them to maintain confidentiality. The plates were sent. New packaging was being produced. No leaks. This was absolutely amazing.

And we scheduled a press conference for the following Wednesday. But before that, the president of SSC&B—the agency that does the advertising for Diet Coke—gets, according to industry sources, an early-morning phone call from Atlanta.

It's from Sergio Zyman, Coke's marketing guy.

"WHAT IS DIET PEPSI DOING?"

The SSC&B guy is asleep. But he's waking up fast.

"DIET PEPSI'S DOING *SOMETHING*. WHAT IS IT?"

"I don't know."

"WELL, I SUGGEST YOU FIND OUT—BY NOON."

Zyman wasn't nicknamed The Aya-cola for nothing.

The president of SSC&B and his staff hustle all morning. By day's end, the Coke intelligence apparatus has twigged that we've masterminded the death of saccharin. That gets their attention. With the tremendous success of Diet Coke, they're not about to just sit around and see what happens. But there's nothing they or The Aya-cola can do about it in twenty-four hours.

Our press conference goes off like clockwork. The press jumps on our move to 100 percent aspartame like dogs on a T-bone steak. It's played as big news. The boys at Coke headquarters in Atlanta don't have much to say except they're keeping their options open.

How long would the Coca-Cola Company contemplate its navel? Not very long, we figured. And for one very good reason. They might not have been willing to take the offensive on 100 percent aspartame, but they, too, could read the research showing that when people have a choice, it's a landslide victory for the brand that has it.

So we produced the new Diet Pepsi commercials *very* quickly—and *very* quietly. They're really hard-hitting.

"Diet Coke has twice as much saccharin as it has aspartame," they say.

We weren't trying to imply there were any health implications in that. We were just informing the public of the facts.

Two weeks before the spots were to go on the air, we showed them to hundreds of bottlers at a Pepsi Bottlers Association meeting in Chicago, in a session closed to outsiders. The bottlers now began to smell the blood we'd been sniffing at for months. Diet Coke blood, to be exact. And still no word from the Coke brass. Would they fall into the trap? Would they sit this one out? Just wait and see what happened in the marketplace?

We didn't know. But if our move was as popular with consumers as we thought it was going to be, we knew they wouldn't sit on the sidelines for long. Still, every day was another day for us to beat them in the consumer's mind.

The following Monday, an industry trade publication ran a very accurate description of our advertising. How'd they do it? Well, their reporter talked to twenty of our bottlers and pieced it all together.

The loose talk of those twenty Pepsi bottlers became one hell of an expensive price to pay to get Pepsi a few inches in a magazine—because just by reading the trade magazine, Coke knew, almost two weeks before air date, exactly what our commercials said. And with this information, Coke quickly decided to go to 100 percent aspartame. No way were they going to hang out there and let Diet Coke get blasted by Diet Pepsi.

Anticipating this possibility, we'd bought much more aspartame than we needed, the better to block Coke. We didn't know how much Coke already had sitting in its warehouses, but we didn't think it was enough to get quick national distribution of 100 percent aspartame Diet Coke; it would take them three months, minimum. We were national with 100 percent aspartame Diet Pepsi virtually right away. Our commercials were all over the tube.

Coke then made a press announcement that Diet Coke was changing to 100 percent aspartame, and sent—by Federal Express—one six-pack of all-aspartame Diet Coke to every grocery store manager in the country. They also made commercials announcing they'd dumped saccharin. Then they demanded that the television networks take our commercials off the air, and sent threatening letters to our bottlers and local TV stations—because, don't you see, the Diet Pepsi ads are all lies. Diet Coke *doesn't* contain saccharin any more.

Nice try, boys. The ole smoke and mirrors trick.

I told our bottlers that 100 percent aspartame Diet Coke was a mile wide and an inch deep. Throw the threatening letters away. We'd track the actual distribution of all-aspartame Diet Coke, and when it reached the point where consumers could find it, we'd change our advertising. And we began to do distribution studies of the new Diet Coke. The independent, outside-company studies came in.

We went down to the networks and showed them: Diet Coke with 100 percent aspartame was available in only 12 percent of the nation's stores. Our advertising stayed. Meanwhile, it was Coke's advertising that was questionable—and ABC pulled Diet Coke's advertising off the air!

This prompted a Coke attorney to call our lawyer Clay Small.

Suggesting that Coke might just sue us for civil penalties. Grounds: false advertising.

"I think you'd be wrong to do that," Clay said.

"Why?" the Coke lawyer asked.

"Because you guys are the ones with a problem."

"How so?"

"You have national distribution in only 12.3 percent of the market, and in the stores where you have *any* 100 percent aspartame Diet Coke, there's a lot more old product than new. Consumers need to use a magnifying glass to find the new stuff."

The Coke lawyer got very quiet. Which leads me to wonder: Were there smoke and mirrors between the Coke marketing types and their own lawyers too?

Coke didn't sue. It did get full distribution—in three months—with the new Diet Coke. But long before Diet Coke was in the stores, Coke once again tried to blunt our lead with a series of teaser ads. "It's coming, it's coming," they said. And saccharin became a non-issue. No matter that people had a hard time finding the 100 percent aspartame Diet Coke—it was coming.

Still, Diet Pepsi got a big boost. Sales surged far above the level we needed to pay back the additional cost of aspartame. So did, when it finally arrived, sales of the reformulated Diet Coke. The Cola Wars, we saw once again, were good for business—this time, both ours and theirs.

But these are not the Cola Wars of yore. Coke has brought something new to the party.

In the old days—really, right up to 1980—except for an ill-fated attempt to discredit the Pepsi Challenge, Coke never mentioned Pepsi by name. To Coke executives, Pepsi was "our imitator." At best, they spoke of Pepsi as "our chief imitator." Now comes the Goizueta era.

In the middle of the 100 percent aspartame battle—at just the point when Coke is distributing its new product a mile wide and an inch deep—Goizueta gives an interview to the *Atlanta Constitution*. This is his hometown paper. In a town where Coke rules. Not much chance he's being misquoted.

"DIET COKE ONE-UPS PEPSI'S COMMERCIAL," reads the *Constitution*'s headline on December 10, 1984.

The article explains how Coke went to 100 percent aspartame several weeks after Pepsi—but just *before* we went on the air with our commercials.

"There must be some reels of videotape and advertising

material in some [Pepsi] file somewhere, because they are not able to use any of them," Goizueta chuckled to the reporter. "We got a big kick out of being in the marketplace in key markets before they were, even though they announced it quite a bit earlier than we did. But that's just the fun of the business—beating your competition to the punch."

Strange, but it looked to me like they were the ones with a problem getting advertising cleared. And, except for those highly-touted sixpacks sent by Federal Express, I'd say we were the ones who made it to the market first.

In October of 1984, as we wait for Phil Dusenberry to bring the storyboards for the 1985 Pepsi commercials up to Purchase, we aren't looking out our office windows at the leaves turning gold on the trees and thinking about how much we've accomplished in a year.

We're thinking: How is it possible to do *better* than Michael Jackson? And: Can *anyone* make a better, more competitive soft drink commercial than "Spaceship"? In soft drink advertising, momentum is the name of the game. Sure, it's nice to have a "Spaceship." But it was also great for Coke to have a commercial as spectacular as the one with Mean Joe Greene.

Quick quiz: What year did the Mean Joe Greene commercial run?

Answer: 1977.

Quick quiz bonus question: Name one Coke commercial since 1977 that is as memorable as the one with Mean Joe Greene. Right. You've got to do it year after year, or people will say, "Wow, Mean Joe Greene—or, for that matter, 'Spaceship'—was way back *then*?"

Dusenberry arrives. He's all smiles. And why not? He knows as well as we do that the "New Generation" Pepsi commercials are contenders for dozens of awards. (He's right; we'll win more than forty in 1984 alone.) The script he worked on for *The Natural* has been made into a film starring Robert Redford. And blissfully, the agency has had time—since February—to work up the Lionel Richie concepts.

"Last year, we announced the New Generation," Phil says. "We gave it the beginnings of a personality—one that lives for the excitement of the cutting edge. This year, we can start to define this generation, to give it depth and character. And Lionel's perfect for what we think we need to do to expand the meaning of the New Generation around Beat and Heart and

Style—we'll get all the excitement of his music, plus his genuine warmth and class."

Phil takes us through the commercials. The first begins simply, with Lionel saying, "You know, we're a whole new generation. A generation of new feelings, new rhythms, new styles." And with that it moves into a classy video with Lionel and the new generation of America, all choreographed to a Richie composition written especially for Pepsi.

Then there's Lionel sitting at his piano. "The heart of the new generation," he says, "is how we feel about each other." And the second spot features Lionel coming home to visit his grandmother. Lionel would like his ninety-odd-year-old grandmother to do the commercial with him. That's guaranteed good feeling. We approve it immediately.

After the magic moment between Lionel and his grandmother, the beat begins—to a reworded version of his colossal hit, "Running With the Night." In the third spot, Lionel will host and sing at the biggest block party ever filmed for a commercial.

All of this sounds terrific to me. It's true to Lionel's character. And it's true to the way we feel—that after the so-called "Me Generation," it's time to reach out again to one another.

These commercials definitely do that. And they'll definitely make history. For one thing, the block party will be the centerpiece of television's first three-minute product commercial. For another, it will be the most expensive commercial ever made.

"How many people are coming to this party?" we ask.

"We could need . . . oh, four thousand extras," Phil says. "Big set."

"Remember the set for 'Spaceship'?" Phil says. "The stage was the size of two football fields. We'll shoot this one on the Universal Studios lot."

"But 'Spaceship' was all effects. This has people—we'll need a big crew, right?"

"Oh . . . maybe two hundred people."

"How will cameras move through that crowd?"

"I thought we'd use a Sky-Cam."

"What's that?"

"A camera that flies."

"How?"

"It's on wires, high above the set."

"Has it ever been used in a commercial?"

"Nope."

"Big production."

"And it's not the only one," Phil says.

"What else is big?"

"'Archeology.'"

"Tell us about it."

"Archeology," Phil explains, features a professor who's taking his Pepsi-drinking archeology students on a field trip. The time: the future. The discoveries: a split-level ranch house, a baseball, an electric guitar. The professor identifies them all. Then a student finds a dusty object. The professor puts it in a machine that cleans centuries of dirt from it. Now we see what it is: the green Coke bottle, a twentieth-century relic. "What is it, Professor?" a student asks as he sips his Pepsi. The professor ponders it once more. "I've no idea," he says.

We crack up.

"This one's a killer," we say. "How complicated will it be to make?"

"We can use models for some of it . . ."

"Yes?"

"But it will probably take two sound stages . . ."

"Yes?"

"And maybe a couple of tons of dirt—to cover the house we'll have to build and then dig up."

"Oh, is that all?"

Phil presents more commercial concepts. "Do it," we say. "Do it all."

One of the things you fear when you start signing celebrities is that the hype begins to outweigh the excitement. "Who will Pepsi sign next?" is a question that can get tired very fast. One way to short-circuit that boredom is not to sign celebrities who can't generate at least a year's worth of good feeling.

Lionel Richie showed us a second way: Sign celebrities who are unique, and whose uniqueness stands in sharp contrast to everyone who came before. For Lionel was certainly different from the Michael Jackson we met in 1983. Yet his appeal was just as great as Michael's. Our sales went up. His commercials also scored tops in the Video Storyboard consumer surveys as the best-liked and best-remembered of the year—the number one advertising in the country in 1985.

And his grandmother, who had inspired Lionel as a child to work at his music, was a truly grand lady. Shortly before she was to appear in our commercial, an unfortunate but minor accident left her with a painfully broken wrist—and a cast that reached nearly to her elbow. Lionel was concerned for her and said there was no need to appear in the ad; we could get an appropriate stand-in.

"Don't worry, Grandma," Lionel told her, "there will be other commercials."

"Maybe for you, Lionel," she responded, "but I'm ninety—this is my big chance."

Grandmother Richie did the Pepsi commercial with an over-sized gardening glove covering her cast. A real trouper; no stand-ins for her.

From the beginning of our relationship to the last date on the contract, Lionel was amazingly cooperative. During his national concert tour before he went on, Lionel would come to a Pepsi reception backstage and meet our bottlers and our customers and their kids. Night after night, he'd stand for as many pictures as people wanted to take. He kissed babies; he kissed women; he signed a million autographs. None of this was in his contract.

Lionel also did something that dovetailed with some long-standing Pepsi interests. In 1984, Lionel was honored as the United Negro College Fund's Alumnus of the Year. Not too many years ago, in 1983, Pepsi-Cola was the first company to donate $1 million to that fund. And that, thankfully, started a tradition that a number of other corporations have followed.

So when Lionel suggested that we join him in some community projects, we were only too happy to do so. Lionel's manager, Ken Kragen, had met Bill Milliken, the founder of an organization called Cities in Schools. This group had done an impressive job of reclaiming inner-city kids who were completely turned off about anything that even suggested school. Now Cities in Schools wanted to set up a model program at a public school in Washington, D.C. Lionel was going to make a contribution; we said we'd match it.

We went down to Washington on an incredibly hot day. Barbara Bush met us at the school. And Marion Barry, the mayor of Washington, dropped in to thank Lionel.

The auditorium was jammed. We were all sweltering. I don't think anyone really wanted to hear a single speech. But there was a piano in the auditorium—and we didn't have to drag Lionel over to it. The kids and their teachers were the greatest audience one could imagine.

In a way, that was the sweetest concert of the whole tour.

CHAPTER 12

Celebrity Roulette

Everyone who's ever run anything knows there's always one area that resists even your most ardent efforts. For me, that's Diet Pepsi advertising.

Thanks to Diet Pepsi's great taste and 100 percent aspartame, Diet Pepsi's sales have been shooting through the roof. By 1986, the brand was almost twice as big as it was in 1983. But Diet Coke just continues rolling along. I'm pretty philosophical about it by now.

And because I'm so hardened to trouble, Diet Pepsi hasn't reared up and bit me for a while. But I know all about that ploy. Diet Pepsi thinks it's got me fooled. *Next* year, when I'm totally focused on something else, it'll get me double.

I'm sure, in your life, you've got one of these. The difference between us is that you didn't hire a very nice woman named Geraldine Ferraro and have your problem in public.

The idea was simple. Pepsi is the "choice of a new generation"—in soft drink terms, people aged fourteen to twenty-four. Now we're going to make Diet Pepsi "the one-calorie choice of a new generation"—which, in diet soft drink terms, means people aged eighteen to thirty-five.

In the fall of 1984, as Alan Pottasch and I talk about this, we feel we're looking at a real opportunity here. Diet drinks are expanding; the generation that prefers them has never been more aware of media personalities—we can do a great campaign that dramatizes the "leading edge" of this generation.

But because of the crunch to get the Lionel Richie commercials filmed and the need to make some quick spots that trumpet our move to 100 percent aspartame in Diet Pepsi, BBDO doesn't get a chance to meet with us about the main 1985 campaign for Diet Pepsi until after the New Year. Shooting 1985 commercials in 1985 is not good planning—and not good news. We'll *really* have to play beat the clock.

When Phil Dusenberry does make the pitch, he suggests three campaigns. The first is good. The second is better. The third is best of all. But then, the third campaign is always BBDO's best—as it is, I bet, at every agency in the world. The agency's favorite invariably brings up the rear. And the client invariably says, "*That* one."

The third idea, this year of 1985, continues the intimate slice-of-life camera technique that proved so successful in '84. It's a distinctive technique, it's associated with Diet Pepsi, and it hasn't—yet—been widely imitated. And it's appropriate.

Because, this time around, the agency wants to use people who represent America's new generation of leaders. They don't have to be super-famous. They do have to be known for an achievement that breaks ground. Some intimate aspect of the character-building it took to break that ground is what we're going to feature. We don't want these people to come out and say, "I love Diet Pepsi." They don't even have to drink the product on-camera. As in the Michael Jackson commercials, the good taste of Diet Pepsi is assumed.

The format is intriguing. Some dialogue between the celebrity and a relative, interviewer, or friend about making a tough choice. Then a product shot, with a voice-over: "When you've got to make a choice, what's right is what feels right. Diet Pepsi. One hundred percent NutraSweet, one hundred percent taste." Then the dialogue resumes and the story gets resolved, with a button—a funny, lighthearted, or tender moment—at the end. And then a final voice-over: "Diet Pepsi. The one-calorie choice of a new generation."

I spark to this idea pretty quickly. So does everyone else at Pepsi. Only one question: Who will we use?

"Peter Ueberroth, the baseball commissioner," says Phil. From Phil—the baseball nut—this is no surprise.

"Who else?"

"Baryshnikov . . . Iacocca . . ."

"Will they do it?"

"I can't ask them until you approve the idea."

"I don't want to approve an idea for celebrity commercials that celebrities may not want to do," I say. "We need to be sure that we have an idea here that can be sustained."

At our next meeting, Phil and the BBDO management supervisor on our account, Gary dePaolo, produce a list of celebrities who are right for this campaign. Geraldine Ferraro's name is on the list.

I get excited right away. The *first* female vice-presidential candidate—talk about a challenge!

"Does anyone at the agency know her?" I ask.

"I've met her," Phil says. "I sat next to her on a plane."

On that flight, I presume, Phil didn't mention that he was a member of President Reagan's "Tuesday Group"—and helped create the President's advertising in the 1984 campaign.

"Do you know her well enough to call her?"

"We talked for a few hours. Yeah."

Good. One down. Thus encouraged, I make a suggestion: Luciano Pavarotti and Beverly Sills. Beverly's been on a wildly successful diet, and she's told me (I'm on the board of the New York City Opera) that she's been drinking Diet Pepsi. So I told her: "Beverly, you are going to do a Pepsi commercial—for a little less than we paid Michael Jackson, okay?" She laughed, which isn't exactly saying yes but isn't a poke in the eye either.

After the meeting with Phil, I call the marketing people at the City Opera and say, more formally, that we might be interested in making a commercial with Beverly. They say they'll check her interest—discreetly.

With one thin woman just possibly on our list, we call the representatives of one large man. But Pavarotti couldn't, they say, be less interested. I drop the idea completely.

Mistake one. We should have asked Beverly to do that commercial solo.

When I'm on a mission—particularly one that has a deadline— I tend to plow straight ahead. And my determination to do this celebrity campaign is so great that I can't let the agency handle it by themselves. Nope, I'm going to call in some chips on my own.

I'm about to call Carl Pohlad, the chairman of MEI Corporation, one of our largest bottlers. Carl's just bought the Minnesota Twins—and if he doesn't know Peter Ueberroth, who does?

Just as I'm reaching for the phone, however, Patti buzzes me. "Carl Pohlad's on the phone," she says.

Maybe the gods drink Diet Pepsi, too.

"Roger, I need a favor," Carl says.

All he has to do is name it.

"We're having this meeting in Minneapolis and Peter Ueberroth has promised to come and speak," Carl says. "Can you possibly fly him out on the Pepsi plane?"

"Carl, I can not only fly him out, I'll fly out with him."

"Hey guys, we're in luck," I tell Phil and Alan at our next meeting. "I'm going to talk to Ueberroth myself."

They're very enthused. And they have some news of their own. Geraldine Ferraro likes the idea of doing a Diet Pepsi commercial.

Now I'm really pumped up. Without knowing a damn thing about the electorate's true feelings, I'm convinced that America has forgotten about that election three months ago. So Reagan won. So he kicked the Democrats almost out the door. That's over now. In victory, grudges die. Gentlemanly feeling returns. Geraldine Ferraro is not, now, a despised Democrat; she's a living symbol of women's possibilities.

I share these views with my colleagues. They've never heard me speak about politics before, so they assume these are deeply held and highly thoughtful opinions. Though they may not agree with everything I say, they certainly are willing to defer to this political pundit who, in his spare time, runs their business.

Also, I have these disarmingly cheery views about Phil Dusenberry's ability to turn political filmmaking into human drama. Remember the film about Reagan they showed at the Republican Convention in '84—the one in which the President walked through the military cemetery in Normandy? Phil made that. And I'm the first to tell Phil that this film was *brilliant Pepsi advertising*. And if he can do the same for Ferraro . . .

In fairness to the PepsiCo staff, there *is* opposition to the Ferraro commercial. It comes from Max Friedersdorf, who was our vice president of corporate affairs before he went on assignment to the Republican White House.

"This is an *awful* idea," Max tells Joe McCann. "Haven't you looked at the polls on Ferraro? People *really* don't like her."

"We don't have to worry about what the polls showed," I tell Joe when he returns from his meeting with Max. "We're not going to present her as a vice presidential candidate or politician. We'll present her as a human being and a mother. We'll make her look beautiful—and people *will* like her."

"Yeah, I told Max that," Joe replies. "And he said, 'That is just what I'm afraid of.'"

Well, Max *is* a true-blooded Republican. So we ignore his concerns. Ignore them so completely that we decide the Geraldine Ferraro commercial will kick off the Diet Pepsi campaign.

"If this commercial does nothing else," I say, "it will be talked about on every news program in the United States. Forget that Phil will make a beautiful piece of film and Ferraro will look terrific—it's worth it just for the publicity. Even if there's a problem and we only run it for two weeks, we'll get our money back a dozen times over in free publicity."

Mistake two: In advertising, scoring free air time is not the objective. Making your sales go up is. I've confused Geraldine Ferraro with Michael Jackson, and celebrity with results.

The agency goes off to make the deal with Ferraro. While we're waiting, BBDO sends word up that another name on the Diet Pepsi list happens to be a good friend of Tom Clark, BBDO's president. And who, in 1985, wouldn't want the BBDO president to call Lee Iacocca?

Now, we can't very well say, "Lee Iacocca for Diet Pepsi." So we come up with a better idea. The commercial will open with a shot of the cover of Iacocca's book—or a shot of Iacocca sitting back at his desk with his hands behind his head in a witty recap of the book jacket picture. That's good for Lee, good for his book, good for us. Lee Iacocca gets a call. And he hears just what we'd like to do with him.

In this commercial, an attractive female reporter will be interviewing him about the hard choices he faced at Chrysler. "Let's go back to 1979," she'll say. "What were your thoughts?"

"The fact is, we were in trouble," Iacocca will say. "And a lot of people were writing us off."

"And then?"

"Well, for us the choice was simple—either go under or go for it. So we rolled up our sleeves and went to work."

At this point, we'll cut to the product shot and the voice-over about choices. Then we'll come back to Iacocca and the interviewer.

"Well, we won," Iacocca will say.

"Was it fun?"

Iacocca will lean back with that cocky look of his we all love.

"Yeah—especially when we run into the people who were writing us off."

He *can't* hate that—and he doesn't.

Ferraro also likes the script the agency's prepared. And why shouldn't she? It starts with her hidden behind a newspaper. Her daughter comes in and says, "Looking for a job, Mom?" The paper comes down. We see who's behind it. Ferraro says, "Very funny," proving for all time that she can laugh at herself. Then her daughter asks for advice. Ferraro tells her that women have a lot of choices now—and they can be anything they want. We sign a contract with her.

Mistake three: When a national politician signs on to do a celebrity endorsement with a prominent company, the first thing the press is going to do is try to find out how much was paid so they can scream, "Sellout!" No matter that the prominent company and the politician have explicitly stated in the contract that the fee will not be revealed. The fee *always* gets revealed— usually inaccurately, usually on the high side. I should have suggested that she make a very public—and unquestionably heartfelt—donation to a nonpolitical charity.

It's now two weeks before the Super Bowl. And, almost as a throwaway, the names of the opposing quarterbacks come up. Dan Marino and Joe Montana? We can really get them? Move over, Mean Joe Greene.

The quarterbacks sign in less time than it takes to throw a sixty-yard pass. They can't shoot the commercial until after the Super Bowl, but who cares? We're officially launched. Three or four more signings, and we'll have a campaign.

Flying out to Minneapolis with the baseball commissioner gives me plenty of time to explain the Diet Pepsi new generation campaign. I get to wax poetic about the intimacy and impact of the film techniques we're going to use. And I go on at some length on the theme of our proposed Ueberroth commercial as a boost to baseball—in much the same way that the Marino-Montana commercial will promote football as well as Diet Pepsi. At the end of all this, I talk about money. My offer is low, but it's clear I can do better.

A few days later I call Ueberroth to tell him that we've upped the fees—and that Lee Iacocca is interested in doing one of these things. Iacocca, I say, will donate his fee to charity.

Maybe, I think, that will suggest a level of class that will appeal to Ueberroth and close the deal. It doesn't. But Ueberroth is interested. He just needs some time to think it over.

Don Kendall invites me to a dinner at his house. And, because I haven't seen him since we signed Geraldine Ferraro, I rush right over and tell him the exciting news.

"Why the hell would you put *her* in it?" Don says.

"Because she was the first woman vice presidential candidate—and she'll get us on every news show in America."

Don falls silent. He's not going to argue about this at dinner. And he knows that because there aren't many Republicans more committed to the party than Don Kendall, anything he says might look narrow and partisan. And one thing Don is not is narrow. Still, I want Don's enthusiasm, not his tolerance. So I run through the rest of the possible Diet Pepsi lineup.

"Ferraro? Iacocca? Montana? Marino?"

Don's looking at me with cool amusement.

"What are you trying to do, Roger—help your brothers and sisters get work?"

And you know, until that moment, I never realized they were all Italian.

"It's a complete coincidence," I say. "But now that I think about it, it's because Italians are doing all the important things today."

Don smiles.

He also says, "We'll see."

The filming of Geraldine Ferraro goes so well that, at the end of the day, Ferraro turns to Phil Dusenberry and says, "You know, during the campaign if we'd had people like you, it would have made all the difference in the world."

Phil now knows that no one has told Geraldine Ferraro that the man who's supervising her commercial is the same guy who helped put her team away a few months earlier. So Phil blushes. And Phil stammers. And Geraldine Ferraro probably goes away thinking that this is a man who gets easily flustered by praise.

The way we make commercials with celebrities is to give them creative approval—sort of. We tell them the concept. If they approve it, we create a script. We show them the script. If they approve it, we shoot the commercial. We show them the commercial. If they have specific suggestions, we try to accommodate them.

But we *don't* contractually let celebrities say, after we've spent anywhere from $300,000 to $3 million shooting a commercial: "I don't like this. You'll have to kill it."

Lee Iacocca tells us: "I like the idea, I like the script—but if I can't live with the finished commercial, it can't run."

What to do?

Hell, it's Lee Iacocca. You say yes. You say it reluctantly, but you say it.

The last time I saw Lee Iacocca was at Babson College graduation exercises in 1965. I was a bright-eyed senior getting ready to grab my sheepskin and take on the real world. Iacocca, the father of the Mustang, was the speaker at my commencement. It is, therefore, a special kick to have dinner with him at Lutèce the evening before we're filming his Diet Pepsi commercial.

Rosemary's with me, and Tom Clark and his wife, and Allen and Missy Rosenshine. Iacocca's brought along Peggy Johnson, then his fiancée and now his bride. It's a lively dinner, and after about two minutes, we're firing questions at Iacocca as if we've known him for years. One of the things we're curious about is—naturally—marketing. How *do* you sell cars?

"You know, men think they make all the decisions, but women really buy the cars for their families," Iacocca says. "So we've been thinking about a woman to be a spokesperson for Chrysler—but it's so damned hard to find one. Why is that?"

I suggest it's because women and men alike can agree on men they admire, but women can be very hard on other women.

"That's interesting," Iacocca says. "Let's try it out here."

And he starts throwing out names of contemporary women for the consideration of the women at the table. No agreement is reached.

"What about Geraldine Ferraro?" Iacocca asks.

Now, the Ferraro-Pepsi connection has still not been announced. The leaks and rumors haven't even started.

Rosemary says nothing. Missy Rosenshine says nothing. Karen Clark says nothing. Like their husbands, they're all thinking: *Lee Iacocca* believes Ferraro is a good idea.

The next morning, Iacocca goes on the set and gives us one of his greater performances. A few weeks later, we send a cassette of the Iacocca commercial out to Detroit. Iacocca loves it.

In New York, Geraldine Ferraro watches a cut of her commercial. Ferraro loves it.

Up in Purchase, we look at a rough cut of the Montana-Marino commercial. It's only one of the best jock commercials we've ever seen.

As it inevitably must, however, with Diet Pepsi and me, the good news starts to unravel.

First, Don Kendall goes to Washington for a high-powered business lunch. And whom should he be seated next to but Henry Ford? If Lee Iacocca sells just a few more books, Henry Ford may well go down in history solely as the man who made the mistake of firing Lee Iacocca. Don sees the opportunity for just a bit of mischief. Don tells Henry that his old buddy is going to star in a Diet Pepsi commercial.

"Really?" Henry Ford says with more delight than Don expects from him.

"Yep," Don says.

"He'll never do it. He'll back out."

The conversation moves away from Iacocca, but Don thinks enough of it to call me after lunch.

"Thanks, Don," I say. "But Lee loves the commercial."

An hour later, Allen Rosenshine calls.

"Iacocca's out," he says.

"You're kidding."

"Nope. His people don't think it's the right thing for him to do."

"They don't like the commercial?"

"They *love* it. But they think it's the wrong move."

"Can you work on him?"

"I'll try."

That afternoon, Iacocca calls. He's not by any means a slave to staff opinion, but he just can't see his way to letting the commercial run.

What am I going to do—yell at Lee Iacocca?

Tom Clark does talk to him again. And Iacocca relents a bit. He'll think it over some more. In the meantime, we can show the commercial at our bottlers' convention, as long as we remember he hasn't made up his mind yet. We do—and he does. Sorry about that.

Later, when asked by a *Time* magazine reporter what happened to the Diet Pepsi spot, Iacocca says flippantly, "I took a powder on that one."

Don Kendall sees the article and calls me. "Tell your buddy Iacocca," he says, "that we just might take a powder on Chrysler cars and trucks." I relay the message—discreetly—through channels. But not, however, to the people who buy our cars and trucks.

News that Ferraro has made a commercial leaks out. Tip O'Neill thinks it's great. He's about the only one.

Every political columnist in the country decides that the "selling out" of the former vice presidential candidate is the biggest blunder since the Bay of Pigs. The press *excoriates* Ferraro. It gets so intense I have to wonder: Why do they really dislike her that much?

I conclude that maybe it really doesn't matter that Geraldine Ferraro ran for Vice President of the United States, lost, and then, four months later, did a Diet Pepsi commercial. Nobody was beating up on former Senator Howard Baker for doing an ad for *USA Today*.

Perhaps if a male former vice presidential candidate was in our advertising, there'd be some chuckling and a few titters, but no great outcry—even if he had the kind of problems Ferraro had during the campaign. I don't know—but you don't suppose all of this was because she was a woman, do you?

Then, as the commercial starts to air, a whole other kind of protest begins. It's about "the choice of a new generation." No, it's about the word *choice*.

One little word. Part of a slogan that predates any idea of an involvement with Geraldine Ferraro. Did it ever enter our minds that, in politics, that word has a very different meaning?

Nope.

So we are very, very surprised when we start getting letters. Angry letters. Letters that say, "Your commercials are 'pro-choice.' You favor the right of women to have abortion on demand."

We answer these letters. We explain that we used the word "choice" instead of "drink" because we want to suggest, as clearly as we can, that people really do think about the diet cola they buy; they *choose* Diet Pepsi. But how do we explain to these people that if we'd known we were going to offend them— or anyone—with these commercials, we never would have made them in the first place? And, more to the point, what do we do when we get 1,200 of these angry letters?

Well, we don't run scared, but we do pull the plug. We take the Ferraro commercial off the air. The mail drops off. In two weeks it stops altogether. This leads us to think that, just maybe, the flap has blown over. So we slap the commercial back on network TV. Five days later the letters pour in again.

These letters criticize Ferraro more than they knock Pepsi, but why split hairs? I feel sorry for Ferraro, who's handled all the furor like a champ, but we take the commercial off the networks—for good—and tell bottlers that if they want to run it locally, that's their . . . Well, we don't use the word *choice*.

And, of course, I learn to keep Pepsi's nose out of politics.

Now it is April. We've got one Diet Pepsi commercial we can run. It features football players—during basketball season. This won't do.

BBDO brings up a revised celebrity list. Peter Ueberroth is on it. This guy owes me a call for two months. The baseball season will be over before he gets back to me. Forget him. All the other names look stunningly familiar.

"Dammit, get Larry Bird and Magic Johnson, and we'll do another jock spot!" I say.

And everybody tells me: "Roger, you'll turn this brand into Miller Lite."

"I don't give a damn," I retort. "We've got to have *something* on the air. It has to show somebody people *like*. And I don't care how much they love Marino and Montana—the football season is long over."

"Okay," they all say. "But no more jocks."

"Why not?" I say. "You can get jocks easy, right? They don't care about touching the product, right? They don't moan to you about overexposure. They don't worry about their political careers. I *love* jocks—so let's go get a few and make some new commercials."

Everybody insists I'm wrong. Maybe I am—I go with the crowd.

Peter Ueberroth calls. *Maybe* he wants to do something with us. We talk about it. We say we'll get back to him. We call him back. He doesn't take the call. He never calls us again. Maybe because he's decided, as we learn a year later, to join the Coca-Cola board of directors. April ends.

We could have had Magic Johnson and Larry Bird in the can and on the air by now—and had a neat fit with the NBA championship playoffs. Instead, for the entire month of May, we approach people who do not, for one reason or another, work out.

New names are proposed. Any time anyone has an idea,

everybody else says, "You're going to use *who*?" One day I call Alan Pottasch into my office.

"Alan, I hope to God this is the lowest point you and I ever have together—because we are really at a low. This is one of the stupidest exercises I have ever participated in, and we're getting into deeper and deeper water. I really think we should find two jocks and get *something* in the can, just for insurance."

Enter Cher. Cher would be terrific. But Cher wants far too much money. Enter Shirley MacLaine. She is, we discover, willing to do a commercial. We send her a script in which, as the star, she talks to some despondent young dancers about having courage to face their disappointments.

Shirley MacLaine doesn't like the script for the commercial. Why? It seems she's seen Geraldine Ferraro's spot and wants to do one like it—with *her* daughter. And she wants a small fortune to do it. Why? Because she's read somewhere that Ferraro got a small fortune.

Does Shirley MacLaine think she's Ferraro reincarnated six months later? I don't know, but everybody agrees that MacLaine is 1) worth pursuing and 2) susceptible to reason in negotiation.

I say go ahead. What the hell, she's a great actress and she looks wonderful on camera—that terrific smile and those great eyes will light up the screen. And I say, "It's *June*. Please, cover yourselves. Phil Dusenberry knows everything there is about baseball. Tell him to pick two players and make a commercial."

The agency comes back with Dwight Gooden and Catfish Hunter. A terrific script is worked up. The commercial is shot. I am—almost—relieved.

What prevents me from feeling completely recovered is the MacLaine commercial. You've never seen it? I'll tell you why. I mean, you think the Ferraro commercial was a mistake? *This* was the worst thirty seconds of film I've ever seen. A complete waste of a great deal of money. Not one good thing can be said for it. The script is dull. And the patented Shirley MacLaine smile? Those great eyes? Do they light up the screen?

Forget it. The only positive reaction you get is relief—when the commercial's over. *That* was the real low point. And yet . . .

The Marino-Montana spot stays on the air for longer than I think credible—and sales go up. The Gooden-Hunter spot goes on network television more times than even I can stand to watch it—and sales go up. And that summer, Diet Pepsi teaches me two lessons.

One is that the advertiser tires of a commercial before the public does. In fact, the public often begins to accept a commercial just as the advertiser thinks it's wearing out—even if the football season ended six months earlier.

The other is something you'd think I'd have learned from signing all those rock stars: If you're going to build a campaign around celebrities, make damn sure the ink is dry on all the contracts before you start.

But these lessons are, this season, mercifully private. Few outside the company notice that we have been flailing about in this advertising campaign. And even on Madison Avenue, no one wonders why we have so few Diet Pepsi commercials on the air.

Because, this season, all attention is focused on Atlanta. For the Coca-Cola Company has decided to avenge—in one bold move—the Pepsi Challenge, Michael Jackson, Lionel Richie, Slice, the three-liter bottle, and Diet Pepsi's pre-emptive strike with 100 percent aspartame. They will return Pepsi to its historical also-ran position—where it belongs.

And all the big ideas and big events we have been first with thus far, all the success we have had in controlling the agenda, all of that will turn out to be . . . just basic training.

CHAPTER 13

Sweet Revenge

Robert Woodruff's obituary appeared in *The New York Times* on March 8, 1985.

Reading it that morning, I sensed that more than a man has passed on. For once, the trite phrase about "the end of an era" had meaning and bite—with Woodruff's death, a large part of a legend that seemed to defy time had gone with him. And with Woodruff's death the mantle had, finally, been passed to Roberto Goizueta. Freed from the need to acknowledge Woodruff—to be the patriarch's good son—Goizueta was now, four years into his chairmanship, completely his own man.

So as I put the paper down, I had a strong premonition that the new Coke management team would now feel free to make some changes in the mother lode—the Coca-Cola brand itself.

You see, we'd known for several years that their marketing and research people had been working on new formulas for brand Coke—formulas that might have a chance of beating Pepsi at its own Pepsi Challenge game. Not infrequently we'd heard of the impending launch of one of those new formulas. None had appeared. When one ultimately did, we'd assumed, it would be a "line extension"—a second, flanker brand.

"Get ready for 'Coke Light,'" our sources would say.

"It's not going to be 'Coke Light.' It's 'Coke II,'" we'd hear.

Though these rumors persisted, neither "Coke Light" nor "Coke II" ever showed up. I always believed that was because Robert Woodruff said, "Forget it. No one's going to fool around with Coke while I'm still here." But now he was gone, and buried with him, I guessed, was his admonition.

As I drove to work, I thought about it some more. By the time I got to Purchase, I was certain. "Coke Light" or "Coke II" would become a reality, and soon. As the world knows, I was wrong. What Coke was about to do was so bold that no one—even a rival committed to bold ideas, boldly expressed—would have thought they'd consider it, much less implement it.

I shared my suspicions with my associates. They gave me strange looks—looks that said, "If they bring out a better product than Pepsi, we're in trouble." But March passes. And nothing happens.

April arrives. And I get a call from a gentleman I'll call "Deep Palate." Deep Palate is a camp follower who is just fascinated with the Cola Wars. And for reasons known to him but not to me, he seems to get Coke news at about the same time the Coke bottlers do. For all I know, there's someone at Coke getting hot Pepsi scoops through him. I don't ask. I just pick up the phone when he calls.

"Roger, it's me."

"Hey. What's up?"

"Something's going on in Atlanta," D.P. says. "They're calling all the bottlers in this weekend, and they've told them to bring along their marketing plans."

"What do you think it's about?"

"I don't know—but it's got to be significant. Maybe it's the Coke line extension I've been hearing about all these years."

"I wouldn't be surprised," I say.

That afternoon, a securities analyst of my acquaintance calls.

"There's going to be a Coke press conference next week," he says. "All the analysts have been invited."

"Really."

"What does 'Really' mean?" he asks.

"It means 'Really.'"

"Roger, do you know what's going on at Coke?"

"Well, I know they have people coming down to Atlanta this weekend."

"I think there's going to be a new formulation of Coke," the analyst says. "And I think they're going to change the sweetener again—this time to high fructose 90."

Now, our R&D people know all about high fructose 90. It has a more concentrated sweetness than the fructose everyone puts in soft drinks, so you can, theoretically, use less of it and reduce the calorie count of your product a bit. But there are two problems: One, there's not enough of it around even to consider using it in a brand as big as Coke. Two, it costs a fortune.

"Impossible," I tell him.

"I have it on good authority," the analyst says.

"No way. When's the press conference?" I ask.

"Tuesday."

"I'll check my facts on high fructose 90 and get back to you," I say, and call our R&D vice president, Bennett Nussbaum, who confirms that I know what I'm talking about.

"You were right," the securities analyst says when we next speak. "Coke isn't changing their sweetener to high fructose 90—they're changing the whole formula of their product! As of Tuesday, there'll be a totally new Coke!"

Am I living in a world in which it is possible that Coke will retire its formula after ninety-nine years?

No. No way.

But is that going to happen?

Yes. I can't believe it, but yes, it seems so.

Is there somehow an opportunity for Pepsi in all of this?

An opportunity? Come on, my little Italian friend, you don't see it?

Oh, yes—yes, I do. Thank you, God. But what *exactly* should I do?

To this question, however, the Lord is silent.

On Friday, around three in the afternoon, I get a call from Joe McCann. Joe has recently been promoted and is now vice president of corporate affairs for PepsiCo, but that doesn't prevent him from taking a continuing interest in Pepsi USA.

"Roger, have you heard anything about a press conference Coke's having on Tuesday?"

"Yes."

"What's it about? We're getting calls from the press about a telegram from Coke. Apparently they're going to announce the most important new development in the history of soft drinks."

"I think they're changing the formula of Coke."

Joe's been, I know, imagining the scenario of the Coke press conference. But this is a show-stopper he clearly hasn't contemplated.

"Why would they do *that*?" he asks.

"They've been working on a new formula. Clearly, they're

going to introduce a new product. And it's fair to assume the product will be more like Pepsi."

"Wait a minute, Roger—you said they're changing the formula. But they're not. This will be a line extension—they're going to have two Cokes."

"I'm not so sure."

"Would changing their formula be a good idea?"

"If it's a terrific product, it's a terrific idea."

"In that case, we'd better get something out there. I'll work on a statement. Let me know if you hear anything more."

The afternoon passes. I take more calls. And learn that invitations from Coke are landing on a lot of media desks this afternoon. Smart move. Late Friday afternoon—they think we'll be caught off-guard.

And as I reflect on it, I see that in fact we are. In the past, no matter what else happened in the market, we could count on one comforting truth: To most people, our product tasted better than theirs. But if they brought out something that tasted better than Pepsi, who knows what would happen?

Around six-thirty, Joe McCann calls again. He reports that the excitement is building as the press and securities analysts start playing telephone tag. For all that phoning, though, no one's sure what Coke will announce. Worse, he hasn't come up with a statement for the press that he has confidence in.

"Everything I try sounds defensive," Joe says. "I can't figure out a way to take the offensive when they're bringing a new product out. And we're having people for dinner tonight, so I can't stick around. But we're all thinking about it. I'll call you Monday morning."

As I drive home, my mood goes like a roller coaster. At the bottom, bleak despair: We're getting a new product to compete with, maybe a product that will taste great. At the top, elation: We've just been paid a great compliment; Coke is admitting defeat by changing its formula. After all these years, Michael Jackson and our "New Generation" advertising have brought Coke down.

Unfortunately, I think, no one outside of Pepsi will see it that way. A new product as a *defeat* for Coke? People will shake their heads and wonder what we've been smoking if we try that gambit. No, the next week's going to be grim. Coke will tell its story in a slick, positive way. And if we try to attack, we'll look like sore losers.

*   *   *

An hour after I arrive home, Joe McCann calls.

"Roger, I almost killed myself on the FDR Drive."

"What?" There are voices in the background. I can picture his wife, Anne, and their guests standing around watching Joe as he tries to talk on the phone and divest himself of his trench coat at the same time.

"No kidding, I almost killed myself on the FDR. I got such a great idea I forgot I was driving. Roger, I have the answer! We can make this into something really big for us."

Joe tugs the phone into a quieter corner.

"We've been looking at it the wrong way," he says. "I can't believe we were too dumb to see it earlier. What we have to do is convince people of one thing: Coke isn't putting out a new product; they're pulling back the old one. They're admitting defeat. The most famous product in the world is coming off the shelves. They're leaving the battlefield, folding their tents. *Roger, we just won the Cola War!"*

Just what I'd been thinking. But I would never have gone public with that idea—who'd take me seriously?

"Joe, who's going to believe that?"

"Everybody!" Joe almost shouts. "Because it's true. And if we tell them loud enough and soon enough . . . Roger, I think we ought to take out a full-page ad Sunday or Monday and tell the world."

Joe's enthusiasm is infectious. I'm *almost* convinced. But we'll have to sell this idea brilliantly, or people will laugh at us. And if we're going to go on the attack, the last thing I want to do is give Coke forty-eight hours notice—or even twenty-four. Whatever we do, I want it to be a surprise.

"Hell, we're not really sure what they're announcing," I say. "Let's not do anything this weekend. But call Alan and see what he thinks—and have him get the agency on it too. And then we'll get together Monday morning and hash it out."

For me, this is the end of the call. Not for Joe.

"Listen, even if we're wrong, a victory statement wouldn't be the worst thing," he says. "Say we run an ad on Sunday that says Coke is pulling their crummy product from the shelves. If we're wrong, we run another ad. We apologize: 'Sorry, everybody, Coke's *not* pulling their crummy product from the shelves.'"

Amusing idea—but why be wrong in public?

"Nope. Let's wait till Tuesday morning—just before Coke's press conference. That way, we might just put them off their stride. They won't have much time to respond."

"Okay. What papers should we put the ad in?"

"The *Times*—New York and Los Angeles," I say. "The *Journal*. *USA Today*. *The Washington Post* . . ."

"How about the *Atlanta Constitution*?"

"Why the hell not?"

Saturday. Contrary to rumors that my idea of exercise is to find a better tailor, I do step outside and cut the grass. I try not to think about the Coke press conference. Weekends are for my family. And if the Coke press conference puts us at our battle stations, the next few weekends won't be. Meanwhile, Joe gets Alan Pottasch on the phone. Alan listens as Joe gets excited all over again about his plan to go on the offensive.

"Joe, that's a *terrible* idea," Alan says. "We'll sound like jerks. Wars, battlefields, winning, losing—I don't see it. It's too militaristic."

They argue for fifteen minutes. Alan's firm—and firmly negative.

Two hours later Alan calls Joe back. And having gone through the same thought process Joe and I did, he now thinks a victory statement might work. But it can't be militaristic—the wording has to change. Which means he and Joe should be in my office Monday morning with their suggestions.

My yard work does not prove to be therapeutic. What's left of the weekend is filled with anxiety. Despite the decision to go with Joe's newspaper ad idea, I'm still not certain Coke's actually going to change the formula of their flagship brand. And if they do, what does it mean for us? Have they just handed Pepsi a big opportunity, or will this be their biggest marketing coup ever?

By Sunday night my anxiety has reached fever pitch. A good night's sleep is not in the cards. Awakening in the dark early Monday morning, I switch on the radio and lie in bed wondering what this day will bring. Rosemary stirs in her sleep. I lower the volume to a barely audible level.

My mind conjures up alternating scenarios of doom and success. Will the Cola Wars end tomorrow—a brilliant frontal attack from Coke pushing the Pepsi upstarts back to their also-ran position? But I still can't believe they're actually going to change their formula. It's too risky, I think. Bold, yes—but also ludicrous. After all, there's more to marketing soft drinks than winning taste tests. More than any other product I can think of, consumers have an emotional attachment to their soft drink brand. Coke wouldn't ignore that fact. Or would they?

Suddenly these self-inflicted mind games come to a screeching halt. The news is on the radio. I hear the word *Coke* and jump to turn the volume up—and I hear a familiar voice. It's Jesse Meyers, the editor of *Beverage Digest*, a bimonthly industry newsletter, and he's telling all.

"This is the boldest move since Eve handed Adam the apple," Jesse declares, confirming that Coca-Cola is indeed about to change the formula of their flagship brand.

"Thank you, Jesse Meyers!" I shout, waking Rosemary.

"What's going on?" she asks, rubbing her eyes.

"They're actually going to do it!" I answer, bolting toward the shower. "And Joe McCann is absolutely right! They aren't introducing a new product—they're pulling Coke off the market!"

Driving to the office, I can't help but notice everything along the way—adrenaline is shooting through my veins; my senses are at a peak. It's a fantastically beautiful spring morning along the Merritt Parkway. I can feel the leaves budding on the ancient oak trees . . . see the grass greening . . . smell the azaleas flowering.

In my office overlooking the sweeping back lawn of the PepsiCo sculpture garden, I switch on my Macintosh. It's time to swing into action. The first step is to write a letter to our bottlers and our employees. I want them to know what our archrivals are up to—and what we're going to do about it.

I'm a pretty fast writer when the mood is on me—and believe it, there's nothing like a Coke reformulation to encourage speed. But still, how do you begin a momentous announcement like this?

With self assurance, I say to myself. That's how. By declaring victory, not defeat. Our bottlers and employees have got to see this as a win for us. This is not the time for them to have doubts about our product, our company, themselves. It's a time for confidence, no matter what the next few days bring.

I begin to type, and, thinking about the intensity of our competitive battle with Coke and feeling now that this is a victory for us, I'm reminded of another competitive battle—the 1962 Cuban missile crisis—and its outcome. A far more serious situation, to be sure, but what was it that Dean Rusk said to President Kennedy when Khrushchev backed down? Something about going at it eyeball to eyeball and the other guy just blinked?

I finish the draft of my letter. Alan Pottasch and Joe McCann arrive and start scribbling copy for our newspaper ad on envelopes. Each of us works alone in his own corner of my office. Finally I finish the draft of my letter. The three of us huddle around the coffee table.

Joe reads his version of the ad. Alan doesn't like it. Alan reads his. Joe doesn't like it. I don't like either one.

"We don't want to be heavy-handed," I say. "We want to hit them hard, but we don't want to appear as if we're taking this too seriously."

In minutes, we're in a quagmire of *don't want to be*s and *can't do*s. A few more minutes and we have a draft written by the three of us.

"I don't like it," Joe says. "It's not tough enough."

"I thought we didn't want to be too tough," Alan says.

In this manner, we start crossing out words. Soon we're back to blank envelopes and sheets of paper. The *do*s and *do not*s begin again.

This begins to wear on Pottasch. After checking his watch half a dozen times, he gets up and walks around my desk to my Macintosh. The computer is humming quietly.

Alan squints at the screen. "What's this?"

"My letter to the bottlers and employees."

"It's not so bad."

"Thanks a lot."

"Why don't we just put this letter in the newspapers?"

Joe looks up as Alan reads off the screen.

"Yeah, that's great," I say.

"It needs to be cut down a bit," Joe suggests.

I take this as a unanimous yes vote and Alan starts paring away.

"How's this sound?" he asks, a few minutes later.

To All Pepsi Bottlers and Pepsi-Cola Company Personnel:

It gives me great pleasure to offer each of you my heartiest congratulations. After 87 years of going at it eyeball to eyeball, the other guy just blinked.

Coca-Cola is withdrawing their product from the marketplace, and is reformulating brand Coke to be "more like Pepsi." Too bad Ripley's not around . . . he could have had a field day with this one.

There is no question the long-term market success of Pepsi has forced this move.

Everybody knows when something is right it doesn't need changing. Maybe they finally realized what most of us have known for years . . . Pepsi tastes better than Coke.

Well, people in trouble tend to do desperate things . . . and we'll have to keep our eye on them.

> Best regards,
> Roger Enrico
> President, Chief Executive Officer
> Pepsi-Cola USA

"That's it," I say.

"Almost there," says Joe. "But it needs one more thing—a capper."

"I've got it," I say. "Let's give everybody the day off on Friday to celebrate."

"Celebrate what?"

"Look at it this way: Pepsi's early history was a rocky road—we've come back from bankruptcy twice. From the beginning, Coke's been king of the castle. Thirty years ago they outsold us . . . what? Three to one? Just look how far we've come. Now they're taking their product off the market. If that's not a victory worth celebrating, I don't know what is. It is a *human* victory—all the hundreds of thousands of company and bottler employees who worked so hard over the years to make Pepsi what it is today deserve to be recognized. Let's let our people celebrate all of that by taking a day off."

So at the end of the letter, I type in one final paragraph:

But for now, I say victory is sweet, and we have earned a celebration. We're going to declare a holiday on Friday.

Enjoy!

Alan calls the agency to confirm the order for newspaper space and calls in the copy to the art director to begin typesetting.

"What about legal approval?" Joe asks.

"Oh, the hell with it," I say.

"What about corporate personnel—can you give the day off without checking?"

"If we tell *anyone*," I say, "they'll want to think about it and give an opinion. We haven't got time for that right now."

"When do you plan to tell them?"

"Let them read it in the newspaper."

Pottasch gets off the phone. "All set," he says.

"Great. Now, on Wednesday, I want us to get together again. I want to be on the tube with a television commercial *fast*, so start thinking about it."

The hard-working people in our public relations department will spend this day working the phones, reaching out to the reporters who have been covering us over the years. Before they do, Becky Madeira, our brave, clean, reverent, and diabolically witty director of public relations, stops by my office.

"You know, Roger, shouldn't we have a little event of our own in New York tomorrow? Like giving out free samples of Pepsi. Say at Columbus Circle? Around noon?"

This is Becky at her hilarious, deadpan best. For Columbus Circle is just five blocks south of the Vivian Beaumont Theater in Lincoln Center, where Coke's press conference will be held. That press conference should be over by noon. If it's a nice day, every media representative who shows up to hear Roberto Goizueta will have to pass Becky's little party on the way back to the office. My laughter tells Becky everything she needs to know.

"I thought we could put up banners that read: 'Taste the *real* real thing—Pepsi.'"

"Sounds good. But let's not push it too far."

"Oh, Roger, don't worry," Becky says, with perfect ladylike innocence. "It'll be in good taste."

Becky goes off to direct her troops. Each has his own distinctive style, but the message that Becky, Ken Ross, and Maurice Cox deliver to the New York media corps is fundamentally this: "Are you invited to the Coke press conference tomorrow? Well, let me tell you what they're doing. As you know, they've been losing market share for years, and they're making a big move to reverse the trend . . . so they've developed a product that tastes as much like Pepsi as possible. They'll put the best face on it—they'll say they're already winning big but want to win bigger—so you might want to have a few statistics to ask them about. Got a pencil? Good, 'cause I've also got some questions you might want to ask them. By the way, after the Coke press conference, come on down to Columbus Circle—we're having a little celebration party of our own. . . ."

Don Kendall's in Japan. But good news travels. And Kendall calls to hear more about it firsthand.

"Roger, what is this rumor?" he asks, over the crackling international line. "Coke's changing its management?"

"No, Don. They're not changing management—they're changing the formula for brand Coke."

"You must have it wrong," Kendall says firmly. "Coke would never change their product."

"Don, they're really doing it. Unbelievable, isn't it?"

Don's silent so long I think the connection's been broken.

"Jesus!" he finally says. "These guys are *nuts*!"

"It's hard to think of another explanation—unless they've got one hell of a new formula."

Don now takes about two seconds to figure out what it took Joe, Alan, and me days to understand.

"Roger, you *can't* let them get away with it."

"I know."

"You've *got* to be assertive. You've got to make it look like they're following the leader."

"That's the plan."

And I read him the newspaper ad.

Kendall goes "Uh-huh . . . good" right up to the last paragraph.

The last paragraph inspires another of his famous silences.

I know what he's thinking: Why the hell are you giving people a day off?

But all he says is: "Okay, keep it up."

Wayne Calloway calls. As president of PepsiCo, he is, in Kendall's absence, the most senior executive in the corporation, but he's not calling to second-guess, just to urge us to stay on top of this fast-breaking news story. Even in a crisis Wayne's calls are a relief. He's always soft-spoken, strong, thoughtful. Today, he checks in every few hours to hear how the plans are taking shape. And every few hours he says the same thing.

"Sounds right to me."

* * *

At noon I attend a briefing and luncheon for securities analysts which our investor relations department has set up. An unusually large number of analysts have made the trip up to Purchase. No mystery why—they want to hear what we have to say about New Coke.

This isn't fun for me. To the world, I have to sound confident and light-hearted. Inside, though, all I'm thinking about is Coke's press conference. If only I could disguise myself and be there—not for the pomp and pride, but for the cup of New Coke afterward. I'd give anything to taste New Coke—to know if this soft drink is so superior that it will bring Coke out of the wilderness and into the Promised Land of unchallengeable cola superiority.

The analysts are just as depressing as my inner monologue. They see New Coke as a big idea—and a big win for Coke. We tell them about our newspaper ad. They think it's cute and strategically shrewd. But as they look at the situation, consumers won't care if Coke is following the leader; an exciting new taste from the biggest brand name on earth spells megabucks.

All the more reason why we've got to make sure there's plenty of rain on Coke's parade. We have to convince everyone—particularly consumers—that Coke is pulling their product off the market because it can't measure up to Pepsi. That way, people will be a lot more skeptical when they try the new formula. Unless it really is a terrific product, Coke drinkers will compare it unfavorably to Old Coke, and Pepsi drinkers will think it inferior to Pepsi.

After lunch, I rush back to my office to work up our marketing offensive with Alan Pottasch and Joe McCann. I stride in with confidence, but immediately sense this is not a feeling in big supply in my office. Alan's down. Joe's down.

"What's the problem?" I ask Joe.

"I'm not sure our moves are strong enough. The securities analysts and the press have a lot of confidence in the Coca-Cola Company. They'll figure Coke management knows what they're doing."

"Well, what do we need to counter that?"

"We need a symbol, something to crystallize our message. So far, most of what we're saying is too complex for the *Nightly* news—even for most business reporters and analysts. Coke has a product, a real live product. We've got numbers. That's no contest. They win."

"What we need," Joe continues, "is you. You have to lead the fight."

"I thought I already was."

"I mean on television. They'll have Goizueta and Dyson. We can't get away with a faceless spokesman. This has to be personal and real—you've got to get out there and bang away."

I'd suspected it would come to this. But no amount of expectations makes hard decisions easier. And this is the hardest of the day. Not because I'm shy in public—after all, I was the kid who wanted to be an actor—but because, when I took this job, I was determined not to run this business in the media. I'd seen John Sculley give over a lot of time to interviewers. I thought it had distracted him—and made him so visible a figure that, in time, he would have become a target.

For that reason I'd turned down all requests for interviews in my first year as president. Then Michael Jackson came along, and I couldn't help but step in front of the cameras. That was both fun and good for business. But when it was over, I was glad to return to a lower profile.

Now, Coke's forcing me out again. But I agree with Joe that there's no choice. I have to state our case as forcefully as Goizueta and Dyson are likely to be pushing Coke's. And I'll have to be someone maybe they can't or won't be: a good-humored winner. No matter how I feel inside.

I take a deep breath. "When do I start?"

"You already have," Joe says, with a short, nervous laugh. "You've got five radio interviews this afternoon. And CBS wants to come up and interview you for tonight's evening news."

"And then?"

"You could be up late with the print media. Then, tomorrow . . ."

I could see what Joe was doing: priming the old war horse for the big race. By this time, though, I don't need priming. I don't really want to spend days and nights saying the same thing over and over—I know I'm going to feel as if I'm throwing my body in front of a train—but this is the biggest moment in our product's history. And when you're facing a moment like that, choice just disappears. "He who hesitates," as a friend of mine says about such moments, "is lunch."

At five P.M., a helicopter carrying the television crew from CBS lands next to the giant Calder sculpture on our back lawn.

Many employees agree that this surpasses even the arrival of Don King.

The camera crew sets up—in a big hurry—in my office. It's rush-rush-rush because the interview is going on the air tonight. I get caught up in the seriousness and importance of the moment and give answers that would make even my wife and son switch channels—facts and figures and logic. The producer is too professional to offer a critique. As the crew is packing up to leave, Joe says, "Tell them about the ad we're placing in tomorrow's papers."

"What about it?" the CBS interviewer asks.

I tell him. The lights and cameras are immediately set up again.

"Mr. Enrico, could you tell me exactly how you see what's happening at Coke?"

"Look at it this way," I say, quoting myself. "Coke and Pepsi have been going at it eyeball to eyeball for eighty-seven years. And it looks to me as if the other guy just blinked!"

That night, there's no sign of Enrico's Business Lecture. Just this one colorful moment. It works—at least in my house. That is, my wife and son don't change channels.

By Tuesday morning, when the Coke executives open the papers, see our ad, and feel their stomachs flutter, we're in a fine mood to have some fun.

Roberto Goizueta has some fun of his own during the "formal speeches" part of the Coke press conference. Before hundreds of reporters and securities analysts assembled in the theater— and hundreds more watching around the world by satellite hookup—he and other Coke executives manage to make New Coke look like the second coming. Then it's question-and-answer time.

From that moment on, Goizueta and his associates are operating at a serious disadvantage. It seems our newspaper ad has not gone unnoticed. The reporters are not on their knees hailing the second coming of Coke. Instead, they're asking tough questions—and repeating them when the answers sound like double talk.

Goizueta is on the defensive. Now is his chance—his only chance—to regain the offensive. If he fails here, he'll have to commit massive resources—muscle, smoke, mirrors, and whatever else is at hand—to justify what will appear to be his betrayal of 70 million loyal Coke drinkers. And it all comes down to one question: "Did you change Coke's formula because of Pepsi's success?"

Goizueta and his associates have clearly rehearsed their answers for days. But they are not, apparently, able to give a straight answer to this question. And, perhaps, they really don't think the *"Are* you following the leader?" question will be asked—or have to be answered seriously.

But there's *no* possibility that question won't come up. And there's no possibility the press will let the Coke brass leave without a serious response. We've made sure of that with our newspaper ads and the hundreds of calls that Joe McCann, Becky Madeira, and our public relations team made to reporters. And Coke's made sure of it as well. Their arrogance—the tell-'em-before-you-tell-'em announcement, the megahype news conference, the satellite feed that's bringing this moment in Coke history to every possible TV-watching cola drinker on earth—*forces* reporters to toughen up their acts.

Of course the press will, as Coke wants, treat the new formula as the biggest marketing story to come down the pike in years—this is Coke, after all—but it doesn't have to be a passive accomplice in the news-making process. Reporters don't see themselves as the people who write the Coca-Cola in-house magazine.

What *should* Roberto Goizueta and Donald Keough and Brian Dyson have said when reporters wondered if Pepsi's success wasn't the *real* reason for the Coke formula change? In my opinion, the truth. One simple word: "Yes."

By trying to sidestep that question and that answer, Goizueta put Coca-Cola in a position that corporations try to avoid—appearing cynical and manipulative toward consumers. *Nobody* loves a bigshot.

And at a press conference, a bigshot is someone who wants you to write down everything he says but won't answer your questions straight.

In my view, that's why corporate executives should always describe their companies in distinctly *human* terms. When you think about IBM, for example, what's the first thing you think of? I'll bet it's not this statistic: In 1985, for the fourth year in a row, IBM had the biggest profit of any company on the Fortune 500 list: $6.6 *billion.*

More probably, you think something like: "At IBM, they give great service to their customers; everybody believes in the values of the organization, they never fire anybody; the employee benefits are terrific. Working there is a bit like being part of a family." That's partly because these things are true, and partly because companies like IBM know a key fact about business-media relations: The press *loves* to take a big guy down.

Now, there were probably a dozen other good reasons—the same sort of Sensible Business Reasons that made me think seriously about dumping the Michael Jackson commercials—for Coke's formula change. But the press wasn't going to accept any of them. They wanted a simple answer to a simple question: Why?

And a complicated, implausible response like "While working on Diet Coke, we just happened by accident to come across this new formula that is *so* much better than old Coke" could only lead to *more* questions.

By accident? Just happened to? Take that route, and it's going to be open season on your company.

Let's look, for a moment, at the way one corporation handled a *real* tragedy: the poisoning, early in 1986, of a young woman in Bronxville, New York. She had a headache, so she took some Extra-Strength Tylenol. But the Tylenol had been laced with cyanide. She died.

A terrible event—made worse by the fact that in 1982 there had been a wave of similar poisonings in the Chicago area. At that time, Johnson & Johnson, the respected and trusted company that makes Tylenol, had decided *not* to stop marketing Tylenol capsules permanently.

I'm sure that decision seemed right at the time to the Johnson & Johnson executives, who had, after all, handled that Tylenol scare with great integrity. Four years later, however, renewed tampering with capsules led to the death of a twenty-three-year-old woman.

How did Johnson & Johnson handle the crisis this time? It did not, citing the possibility of lawsuits from the young woman's family, clam up. It did not pussyfoot. It did not shift blame. The chairman, James E. Burke, stepped out front. When he was asked if he was sorry that Johnson & Johnson hadn't stopped making Tylenol capsules after the Chicago poisonings, he told the truth.

"Yes, indeed I am," James Burke said.

Then he pulled every bottle of Tylenol capsules off the market and had them destroyed. Johnson & Johnson doesn't make Tylenol in capsule form anymore.

And what was the reaction to Burke's unusual candor? "I give him high marks for the way he has handled this situation thus far," said Stephen Greyser, a marketing professor at the Harvard Business School.

More to the point, President Reagan said that James Burke "has lived up to the highest ideals of corporate responsibility and grace under pressure."

And the press treated Johnson & Johnson fairly, as well they should have.

But Goizueta and Keough and Dyson cannot say the one word that might fend off their worst nightmare. They cannot say that as late as mid-April—just a week earlier!—they were so unsure about dumping the old Coke formula that they debated keeping it on the shelves and introducing New Coke as a line-extension.

So, at the press conference, Goizueta says the improbable: that changing Coke's formula was "the easiest decision I ever made." Then he intones the debatable: that all the research—the expensive, three-year taste-testing process—supports the formula change. And finally, the laughable: that he has had the old Coke formula placed in a vault at the Trust Company of Georgia, where it will reside, in perpetuity, unused.

"Describe the taste of the new Coke," someone asks.

"It's . . . uh . . . rounder . . . smoother . . . uh, uh . . . more harmonious . . . uh . . . yet bolder."

This is perhaps the most amazing moment of the press conference: the former chemical engineer who was once head of Coke's technical operations can't quite get it together to describe the product that, as Coke's chairman, he's presumably been drinking for some time. Why? What about this question rattles him? Or is it the prospect of the follow-up questions that causes him to swing wildly at an easy pitch?

Whatever the reasons, the Coke executives do not, at this press conference, hit a home run.

While Roberto Goizueta and his associates are presenting New Coke as the greatest thing since—well, since Old Coke— Becky Madeira and our PR staff are watching a little Pepsi robot run around Columbus Circle.

Soon they're not alone. Hundreds of people, lured by the robot and the offer of a free Pepsi, surround them. So, fresh from the Coke press conference, do some reporters and film crews. And the people on the street give those reporters a very different story than the one they've just heard.

"Coke finally gave in," a man says.

"They can't keep up with the competition."

"Pepsi's the best."

"Pepsi's number one—hey, you're not Coke guys, are you?"

A member of our PR team, Nora Slattery, has worked at Pepsi for exactly one day. She's from a small town in California—she's even brand-new to New York. She's bright and quick and funny, which is what you want your PR people to be. And, of our whole PR staff, she has the most beautiful smile.

Nora Slattery, a private in the Pepsi media corps, is therefore asked to stand in front of any TV camera around, and, as Pepsi's representative, smile and say: "Victory is sweet."

Nora does this brilliantly, over and over again. That night, she appears as Pepsi's spokesperson all across the country.

And, for this night, anyway, victory is indeed sweet. Every network news show carries the Coke announcement. Not, however, without a little topspin. My favorite was Tom Brokaw's report on NBC.

"Coke today announced a new real thing—a change in its formula," Brokaw reported. "And Pepsi said, 'Baloney.'"

Later that night Johnny Carson had a few choice words on the subject. "Coke is changing its formula," Johnny said. "Why? That formula is the best-kept secret since what—what Dick Cavett does for a living.

"This change," Johnny continued, "sounds like an idea that Reagan's travel aides would think of. [The President was then in the throes of an enormous controversy about his proposed visit to the cemetery in Bitburg, Germany, where Nazi officers were buried.] Next they'll change Twinkies and put in a spinach filling."

Still later that night, David Letterman put it all into a deadpan one-liner. "Coke's decided to make their formula sweeter," Letterman said. "They're going to mix it with Pepsi."

That's when I knew that Coke was going to have a hell of a time regaining control of the agenda.

No reason to fudge it—the morning after the Coke press conference, I'm feeling pretty good. Congratulatory calls from bottlers who've seen the ad are flooding in. So are "way-to-go" calls and telegrams from civilians who enjoy watching the battle. A Pepsi pollster would never draw conclusions from so small a sampling of opinion, but the fervor we hear this morning certainly suggests that, for now anyway, we're running the show.

The battle, however, is just beginning. Coke has yet to introduce the new formula to the American public. And I am intimately familiar with their marketing, distribution, and financial power. Soon, I know, they will have New Coke available in hundreds of thousands of retail outlets. Huge displays will be built, special prices will be offered, coupons handed out, free samples given—and millions of dollars will be spent advertising the product. All of that marketing activity could still turn the beginnings of a defeat into a resounding victory for them.

I ask Richard Blossom and his marketing team for their recommendations on an offensive program to make sure the uphill slope becomes so steep that Coke *can't* possibly regain the initiative. In hours, their proposal is on my desk. It's sound, well conceived—Richard has covered all the bases. His recommendations will activate the entire Pepsi system, get the army pumped up and moving in step. The only problem is the cost.

"Terrific job, Richard," I say, "but this adds up to *eighteen million dollars*! Unbudgeted! Where in God's name are we going to find that kind of money at this late date?"

"I don't know," Richard responds. "I certainly don't have that kind of flexibility in my marketing plan. But I do know one thing: We've got to do something fast before Coke regains the initiative."

He's right, of course. But $18 million? This is one decision I need support on.

I call Wayne Calloway's office for an appointment. Wayne answers the phone himself. A few minutes later I'm in his office with Richard's plan for going on the offensive. Wayne's no stranger to tough decisions; he ran Frito-Lay for seven of its most successful years, and after that, as PepsiCo's chief financial officer, he conceived and executed the strategy for divesting the company of Wilson Sporting Goods, Lee Way Motor Freight, and North American Van Lines. Now, as PepsiCo president and chief operating officer, he's been focusing the corporation on building its three most important and most promising businesses: soft drinks, snacks, and restaurants.

Wayne listens attentively but says nothing and asks no questions. Silence in his office, except for the loud pounding noise emanating from my chest. He looks thoughtfully at the serene setting beyond his windows, turns to me, and declares, "This is a big opportunity and I think you've got to move quickly and forcefully to capitalize on it. I trust you to know what that takes—how much we should invest. And we'll find the funds to support you."

Armed with Richard's proposal and Wayne's support, I return to my office and begin hammering away at my Macintosh—another letter to our bottlers.

"Twenty-five percent of cola drinkers are loyal to Coke, twenty-five percent to Pepsi, and fifty percent swing back and forth," I write. "Until now, people haven't had to think much about the cola they drink. Today, Coke has given them a reason to. And loyal Coke drinkers are now going to have to make a decision: 'Do I like the taste of New Coke?' We have reason to believe that Coke's own research shows that almost half of its users will be unhappy with what they taste."

With that, I lay out a three-point plan.

First, we must communicate to consumers. But we don't have to lean too hard on Coke. All we have to do is show some sympathy for the loyal customer Coke has just abandoned. To do that, we'll produce some new advertising and we'll have it ready by May, so it'll be on the air a week before Coke has its new formula out. Bottlers will convert all the television time they've already bought to the new advertising. In addition, Pepsi USA will buy more network time: an additional $4 million for the months of May and June alone.

Second, we have to get *really* competitive. We've got to make sure our product is out there, in massive quantities, prominently displayed. To help bottlers step up their in-store merchandising activities, Pepsi USA will fund another $8 million, to be matched by the bottlers.

And third, we must offer purchase incentives to pull customers over to Pepsi. So we'll adopt a two-coupon system—a trial offer for uncommitted Coke drinkers, an equal refund for loyal Pepsi drinkers. Bottlers should take out 1,000-line newspaper ads to announce this. Pepsi USA will absorb 100 percent of the cost—a further $6 million investment.

Then I decide not to send all this out in letter form but to make one of my not infrequent videograms instead. Compared to the hoopla of the Coke press conference, a videogram may seem like a puny effort. It does, however, enable me to look into a camera—albeit a small one—and talk directly to every bottler and employee in our system. And it gives me a chance to end on a personal and unscripted note.

"Thirty years ago, we were burning furniture just to stay alive," I say. "Now we're so successful that Coke has changed its formula. Think of how far we've come! And of how much fun we're going to have from this day on."

Later that Wednesday morning, Allen Rosenshine drives up to Purchase. Phil Dusenberry is away at a meeting in California, but the agency has worked overtime and, in a day and a half, has a script for a new commercial. Alan Pottasch, Joe McCann, and I aren't crazy about it.

"Okay, we'll have another go at it," Allen Rosenshine says.

"Let's take a crack at it right here and now," I say.

The way I figure it, we've got assembled in my office the head of a great agency, a very creative PR executive, the father of the Pepsi Generation, and a Pepsi president who doesn't, when the advertising needs work, look to Madison Avenue for *all* the answers.

And, hell, we survived all the misunderstandings with Michael Jackson. We can *certainly* come up with a concept for a thirty-second commercial to respond to Coke's reformulation. Alan Pottasch does not, today, look at me as if I'm interfering in the creative flow. Neither does Allen Rosenshine.

"Let's make it easy on ourselves. What's on Roger's Macintosh?" Joe says.

"Very funny."

"Seriously . . ."

"You really want to hear the script of my videogram to the bottlers?"

Joe shakes his head. Allen Rosenshine breaks out a yellow legal pad. "Let's start from the beginning."

"We've always come at advertising from the point of view of our consumers," Alan Pottasch says. "Let's do that here—only let's do it from the point of view of a *Coke* drinker."

Instant smiles all around. This isn't going to be the *hardest* thing we've ever done.

"A guy?"

"A girl."

"Why?"

"A guy who's disappointed by a cola could look like a wimp."

"But if a girl's betrayed by a cola, it's like she's been dumped on prom night."

"Makes the dumper look worse."

"Heartbreaking son of a bitch."

"She's talking to the camera."

"A message to Coke."

"To other Coke drinkers."

"No—to *anybody* out there who might have the answer. Because she's sad, but even more she's *confused*."

"Why *did* they do this to her?"

"What will they do to her *next*?"

"No, let's stay in the here-and-now."

"Okay, she's searching. She wants to know *why*."

"And while she's trying to figure it out . . ."

"Listen to this," Allen Rosenshine says, looking up from his scribbling. "I think this is the sense, anyway, of what we're trying for."

He reads from his legal pad. "She's looking forlornly at a can of Coke. 'Can *somebody* out there tell me why they did it? They said they were the Real Thing. They said they were it. And then— kablooey—they changed.'"

Allen pauses.

"Now she reaches for a Pepsi. And when she takes a sip, this is the 'drink shot' of a lifetime. *Lots* of surprise. *Big* satisfaction. She looks at the camera again. 'Now I know why,' she says. And that's it."

"That is *exactly* it," I say.

"Take out *kablooey* and you got my vote," Alan Pottasch says.

"How quickly can we have this on the air?" I ask.

"Oh, a couple of weeks."

"I was thinking of this Sunday night."

"My God!" yells Pottasch.

"A couple of weeks is way too slow. We have to take advantage of this situation before Coke throws millions behind advertising that just might get them over this hump."

"Fine, but Sunday's just not possible."

"Sure it is. You and Alan cast tomorrow, videotape it Friday, edit Friday night and Saturday. I'll come in and look at it, and it's on the air Sunday night."

"Give us one more day," Alan pleads.

Joe McCann sees an opportunity to be both diplomatic and media-savvy.

"Roger, if we wait until Monday," he says, "we'll have enough time to be sure the commercial's okay *and* get out a press release. It'll be better news than the Coke press conference:

'Five days after Goliath shows off his new club, David makes a new slingshot.'"

"Okay. Buy time on Monday night."

Alan and the BBDO people spend Thursday interviewing actresses with the girl-next-door look. Richard Blossom and his marketing team are busy getting the materials for the "offense" program to the bottlers. Joe McCann and his PR staff are still working the phones with the press.

I pace and get in everyone's way.

By late Thursday afternoon, I decide we have to make a second commercial.

On Friday—the day I've declared a holiday—the last thing I'm up for is a day off. I'm much too wired to stay at home. It doesn't bother me that I might be roaming around an empty floor. The bottlers are out there working—and the telephones aren't on holiday. And then, too, there is that commercial to think about.

But there's something I've forgotten: The rest of my team is as wired as I am. Most everybody's in.

A good time to blue-sky with Alan Pottasch and Ron Tidmore, who's president of our fountain syrup division. Ron was born in Alabama. He played football at the University of Georgia. He is, indisputably, our senior resident Southerner.

"Remember that IBM commercial—the three old guys sitting on the park bench?" I say. "Well, as I was driving in today, it occurred to me that we could do something like that. We've done out-of-the-mouth-of-babes. Now we can take the same shot, but from a different angle."

"*Southerners*," Ron says. "We really ought to make a commercial for the South. For the good old boys who have been drinking Coke ever since they climbed out of their cradles."

I've always thought that great ideas come to people out of the blue. In a flash. Well, the only thing faster than Ron today is a speeding bullet.

"You're right!" Alan says. "To them, Coke's like the local banker. They've known him all their lives, have had him over for harvest suppers—now they've just discovered he quietly foreclosed on their farm last week."

Alan doesn't use computers; to him, they're much inferior to the backs of envelopes. Working with Phil Dusenberry, he's back a few days later with the script for a commercial called "Wilbur."

"Wilbur's sitting on a bench in the town square with two old friends," Alan explains. "He's drinking a Coke, and clearly he's in a rotten mood.

"'What's the matter?' asks the first friend.

"'They changed my Coke.'

"'Somethin' wrong with it?'

"'They coulda asked,' chimes in the second friend.

"'I stuck with them through three wars and a coupla dust storms, but this is too much,' says Wilbur. 'Wonder what made 'em change? Musta been somethin' big.'

"'Right big,' says the first old buddy as he hands Wilbur a Pepsi.

"'They coulda asked,' states the second friend.

"Wilbur drinks and smiles and, just like the teenage girl in our first commercial, he comes up with the answer. 'Right big,' he says.

"'Still coulda asked,' says the number two friend."

The first commercial with the teenage girl runs Monday night and gets lots of attention. The agency takes two weeks to shoot and edit "Wilbur."

Meanwhile, remember the "Archeology" commercial? The one with the professor who can't identify the old hourglass-shaped Coke bottle—the ancient relic from the twentieth century?

Well, a lot of people thought we shot that one in response to New Coke. Not so. It was done earlier that year—in January. But the way it fit as a response to the New Coke fiasco made us feel as though we had been clairvoyant. Our bottlers saturated the airwaves with it. And at the Cannes Film Festival, it was voted the best commercial in the world, winning the Grand Prix in competition with more than two thousand ads from over a hundred countries.

A few days after Coke's ninety-ninth birthday, New Coke was formally introduced to a curious America.

In New York, the chairman of the Coca-Cola Bottling Company of New York presented a can of New Coke to a construction worker on the Statue of Liberty restoration project.

In Atlanta, a three-ring circus was set up in a downtown park. "Step right up to the greatest taste on earth," cried the barkers, while overhead, Coke released 25,000 red and white balloons and skywriters plied their trade.

In advertising too, Coke went all out. But *twenty* commercials with Bill Cosby?

I don't even want to guess how much they cost. And he's now declaring the sweeter New Coke is simply magnificent—just a few weeks after he was on the air saying Old Coke was better because it was *less* sweet than Pepsi.

Still, the proof is in the product. *We* haven't tasted it yet. If New Coke really is as magnificent as Cosby claims, everything up to now, we know, will be for naught. The press conference that backfired on Coke? The positive response to our newspaper ad and our TV commercial? Richard Blossom's $18 million offensive program? All those things will be meaningless if Coke's new formula is a winner.

The first morning New Coke can be bought in Atlanta, Bennett Nussbaum, our R&D chief, just happens to be there. He gets the idea of buying up an armload of six-packs. Then he conveniently hops a plane for New York.

That afternoon, Pepsi employees—senior managers and secretaries, mailboys and executives—begin to gravitate toward Don Kendall's office. The cans of New Coke are opened. Paper cups are filled.

All this happens in total silence. As everyone here is well aware, our future prosperity resides in those paper cups. Nervously, we all pause, cups in hand. Don Kendall takes the first sip.

While he does, we sniff those paper cups as if they held prewar Chateau Lafite. Then we sip, letting the flavor expand on our palates. Seconds go by. We savor the carbonation. Only then do we swallow, reach for cups filled with water to refresh our taste buds, and start again.

Still total silence.

But now, slowly, one by one, face after face lights up with a huge smile. For the impossible—the one thing so remote that no one has even dared to speculate about it—has actually happened. The Coca-Cola Company, famous, loved, and universally respected, has just made a major miscalculation.

It's not that the product is terrible, just that it *isn't* a winner. It's flat and uninteresting. To us, it doesn't matter if New Coke does or doesn't taste better than Old Coke—it clearly doesn't taste better than Pepsi. Doesn't, in fact, even taste *like* Pepsi.

Still total silence.

Don Kendall stares at his cup. At the can. At the label. Then he shakes his head.

"Unbelievable," he says.

And from that moment, there was never any doubt in my mind that New Coke could be beaten. Not that it would go away all by itself. We'd have to help it a bit.

By May 13, New Coke has national distribution.

According to Coca-Cola executives, 150 million people try it—the widest trial of any new product in American history—and 50 percent of those people say they'd try it again.

According to Coca-Cola executives, shipments of New Coke have taken Coke sales to an all-time high. No one should have any trouble making a preliminary assessment: New Coke is a monster hit.

Our R&D department doubts that. New Coke has, our R&D team believes, about a third the level of expensive flavor oils of Old Coke. And only about 10 percent of the also-very-expensive vanilla Old Coke had. Which means that the taste of New Coke disappears long before you swallow.

"Is this what it's all about?" I ask. "Is Coke's reformulation just a cost-reduction project dressed up to look like a new product?"

"Don't know," the R&D folks say. "But we do believe this formula will save the Coca-Cola Company about fifty million dollars a year worldwide."

But give it its due: It *is* sweeter than Pepsi. Which leads us all, as one, to the big question: If New Coke is sweeter than Pepsi, how can Coke possibly claim it has fewer calories than Pepsi? Sweetness and calories do, after all, tend to go hand in hand.

We're curious. And not entirely confident that Coke cares to be even-handed these days. So we ask an independent lab to measure what's called the brix level—the amount of sweetness—and the calories in New Coke and Pepsi.

Pepsi weighs in as it always does, with a brix of 11.3 and eighty calories per serving. New Coke scores a brix of 11.7—about 4 percent more sugar than Pepsi—and eighty-three calories per serving. Guess what? New Coke has more calories than Pepsi in exactly the same proportion as it's sweeter than Pepsi.

So how can Coke claim to be both sweeter and *less* caloric? Well, there are, you see, several ways of measuring calories. The method used by Pepsi assures that we don't understate caloric content. Coke publicly cited that calorie count—for Pepsi. For New Coke, it used a less conservative method—that just happens to yield a lower calorie count. And lo and behold, thanks to that juggling, New Coke has fewer calories than Pepsi.

As it turns out, we're not the only ones who question how the cola that's sweeter can also be less caloric. Jesse Meyers, the peripatetic editor of *Beverage Digest*, is also on to this. He makes loud noises—something doesn't add up, and he's going to get to the bottom of it. We know he does, because we give him the independent laboratory tests.

Jesse dutifully prints the results. But the whole issue fades away. After all, why worry about something as trivial as a few calories when a much bigger story is about to break.

And something more was indeed coming.

It all happened so quickly that there was really nothing anyone at Coke could do about it. The mood of the nation just . . . poured out. And the nation, it seemed, was in the mood to pour New Coke down the drain.

Suddenly it seemed that every stand-up comic, cartoonist, and columnist in America was now doing for Pepsi much, much more than we could possibly do for ourselves.

The Tampa *Tribune* ran a cartoon which showed an executive rushing into the Coke marketing director's office. "Our taste test proves it," he says. "Ninety-seven out of 100 people like the new Coke. The other 3 preferred the milk of magnesia!"

A New York *Post* cartoon showed the Coke bottle standing in a graveyard as if it were a tombstone. The inscription read: RIP, COCA-COLA, COKE WAS IT, 1885–1985. UNTIMELY DEATH DUE TO ACUTE PEPSI ULCER.

In Atlanta the staff of *Southern Accents*—a magazine edited by a veteran Coke drinker—voted to have the Coke machine pulled out. Only a promise from the local bottler that he would make up special batches of Old Coke kept them from calling Pepsi.

In Beverly Hills a wine merchant named Dennis Overstreet bought five hundred cases of vintage Coke and started selling them at $50 a case. Celebrities flocked to buy it. Overstreet soon had to start looking for an overseas supplier of Old Coke.

But our best helpmate was a civilian. Gay Mullins, a retired Seattle citizen who seemed to have both some time on his hands and a powerful desire to serve his country, founded the Old Coke Drinkers of America. Instant publicity for Mr. Mullins! And instant membership—8,500 people joined his organization. Millions more cheered him on as he filed a consumer protection lawsuit against the Coca-Cola Company.

The lawsuit was thrown out by a federal judge who ruled that he didn't have jurisdiction—and besides, he liked Pepsi anyway.

Despite our delight with Mr. Mullins's antics, we quickly determined that it was in our best interest to keep our distance. After all, he *did* have difficulty picking out his ostensibly favorite cola—Old Coke—in a blind taste test.

Anyway, it was Coke-bashing season now. The best thing we could do was take light little jabs and keep out of the way.

Every week we conduct national telephone surveys to gather data on consumer experience and attitudes about New Coke. The surveys tell us it's a turkey. The overwhelming majority see it as inferior to Old Coke—and to Pepsi. Large numbers of people intend to stop drinking Coke altogether. Most of them will switch to Pepsi. But, out of Atlanta, a different story.

"Our research," say Coke executives, "shows overwhelming acceptance of New Coke—and shows that New Coke has already passed Pepsi's share of market."

"Is it possible," I ask John Almash, our market research director, "that our surveys are wrong? How can their information be so different from ours?"

John looks at me as though I still had diapers on.

My small uncertainty as to what consumers really think is soon eliminated. *Advertising Age* publishes the results of a consumer survey. The data on the public's rejection of New Coke mirror ours. So much so that I call Becky Madeira, thinking she's leaked our consumer research to one of their reporters.

"I didn't give them anything," Becky replies. "But I'll find out who did."

Later she calls back to tell me no one leaked the data from our research because the consumer attitudes published in the *Advertising Age* story were gathered through their own independent studies.

"So Coke's back to the old smoke and mirrors routine," I tell Becky. "Let's get ready to release our research to the press. And, by the way, let's release our May sales results too. They look like they're going to be spectacular."

Now, releasing confidential research data and monthly sales figures to the press is not our normal practice. In fact, under normal circumstances it's something I'm violently opposed to. But I thought at the time: These guys are likely to do absolutely anything to pull this one off on the American public—and I'll be damned if I'm going to stand by and let them get away with it.

We sent out a press release and placed another newspaper ad.

TO ALL NEW PEPSI DRINKERS:

The Pepsi-Cola Family extends its sincere appreciation and warmest welcome to the New Pepsi Generation.

In a nationwide survey, nearly half of those who have tried New Coke say it's time to switch from Coke . . . and the overwhelming majority say they'll switch to Pepsi.

And you've already begun. Our May sales were the highest for *any* month in our 87-year history . . . up a whopping 14% over last year.

So thanks for your support and welcome to the Family!

> Sincerely,
> Roger Enrico
> President, Chief Executive Officer

Coke called every reporter they could get, complaining that I wasn't playing fair. That 14 percent sales increase, they said, was for all Pepsi USA products—not just Pepsi-Cola. Then they told them that sales of New Coke alone were up 8 percent.

What they said was true. Our 14 percent sales increase was for all Pepsi USA products. And perhaps New Coke sales *were* up by 8 percent.

But here's the catch. Coke's numbers didn't reflect actual case sales by bottlers to retail stores. Ours did. What Coke reported was concentrate and syrup shipments to their bottlers. The difference: millions of cases of New Coke their bottlers had produced to fill one very large product pipeline. Those cases hadn't yet reached supermarket shelves—or consumers' refrigerators. Mostly, they represented concentrate and syrup inventory in the bottling plants, finished-goods inventories in the warehouses, and a lot of cases sitting on Coke's thousands of route trucks.

Irrespective of our battle of the numbers, the press by now was having a field day. A columnist called Coke executives "soda jerks." Cartoons proliferated. Comedians had fresh material every night.

Coke took out newspaper ads declaring "It's a Hit"—and quoting press reports gushing positive about New Coke as though it were the latest Andrew Lloyd Webber musical blockbuster.

The reporters and columnists listed in that ad went public, castigating the Coca-Cola Company for taking quotes out of context from their otherwise negative reports on New Coke.

The Coca-Cola Company apologized, telling the world they didn't realize that what they were doing was wrong.

In mid-June, I start getting phone calls from very excited Pepsi bottlers.

"Roger, I can't *believe* these sales figures."

"I've never sold so much Pepsi in my life."

"Roger, is *anybody* drinking Coke?"

These calls tell me that Coke has a disaster of major proportion on its hands. No more consumer-attitude surveys now. No more "My numbers are bigger than yours." This *is* the real thing: Coke is going to hell in a handbasket.

And, later, when the Nielsen market share data roll in, we discover—not to our great surprise—that Coca-Cola has dropped to the lowest share in its history. The brand is off 2.5 share points. In just the take-home portion of the soft drink market alone, that's a sales drop of about *$625 million.*

What would *you* do if you were running the second-largest company in your industry, and the largest company trashed its biggest-selling product? First, you'd be amazed.

We were.

Then you'd have some fun at the giant's expense.

We did.

But what if your surveys showed that 80 percent of the people who tasted the giant's new product thought it was a lousy idea? What if your surveys told you that 70 percent of the people who tasted the giant's new product just plain didn't like it? And, knowing all that, what would you do after two or three weeks went by and it was clear that a lot of consumers *really* wanted the old product to be returned to the marketplace?

Right. You'd do what we did: You'd wait for the giant to change his mind.

But what if—knowing all that—the giant *still* refused to bring back the old product everybody was now demanding? What would you do *then*?

No, you say. You wouldn't. Not *that*.

But you would. You're damn right you would. If the Coca-Cola Company won't make the real thing, you'd say, we'll have to do it for them.

That's why I ordered the Pepsi R&D lab to reinvent Merchandise 7X—because if Coke wouldn't make Coke, I decided, Pepsi would. In about two minutes, we even had a name for it.

Savannah Cola. Savannah "Classic" Cola, to be exact.

It didn't take us long to crack the Merchandise 7X code. Or to come up against a problem. To make Old Coke just like the Coke many people knew and loved and were now mourning, we'd need some coca leaf—with the cocaine extracted, of course. Unfortunately, there's just one company I'm aware of that specializes in this product. And guess who its biggest—and practically only— customer is?

If we ordered that coca leaf, Coke would know what we were up to in *seconds*—and even the most stubborn New Coke supporter at Coke headquarters would vote to bring back the old formula. So R&D went back to work, trying this time to simulate the taste of cocaine-removed coca leaf.

We imagined that we'd have Savannah Classic Cola ready for the world by mid-September 1985. With that timetable, we'd be able to announce it on Labor Day. Happy picnics, America! Have a Coke and a smile—compliments of your friends at Pepsi!

PepsiCo's board of directors is an unusually distinguished group. At that time the outside directors included Robert Strauss, former chairman of the Democratic National Committee; Thomas Murphy, former chairman of General Motors; Clifton Garvin, chairman of Exxon; Frank Cary, chairman of the Executive Committee of IBM; Robert Stewart, chairman of Interfirst Bank; Jack Murphy, chairman of Dresser Industries; William Coleman, former secretary of transportation; Arnold Weber, president of Northwestern University; and Andy Pearson, former president of PepsiCo and now a professor at Harvard Business School. It is also a tough-minded, hard-nosed group.

On the afternoon of Pepsi's June directors' meeting, though, these are just ordinary citizens, asking the same questions that cab drivers, homemakers, students, and newspaper columnists have been asking for weeks.

"*Why* did Coke do it?"

"Is this some kind of *ploy*?"

"How could Coke have made such a mistake?"

I offer some answers. But there aren't any really good ones. So Robert Strauss—who ran the Democratic Party during the Jimmy Carter years—interrupts. "I don't understand this thing at all," Strauss says. "Pat Caddell must have messed them up something awful."

This gets a laugh. Caddell had done some of the polling that led to New Coke. And everybody knows that Caddell's polling for Carter didn't, in 1980, suggest the depth of the public's dissatisfaction with the Democratic candidate.

"Perhaps," I say. "But people are rejecting the product as well as the marketing."

"Why didn't Coke anticipate that?" someone asks.

I explain how they claimed their blind taste tests indicated that New Coke was better than Old Coke.

"Come on," Bob Strauss says. "How much of this is really due to problems with their product and how much is due to your astute response?"

"Now that you put it that way, Bob," says Mike Jordan, then PepsiCo's chief financial officer, "I'm sure Roger will tell you one hundred percent was due to his astute response."

Another easy laugh. The boardroom feeling's long gone. Now we're just another bunch of fascinated Americans trying to figure out what's really going on at Coke. As someone said, it's like watching the Super Bowl every day.

At this, Frank Cary, who hasn't said very much during this meeting, leans over to me. "Yours is a fascinating business," he whispers.

And I think: This man has run IBM and he believes *ours* is a fascinating business? Finally, the inevitable happens. Somebody asks, "What are you going to do next?" So I tell them about Savannah Cola.

And these astute, thoughtful, always-in-control gentlemen simply break up laughing. But they don't hate the idea.

No, they don't hate it at all.

CHAPTER 14

"We've Hurt You. We're Sorry"

When it was all over, Coca-Cola executives finally acknowledged the real reason for the Coke formula change.

"The product and the brand had a declining share in a shrinking segment of the market," Roberto Goizueta said, looking back to 1981, the year he became chairman. "The value of the Coca-Cola trademark was going downhill."

In an interview with an Associated Press business writer, Brian Dyson said much the same thing. "What we did as a system was we faced up to a problem and we made a decision," Dyson said, in answer to a question about the reformulation. "There was a slowly eroding share position that had taken place over a number of years. That was unacceptable."

Goizueta's remarks appeared in *The Wall Street Journal*—on April 24, 1986. Dyson's appeared in the business sections of a number of Sunday newspapers—on April 20, 1986.

It took a year, almost to the day, after the press conference announcing the formula change for the men behind New Coke to admit that the truth of the matter was exactly what we were saying even before New Coke was officially announced.

As Coke's fiercest competitor, it's probably not my place to comment on their errors. All I know is what I read in the papers, saw in the independent sales reports, and heard through the grapevine. What went on in the Coke boardroom, who said what to whom, the alternative plans that may have been considered— these remain as mysterious to me as they are to you.

But just looking at the public record and stringing the known events together in a loose scenario of Coke's summer of agony, it's hard not to conclude that Coke's biggest problem came to be not its product but its credibility as a company. You can, after all, fix a product. But damage an intangible, and you're condemning yourself to years of distrust.

I don't know why Coke's senior management had trouble with the facts. Was it deliberate? Were their marketing people so anxious to give them good news that they consciously left out the bad news? Or was it because Coke feels it has to win *every* battle, that the only philosophy which makes sense in Atlanta is "Take no prisoners; kill the cattle"?

Unless some Coke executive makes off with the files and pens a tell-all book, I doubt we'll ever know the answer to that one. But I do think that, just by looking at the scenario of responsibly reported events, a pattern does emerge. What follows, then, are not just the bare bones of a fascinating story about how a bad business decision gets reversed. It's a small morality play, in which people who insist that reality is one thing when the facts suggest it's another are, rather painfully, finally forced to acknowledge things as they are. And then—as though in an ending right out of a fairy tale—they claim to discover a pot of gold at the end of the rainbow. But I'm getting ahead of our story. . . .

As early as the first week in June 1985, the consumer hotline at the Coca-Cola Company was so swamped with complaints that Coke started asking beleaguered employees to put in some overtime.

Coke was, however, announcing that 75 million Americans were so pleased by their first taste of New Coke they'd gladly try it again.

By the second week of June, *Advertising Age* reported, the Coke consumer hotline was handling about 1,500 calls a day. To prayerful requests that the company bring back the classic formula, spokesmen were semi-encouraging. That is, they told callers: "We never say never." Coke executives denied the *Advertising Age* report.

In mid-June, at a regional convention in Dallas, Coke bottlers—guys who were suffering twice, once by losing business, once by being shunned in their hometowns—signed a petition *demanding* the return of the old formula.

When your own bottlers turn on you, it's no longer a matter of smoke, mirrors, and PR. You get on the stick and *do* something to placate them. What Coke's marketing department did was to start paying attention to consumers.

Sergio Zyman—who had probably been pooh-poohing the consumer complaints as the normal dissatisfaction of the usual vocal minority—now ordered all members of his staff to monitor phone calls from consumers.

Zyman himself went to watch some focus groups talk out their feelings about New Coke. After one session, he apparently asked the participants what Coke could do to make consumers better pleased with New Coke. They were happy to give him some advice.

"Kill it," they said.

Meanwhile, Coke shipments fell dramatically in many markets—the South among them, as we observed by watching Pepsi sales rise in Coke's home territory. But it took until the end of the month, with water seeping through every weld and the ship visibly sinking, before Coca-Cola finally began to feel that it no longer had control of the way the public perceived New Coke.

At that time, Roy Stout, head of Coke's market research, started preparing regular briefings for Coca-Cola President Donald Keough. Keough's response was to wonder if nine hundred people were a representative sampling of the American public. Stout dutifully expanded his polling base. But when five thousand people were asked about New Coke, they were just as negative as the nine hundred were.

If you think back to July of 1985, you'll recall that the one name you couldn't avoid that month was Madonna.

Her tour was selling out across the country, turning her impressionable young fans into "wannabees"—Madonna clones. Her film, *Desperately Seeking Susan,* was doing well at the box office. And at the newsstand, nude pictures of Madonna, taken during her struggling years, were selling untold millions of copies of *Playboy* and *Penthouse.*

Another big story was Ronald Reagan's polyp. America's attention turned—for some days—to the President's health, and to what we might do to keep ourselves healthy.

These stories—the dominant news stories of midsummer—all focused the attention of Americans on America. Nothing could have been less useful for Coke.

Coke surveys showed that New Coke was not only less loved

than the drink that used to be America's drink—Old Coke—but it was losing to Pepsi as well.

A little more of this, and Coke, that bastion of Americana, would look like the enemy within. What would have done that?

One more guerrilla strike from Pepsi—say, the announcement that Savannah Cola was coming. But because I wanted to get the formula *exactly* right, we held back.

This was probably a mistake. Maybe I should have done what Coke had done with Minute Maid: announce a product long before you're ready to roll it out, just for the sake of the publicity. Obviously, if we'd suspected that Coca-Cola would condemn its new wonder drink in less than ninety days, we'd have made a big deal out of a few almost-there cans of Savannah Cola just for the PR value. But we really believed Coca-Cola would stand by New Coke through thin and thin. For our caution—and for our rather too conscientious concern that Coke drinkers get a product that tasted precisely like Old Coke—we lost a big opportunity.

And America missed out on a lot of dinner table arguments: "It's the real thing, Mom!" "No, it's not!" "Yes, it *is!*" That would have been a lot of fun.

You may be wondering: The PepsiCo board of directors knew all about Savannah Cola, a drink that Pepsi never even introduced. What was the Coca-Cola board of directors doing during this period?

According to Coke director James B. Williams, president of the Trust Company of Georgia, the topic of bringing back Merchandise 7X was discussed at *every* board meeting *after* New Coke was introduced. I read that as concern. Not, however, concern as urgent as the bottlers felt.

Directors are powerful people who have accomplished much in their lives. They don't serve on boards for the money. Compared to what most of them earn elsewhere, the remuneration they get for attending board meetings and overseeing companies isn't worth talking about.

Bottlers—even the most successful ones—look at the business differently. As they see it, every time a customer buys a rival cola, it's money out of their children's inheritance. And, because they're on the front lines, they're the first to notice their customers' defection.

That's why, early in July, five key Coke bottlers told Coca-Cola executives what the directors, with their better manners, probably couldn't bring themselves to tell Goizueta—that if the trend away from Coke continued, it could become *irreversible*.

Why did it take Coke's bottlers, rather than the company's marketing staff, to convince Coke executives of the extent of the problem?

I have to think it's because they were *still* looking at research and sales projections—at numbers. For all their marketing savvy, they must have completely ignored one of the most common truths of human nature: We tend to love what we can't have. And because original Coke was no longer obtainable, it seemed to taste better and better with every passing day; in memory, at least, it was a far, far sweeter drink than New Coke could ever be.

I don't know when Coke's marketing staff finally came to understand this. But I do know when they got factual confirmation of this psychological truth—in late June when their own polls showed only 30 percent of the people interviewed preferred New Coke. A whopping 60 percent preferred—in memory, anyway—Old Coke.

That data gave the bottlers all the ammunition they needed. And as soon as the bottlers turned en masse against New Coke, Goizueta and Dyson and Keough had the face-saving rationale they needed to make the necessary decision. For with those figures in hand, they were positioned to make a breathtaking turn. Having forced New Coke on loyal Coke drinkers, they now had a mandate to represent those customers against the company—really, against themselves.

And for Coke executives, the challenge was now to coat themselves in Teflon, beg the consumers' forgiveness, and get back to business—the business of taking the momentum back from brand Pepsi. But how to do that? There's really only one first step.

You have to stand at the microphone, look right into the cameras, and say, "We're sorry, we were wrong." And, because the press is inclined to regard any data you may present as just more disinformation, you've got to humanize the story; you've got to let reporters in, pour a glass of Coke, and bleed for them.

That's not easy to do—particularly for captains who have been standing on the bridge of their sinking ship and insisting that the stuff slopping over the deck isn't water. But . . . there's no choice. If they don't eat crow for lunch, it's very clear that they'll have it again—with a second helping served up by Pepsi—for dinner.

Coke's prideful executives, to their credit, do their distasteful duty well.

The story of Old Coke's return, as Coke executives tell it in July, begins in Argentina, where Brian Dyson has gone in late June for a family reunion.

Dyson is no absentee president. He wants to continue to monitor the overnight and weekly reports on consumer reaction. So aides phone these reports to Buenos Aires, where they are tape-recorded and driven to the Dyson ranch, six hours away.

In this remote location, while Dyson is, as *Time* magazine put it, "dining on a freshly slain and roasted heifer," the president of Coke USA gets all the perspective he needs. Upon his return, Dyson begins polling his associates about the correct way to extricate the company from this mess.

Dyson and Don Keough agree that July 8 will be Decision Day—if New Coke sales don't rally over the July Fourth weekend, they'll go to Plan B. Sales continue to fall.

That weekend, Keough decides Old Coke must be brought back. That weekend, while training for a triathalon in Georgia, Dyson comes to the same decision.

On Monday, July 8, five key bottlers meet with Coke executives. Some executives say that the removal of the word *new* on Coke's packaging will cool the controversy. The bottlers say, "Bull." They've heard enough. They demand—so the Coke executives say—a two-cola policy.

I hate to butt into another man's story, but I don't know that I buy this.

I do know how Pepsi bottlers would feel if I tried to pass off promiscuous product segmentation as shrewd marketing. They'd threaten my wife and child. So I just can't see Coke bottlers saying: "In addition to producing and delivering Diet Coke, Caffeine-Free Diet Coke, Tab, Caffeine-Free Tab, and Cherry Coke, we *really* want to bottle, transport, and fight with supermarket managers for shelf space for *two* Cokes."

No, it seems more likely that Coke bottlers asked to champion two Cokes would be more inclined to say: "Then what? Will we also have New Diet Coke, Old Diet Coke, New Caffeine-Free Coke, Old Caffeine-Free Coke, New Tab, and Old Tab? And what about Caffeine-Free Diet Cherry Old Coke?"

But maybe Coke bottlers were so glad to get Merchandise 7X back, they'd agree to anything Coke management wanted. In any event, they do agree to bottle and distribute old and new Coke, and Dyson goes off to huddle with Keough. Keough then huddles with Goizueta. Keough and Goizueta decide that Coca-Cola "Classic" is a better name than "Original" Coke. New packaging is ordered.

On Tuesday, Keough rushes to an Atlanta television studio to tape a commercial announcing the happy news. Then, exhausted, he goes home. At nine P.M. he falls asleep. At eleven, his wife wakes him to say she likes the new name. And Keough sits up for the rest of the night pondering his decision.

On Wednesday afternoon, leaks on Wall Street force Coke to make the announcement a day earlier than they've planned. And as Coca-Cola stock rises over the next two days to a fifty-two-week high, Goizueta and Keough step out front for their one-time-only, three-course meal of crow.

"We want people to know we are sorry for any discontent we have caused them for almost three months," Keough says. "Coca-Cola Classic is truly a celebration of loyalty . . . a vindication of their cause."

"We have hurt you," Goizueta says. "And for that we are sorry."

Keough calls the outcry over New Coke "a wonderful American mystery."

"We knew we would hear concerns, but the passion for original Coke flat caught us by surprise," Keough says. "This has been a lesson in humility."

No, Keough says, this is not "Cokescam," a cynical scenario engineered months earlier to create enormous interest in Coke.

"We're not that smart," he says, "and we're not that dumb."

But, for a few minutes anyway, they are that humble. To prove it, Keough reads a selection of letters from consumers.

"Dear Chief Dodo," one begins.

"What ignoramus decided to change the flavor of Coke?" goes another.

But Goizueta and Keough don't intend this meal to end with a glass of crow liqueur.

"We do not see this as a defensive move," Goizueta says. "This is an offensive move to satisfy more customers and sell more gallons of soft drinks."

And so they introduce a new word—for the language is not rich enough to express the magnitude of a soft drink company that has in its arsenal both old and new Coke. Coca-Cola is no longer a single trademark fighting against all others for soft drink dominance.

Now it's a "megabrand."

Megabrand is a word that sounds best in the basso tones of one of those voice-over actors who do coming-attractions narrations for horror films. Spoken that way, it conveys more than bigness—it suggests indomitability. I hear the word and I picture a brooding giant, a monster wearing seven-league boots and carrying a club. This brute can read consumers' minds. He can create and distribute as many different products as he wants. And as he goes about his business, competitors had better watch out—if he sees one of their products on supermarket shelves, he'll convey it into the next county with a single angry sweep of his hairy hand. It's folly for other soft drink companies to try to fight him. He's too big, too smart, too strong, too hungry.

It's an intimidating word and image, all right. It impresses reporters and securities analysts who suggest that Coke may have backed into a powerful competitive position, with Old Coke holding court above the Cola War fray while New Coke hammers away at Pepsi's loyal user base. Unfortunately for the vice presidents of synonyms at Coca-Cola, it does not produce the desired effect at Pepsi.

Instead, it forces me, once again, to throw my body in front of the Coke freight train. For it's clear that the battle isn't over yet. New Coke may have lost the initial skirmish, but Coke executives are not admitting defeat. Rather they're hoping consumers will not only forgive, they'll forget their dissatisfaction with the new formula. Reluctantly, I rush to New York for network news interviews and a special edition of ABC's *Nightline*. The next morning, viewers of *Good Morning America* and the *CBS Morning News* also get to hear Pepsi's side of the story.

Later that day, Coke holds a press conference at the Pierre Hotel to make the official announcement of Coca-Cola "Classic." They also offer reporters a lavish buffet lunch. But a free lunch doesn't, today, have its usual appeal—not when Pepsi's having a press conference in a crowded meeting room at BBDO. I call it a press conference only in an effort to give it some dignity. Actually, it was more like a comedy show, but it had a very serious purpose: to reinforce the public's rejection of New Coke.

"What are they going to say—Coke *are* it?"

"Coke should adopt Dr Pepper's slogan: 'The most misunderstood soft drink in America.'"

"Maybe Coke should start a Cola-of-the-Month club."

"I don't understand why they used 'Classic' and 'New' Coke—'Confusion' Coke would have been much simpler."

"If they keep this up, we're not going to need a marketing department."

"Consumers weren't screaming for a new Coke. They're not screaming for two, either."

"No, we won't run ads against New Coke. There's not much sense directing advertising against something that has flopped."

"New Coke is the Edsel of the '80s."

I do make one completely serious remark. "I welcome the opportunity to match the single preferred taste of Pepsi against the split personality of our competitor."

After seemingly hundreds of radio, television, newspaper, and magazine interviews, our entire Pepsi team is exhausted. But there's one more thing to do before calling it a day—meet with Phil Dusenberry to discuss a new commercial. But Phil's way ahead of us. He's already got a script.

"I know you want to move quickly, Roger," he begins, "so let's feature a character we've used before."

"The teenaged girl?"

"Nope. Wilbur."

Coke may try to rise again, but their neighbors will be right there to remind them of their betrayal. As Phil explains it, Wilbur comes into a soda fountain and orders a Coke.

"Which one?" the counterman asks.

"Just a Coke," Wilbur says.

"Well, there's lotsa them. See, the old Coke is the old Coke before it became the new Coke. The new Coke is the one that used to be your old Coke . . . which became your new improved Coke. Except for your Classic Coke, which is really the old Coke, but now that's your new Coke. Know what I mean?"

Wilbur doesn't.

"What do you like best?" he asks the counterman.

"Easy," the counterman says.

And hands Wilbur a Pepsi.

Phil looks up. "You like it and you want it on the air Monday?"

"Yes."

"Can't do it."

He's right. Ray Guth, who played Wilbur in the first commercial, is in a Los Angeles hospital. A crew can't be assembled overnight. So it takes BBDO until Monday to shoot. Tuesday, the commercial is edited. At midnight on Tuesday, Alan and I see the finished commercial. On Wednesday, July 17—just a week after the Coke announcement—the commercial airs.

We're glad that Coke executives have discovered humility and rejoined the human race—but we're determined not to give them a chance to save New Coke.

What is Coke going to do with all the New Coke syrup that nobody really wants? Of course, they insist that they're *firmly* committed to making New Coke work in America.

But . . . they're also going to introduce it overseas, where Coke is not so deeply identified with quintessential Americana. And in countries where the news of the American uproar over New Coke hasn't made much of a dent, New Coke might just be the success that Coke researchers swore it would be.

That's pretty good thinking. But there's a flaw in it. They've forgotten about Pepsi.

On August 19, Bob Beeby, head of Pepsi's international division, announces that *we're* going to introduce New Coke at press conferences in thirty cities around the world before Coke can deliver its first batch of syrup overseas. And by "introduce," Bob means that we'll serve up samples of the drink that America has rejected—and that, rumor has it, Coke's overseas bottlers are resisting.

The president of Coke's international division promptly fires off a heated memo. "It is highly unprofessional and a blatant attempt to manipulate the press for a competitor to start an early sampling program for us," he writes.

Highly unprofessional? I suppose so—that is, if people who try it at our press conferences actually believe New Coke is tastier than Pepsi.

A blatant attempt to manipulate the press? Sorry. That's impossible. The nature of the Cola Wars doesn't permit media manipulation. The press loves the Cola Wars too much for that— loves calling Pepsi for a reaction to the latest Coke move, loves telling Coke what the people at Pepsi just said. All this makes for exceptionally well-balanced coverage—and for lively reading.

As Bob Beeby's gutsy move proved.

And there, for the moment, the New Coke story just . . . faded away. And both Coke and Pepsi got down to the nitty-gritty of marketing.

How'd Coke's two-cola cola do in that bottom-line warfare?

According to John C. Maxwell, a much relied-upon beverage analyst for a New York investment firm, New Coke finished 1985 with a 14.1 percent market share and Classic Coke with 7.1 percent. Taking these figures together, the two-Coke strategy resulted in a loss of 1.3 points from the 22.5 share Coke enjoyed the previous year.

Even though that doesn't sound like an improvement in Coke's fortunes, Brian Dyson insists that it was. "Don't forget," he reminded an Associated Press reporter, "that it [Coke's market share] had been changing in a negative sense."

Yes it had. And it looks to me like New Coke made things worse.

How did Pepsi do?

According to Maxwell, Pepsi grew at a 5.1 percent rate in 1985 and became the largest-selling individual soft drink brand in America. It still is. I'm not unhappy with that rate of growth—or with the plus 7 percent Pepsi grew in the first quarter of 1986—especially when Coke, for all the attention it got in the year of New Coke, managed only to accelerate its skid.

But I think the detailed surveys reported by the A. C. Nielsen company for February and March of 1986 are much more telling. Those figures don't include the "captive" market: vending machines and restaurants, where, usually, only one cola is served and where, for decades, Coke has ruled. They do include the places where the consumer can choose between Pepsi and Coke—in grocery and convenience stores. And in those places, the Nielsens show Pepsi with 18.7 percent of total soft drink sales. Classic Coke has 14.6 percent. New Coke has 2.6 percent. By that survey, then, Pepsi beat both Cokes by 1.5 percentage points—or about $250 million in sales.

But in this age of segmentation, with each soft drink company offering six or eight products to the consumer, it's no longer meaningful to focus solely on the flagship brand. Cherry Coke, for example, was a 110 million case business for Coca-Cola in its first year on the market. An impressive launch—but not, I think, nearly so meaningful as the 90 million cases Slice racked up for Pepsi-Cola in its first year.

Now, how does 90 million turn out to be more significant than 110? Because Slice—the 10 percent juice-added soft drink—is not just a single product; it's a whole new product category. In 1986, it should grow to over 200 million cases. Cherry Coke, meanwhile, began a downward slide just a few months after its introduction.

And while Coke is wrapping itself up in its Cherry Coke–New Coke–Old Coke dilemma, we are pushing and prodding Slice to a sales level that suggests it can indeed grow up to be, after Pepsi and Coke, the number three soft drink in America.

No, I haven't forgotten Coke's Minute Maid orange and lemon-lime sodas with 10 percent juice. But it doesn't appear they are setting the world on fire. It seems that Minute Maid isn't such a terrific trademark for a fruit-flavored soft drink, after all. And, of course, Coca-Cola bottlers are awfully busy with that Coke "megabrand," you know.

In July of 1985, before all these figures and sales trends were mine to quote, I was often asked to take the long view and assess the historical impact of New Coke on our business.

Fast-paced marketing businesses like soft drinks don't encourage you to look several years down the line. A year is about the most anyone can reasonably discuss—and in an industry where one decision or one commercial can change an entire nation's attitude toward a soft drink, you can't be too confident even about a year. Still, I decided to answer the question.

In a year, I said, whether the Coca-Cola Company kills New Coke or spends tens of millions trying to prop it up, we'll find ourselves in pretty much the same place we are now.

Coke, which has been losing ground in the regular cola business since 1980, will continue to confront the reality of a shrinking market share. Pepsi, which has been growing steadily, will gain another share point or so in the regular cola segment. And that's pretty much the way it's worked out.

But that's not an answer that people find very satisfying. All that excitement for a whole summer, all those commercials and press conferences and promotions at the supermarket—and when it's all over, things stay about the *same*?

Yes.

Then the New Coke blunder really wasn't very important, you say. Oh, no, it was *very* important. And not just because Coke's managers had to sit on their hands and watch us take a huge, uncontested lead in the juice-added category with Slice *and* gain more ground with Pepsi while they blew as much as $80 million on New Coke.

The New Coke blunder was important for a reason that's all-important in the soft drink business: imagery. Lord knows I'm partisan, but to me, the New Coke blunder revealed that just about everything Pepsi has said about Coke has turned out to be true.

We said Coke—*Old* Coke—was no longer the preferred cola in America. By changing the formula, the Coca-Cola Company acknowledged that.

We said Pepsi was rapidly becoming the most popular soft drink in America—and now, thanks to Coke's tacit admission of the fact last year and its open acknowledgment of it in the press this year, the public recognizes that's not just hype.

We said that Pepsi was for people who like new things and are willing to have some fun. We demonstrated that with our advertising. And—without being too brash or self-congratulatory about it—I think we proved those commercials weren't the creation of some Madison Avenue slicksters by stepping out front ourselves and having a ball running our business. I don't think, in contrast, that our friends at Coke headquarters in Atlanta looked as if they were enjoying themselves defending New Coke.

And we said something else—something about America. It's been said in movies and bestselling books and business seminars a lot in the last few years, and in the process it's become a bit of a cliché. It's still true.

I'm talking about the power of a single person with a good idea—and of what can happen when that person teams up with a few others who share that good idea. The little guy *can* change history. He's just got to keep on coming.

Now, Pepsi-Cola is not exactly a little guy. Each year, after all, we sell enough Pepsi to float an armada. But compared to the awesome global reach that Coke has had at its disposal, compared to the enormous advertising budgets that Coke has had to play with, we've been pretty small change for most of our existence.

Except in one key area: consumer preference for the taste of our product over theirs. I think, after the summer of 1985, people got that message, loud and clear.

And, in the summer of 1985, I think everybody got a chance to see how important imagery is to a company's health. A few days after Coca-Cola brought back Merchandise 7X, Jonathan Yardley wrote a column in *The Washington Post* that suggests how much Coke's image had been damaged:

From the outset, it [New Coke] was, of course, nothing except a "business decision," which was precisely what was wrong with it. It was not enough for the accountants and market survey experts who now run Coca-Cola that their company was in possession of one of the few commodities that had transcended the marketplace and entered national legend, one that had actually become the truly ubiquitous representation of American values and tastes to the rest of the world. This, plus clear dominance in the soft-drink market, wasn't enough for the new entrepreneurs in Atlanta and their mouthpieces in the advertising industry; they wanted more.

Accountants! Market survey experts! "New" entrepreneurs and mouthpieces! That's strong stuff—light-years away from the images we have of "Mr. Bob" and those great ads showing Santa Claus having a Coke by the Christmas tree, and Mean Joe Greene tossing his game jersey to a boy who idolizes him.

Now I've never met Roberto Goizueta, and I've only spent a little time with Brian Dyson and Don Keough, so I don't presume deep knowledge of their souls. Still, I'm certain that they're better men—and better executives—than the parodies of corporate leaders that Yardley describes.

While they did preside over one of the biggest marketing blunders of the century, Coke's top executives also had some successes—notably Diet Coke. The problem was, those successes probably gave them a feeling of invincibility, confidence that their sophisticated research, marketing prowess, and powerful bottler distribution system would make a risky move—like changing Coke's formula—a sure thing.

Painful as it was, though, I think the crisis of New Coke was good for Roberto Goizueta and Don Keough and Brian Dyson. I think, by the end of their nightmare, they figured out who they really are. *Caretakers.*

They can't change the taste of their flagship brand. They can't change its imagery. All they can do is defend the heritage they nearly abandoned in 1985.

The wheel, for them, has come full circle. However much they resent it, they *are* Robert Woodruff's children. If they're going to innovate, they're not likely to do it successfully with Coke.

* * *

But lest I lose my competitive zeal, let's not feel *too* sorry for the architects of New Coke. They're not, I assure you, feeling sorry for themselves.

As Don Keough explained the summer of New Coke to *The Wall Street Journal*: "It's kind of like the fellow who's been married to the same woman for 35 years and really didn't pay much attention to her until somebody started to flirt with her."

Viewed that way, was the controversy over New Coke harmful? Nope—as Coke executives tell it these days, all the attention was positive. Those angry phone calls? Showed that people cared. McDonald's—New Coke's biggest syrup buyer— giving New Coke the boot in the spring of 1986? They switched to Classic Coke, not Pepsi, didn't they? In short, from Coke's point of view, they beat us again.

In fact, a year after New Coke's ignominious failure, Don Keough announced at a shareholders' meeting, "If people aren't drinking it, they must be watering their lawns with it."

And a Coke ad in *USA Today* trumpeted New Coke as "One Year Old and Still Growing!"

Watering lawns? Maybe.

But still growing! Who's going to believe that? New Coke's share of market in food-stores alone was almost thirteen points below its introductory level—that represents a retail sales drop of about two *billion* dollars!

Now, I'm sure the gentlemen in Atlanta can find statistics to prove Coke's superiority. And, if we laid those statistics side by side with the statistics I've cited, you probably wouldn't know whom to believe. So let me concede, right here, one area in which I know Coke whipped us.

Executive paychecks. How *did* Donald Keough and Roberto Goizueta do in 1985?

Each year, *Business Week* puts out an issue on "Executive Pay."

"Who Made the Most?" the cover line asks. "And Are They Worth It?" In 1986, *Business Week,* under the headline "Golden Mistakes," had this to say about Coke:

A few fortunate executives were even rewarded for strategic mistakes. Coca-Cola Co. is a case in point. The compensation committee granted "performance units" to Chairman Roberto C. Goizueta and President Donald R. Keough potentially worth millions of dollars last year. The reason: their "courage, wisdom and commitment" in introducing new Coke, the most publicized new-product flop of the year.

Goizueta, 54, won't be able to savor any of these benefits until at least 1991 and Keough, 59, not until he retires. On paper, however, they are worth $6.4 million and $3.5 million, respectively. That's a considerable pop for a product that has fizzled so far. How could Coke's board justify such a generous new benefit?

"They had the courage to put their jobs on the line, and that's rarely done today at major American companies," says Herbert A. Allen, president of Allen & Co. and chairman of Coke's compensation committee. . . ."

The more cynical among you may be thinking: Wait a minute! I can see rewarding executives for taking risks and putting their jobs on the line. But when they make a giant mistake, they don't usually get a bonus—they get *fired*.

Yes, they do. But let me defend my competitors for a brief moment. To fire them because of one mistake—no matter how huge—is to put everyone who works at Coke on notice: One slip, and you're out. That wouldn't yield better performance; it would only eliminate all risk-taking.

As I see it, one of the most valuable services a CEO can render his company is to provide a safety net for his people. If he wants his business to grow, he's got to encourage them, over and over, to look for and take intelligent risks—and if those risks sometimes don't pan out, he's got to help his associates through those hard times. If he's not supportive, if failure is intolerable to him, it doesn't really matter how successful his company is right now; it won't be tomorrow.

So the directors of Coca-Cola were right, in my view, to send a message to Coke employees that risk-taking is still the name of the game in Atlanta. On the other hand, I'm not sure that a less expensive message wouldn't have been just as effective—and a bit more appropriate.

Which leads me to the cynic's second thought: I get it. What Enrico's really agitated about is the paltry bonus *he* probably earned. Sorry, cynics. It's not that way. I did get a bonus. And, in addition to hard currency, I got some other, equally rewarding, bonuses.

I got to see the Pepsi team work together as it never had before. The Cola Wars paid off for us. Competition had, as we'd been saying all along, made us stronger. And once we took the lead, our employees—thousands of people at every level of the company—didn't choke. We really proved, I think, that it's possible for Pepsi to win, and win big. And, just as important, to win graciously.

I also got to see the PepsiCo system—the big company that acts like a small one—work flawlessly. In any corporate environment with lots of executives and diverse points of view, second-guessing is natural. But Don Kendall and Wayne Calloway gave me absolute support, total encouragement—and not a single "Roger, what I'd do now . . ." It was a great feeling to prove that we were worthy of their trust.

And I got to see that we had learned the one lesson that Coke's present senior management had to teach us. Over the last three years, they had indeed become public relations experts. Their press conferences and news flashes often produced a distorted vision of reality. No matter—Goizueta, Keough, and Dyson were extremely skillful at getting the message out. With New Coke, we proved we could get out there first and beat them at their own game. And, in the process, I think we proved that the American public is more intelligent than its critics would have us believe—all the hype in the world won't make Americans buy what they really don't want.

Finally, I had the best bonus I can think of. I got to write these last two chapters. Believe me—I feel rewarded.

Which is not to say I have taken to spending my days and nights gleefully fantasizing about *another* giant Coke mistake. I don't. I *like* seeing my family at night on a more than occasional basis. And I think, by now, I can generate quite enough Cola War excitement without Coke's help, thank you.

And then too, as a veteran Cola Warrior, I'm reminded of a story I once read about British Prime Minister Harold Macmillan and the great British World War II commander Field Marshal Sir Harold Alexander.

Long after the war, Macmillan and Alexander ran into each other as they were walking into a London theater.

"Alex, wouldn't it be lovely to have it all to do again?" Macmillan asked.

"Oh, *no,*" the field marshal replied. "We might not do *nearly* so well."

As a fellow victor, I know just how he felt.

CHAPTER 15

Riding the Wave

There's an old story about two Buddhist monks walking from one monastery to another. On the way, they reach a stream. It's the rainy season, and the bridge has been washed away. But they know they can easily wade across the stream.

A peasant woman approaches the stream at the same time. She explains that she's been trying to cross but is afraid the current will carry her away. And yet she must get home as soon as possible.

At this, one monk lifts the woman onto his back and carries her across the stream. He sets her down on the far side, acknowledges her thanks, and watches the other monk cross the stream. The monks walk in silence for several miles.

Then the second monk turns to his friend. "You know monks are never supposed to touch women," he says. "Why did you carry that woman across the stream?"

"Oh, I put her down miles ago," his friend answers. "But I see that you're still carrying her."

That story is a paradigm of the Pepsi-Coke relationship. We'd both like to be the high-minded monk who does his duty, keeps his head clear, and moves on. For better or worse, though, we're both like that worldier monk—tightly bound to the do's and don'ts and got-to's and better-not's. Clear sailing? For Pepsi USA, in the hot summer of 1985, only blue skies, gentle winds, and open seas lay ahead of us. But for Pepsi executives— well, for a lot of us, we were so busy competing with Coke that summer we never had a chance for the R&R we'd earned.

* * *

The problem of keeping astronauts refreshed in space is not one that deeply engages executives of soft drink companies. At best, providing astronauts with soft drinks is a two- or three-case business each year—and in an industry that produces retail sales of $39 billion annually, it's hard to get worked up about anything less than 30 million or 40 million cases.

So, in 1983, when engineers at a Pennsylvania company called Enviro-Spray Systems, Inc., suggested that Pepsi commission them to develop a technologically advanced can that could be used in a zero-gravity environment, our people really weren't all that interested.

But a year later, at a Coca-Cola bottlers' convention, Brian Dyson announced to the gathered brethren that Coke was negotiating with NASA to send some "space cans" on the space shuttle. That, of course, got us interested.

We checked with the folks at NASA headquarters—and got blank stares. No negotiations going on. We'll call if there's any change. NASA didn't call. A year later, however, we learned that Coke was indeed sending their product up on the nineteenth mission of the shuttle, scheduled to launch on July 12, 1985. The purpose, in NASA terminology, was "carbonated beverage container evaluation."

This was not just NASA jargon. As you know if you've ever been on a very long airplane flight, the best way to feel good in a pressurized cabin is to drink plenty of nonalcoholic liquids. In the zero-gravity environment of the space shuttle, preventing dehydration is just as important—but the challenge of drinking anything is much greater than that of getting the stewardess's attention. In space, the liquid must be carefully packaged, lest it escape the container and float around the cabin in the form of droplets. But even a pressurized container can cause problems—because it's very difficult to swallow in a zero-gravity environment, the liquid must be delivered, in small amounts, to the back of the throat.

Joe McCann and Clay Small not so gently reminded the folks at NASA of their prior commitments to us. NASA acknowledged that they did seem to have broken their promise to call Pepsi. And in the spirit of fairness they gave us an equal opportunity to go up on the shuttle. But this is mid-June. The mission is scheduled to blast off in a month! With so little time to build a space can and get it approved, how could *anybody* catch up?

At Coke headquarters, in the season of New Coke, this must be one victory Coke executives are certain of.

Fortunately, we remember those Pennsylvania engineers we had cold-shouldered two years ago. Well, those days are gone. We send the company plane for them. Tom Williams, our vice president of technical services, quickly coordinates Enviro-Spray, the Crown Cork & Seal Company, and Precision Valve, Inc., into a team that's committed to working around the clock until a prototype of the space can is perfected.

Soon Tom Williams and his team are winging their way to Houston in our company jet to meet with the engineers at the Johnson Space Center who will evaluate our just-out-of-the-lab package.

Tom has tried our space can many times—on the ground—and it seems to work fine. But what if it doesn't work in zero gravity? Figuring one of our pilots might know something about such things, Tom asks his opinion.

"We can find out right now," the pilot says. "Strap in and we'll put the plane in a zero-G maneuver. When you see things begin floating in the cabin, try out your can."

Tom straps in. Magazines begin to float in the cabin. Tom presses the lever on the can. Pepsi comes out—just as it's supposed to. It hits the back of his throat—just as it's supposed to. Everything works fine—except for Tom. He's so excited about the brief feeling of zero gravity, he forgets to let go of the lever.

Pepsi now hits more than the back of his throat. It hits his face . . . his neck . . . his white shirt . . . his pants.

Tom and his associates arrive at Johnson Space Center. A team of NASA evaluation engineers is waiting for them. Tom begins to demonstrate the space can. He removes the cap.

"What's that cap made of?" asks a NASA team member.

Tom's answer leads to a "that material can't go up" retort.

"Oh, you don't really need the cap," Tom says, pocketing it.

"What's the label on the can made of?" asks another NASA engineer.

Tom's response generates frowns on the other side of the table.

"Oh, we just put that label on the can for the test," Tom says. "For the launch, we'll have a permanently affixed logo."

With that, he takes out a pocket knife and begins scraping away the temporary label. As he does, he discovers that someone lacking a Pepsi can with the correct dimensions to fit the specially designed space top has used, instead, an empty

Gillette Foamy can—filled with Pepsi, but with the Foamy logo fully intact.

Audible groans from the NASA side of the table. But they agree to test our can anyway.

It passes with flying—albeit not Pepsi—colors. Later, with a few more twenty-four-hour workdays to do the impossible, Tom Williams and his team acquit themselves with the engineers at the Johnson Space Center. The detailed volumes of data and our new space can have suitably impressed the NASA folks, who tell us they'll use them as the model for future supplier proposals of this sort.

Four days before the scheduled launch, NASA gives us the okay. Considering that this is July 8—the same day that Coca-Cola executives are preparing for the relaunch of Old Coke—we may assume that no one at Coke has much time to deal with this latest coup.

Except, perhaps, to look over their shoulders in the manner of Butch Cassidy and the Sundance Kid and wonder, as we get closer and closer, "Who *are* those guys?"

Technical problems keep the shuttle on the launching pad on July 12. The new date set is July 29. Fine with us—by July 29 there's no more news coming out of Atlanta, and the press is happy to come to Florida in search of the next Pepsi-Coke face-off. As launch time approaches, it's pretty easy to see who's on what team.

The Coke people are intense and earnest. When the news cameras are turned on them, they talk about Coke-in-space as if they're planning to put Coke machines on the moon tomorrow. They actually speak of space as the next frontier for Coke.

Our people wear T-shirts with a slogan on the front: ONE GIANT SIP FOR MANKIND. It's pretty hard to be overly serious wearing a shirt like that.

The press gets right into the Pepsi spirit. Sure, there are fourteen other experiments being conducted on this flight, and $72 million in scientific equipment—but reporters have to be reminded of that.

"We're not up there," astronaut Charles Fullerton says with considerable bite, "to run a taste test between the two."

He's right. And yet all anybody wants to talk about are those four cans of Pepsi and four cans of Coke.

Which will win?

Then the reporters ask the key question. Which Coke is going up—New or Classic?

It's New Coke.

After the mission, reporters asked the other key question. Which cola did the astronauts like best?

"Neither," was the response. Seems they didn't feel that warm cola did much to refresh their parched palates. I couldn't say I blamed them.

Early in the summer, Jay Coleman is approached by the organizers of what, they say, is going to be the most-watched concert in the history of the planet. Every rock star you can think of is going to perform in Philadelphia—or at an earlier, sister concert in London. MTV, a couple of hundred independent television stations around the country, and ABC are going to televise it. And the fortune this music festival will raise will go to the same cause that has already galvanized America once this year: the hungry and homeless of Africa. Who wouldn't want to be part of "Live Aid"?

And—being practical now—what soft drink company wouldn't consider a hundred thousand thirsty kids and a hundred parched performers in a Philadelphia stadium on a steamy summer day a splendid sight? Jay Coleman has an easy sell with me.

The plan is for MTV to broadcast the event from start to finish—from nine A.M. to some time deep in the evening. The independent stations will broadcast from the start to about six P.M. In the evening, ABC will join the party. This gives corporate America several ways to participate.

One is to become a sponsor of "Live Aid" itself. For a little over half a million dollars, this sponsorship entitles a company to display signs in the stadium and onstage. And, as a bonus, MTV and the independent stations are giving commercial time, free of charge, to those companies every hour.

The ABC deal is pricier. For several million dollars, ABC is creating "exclusives"—only one company per industry can advertise during its coverage of the event. ABC calls BBDO and asks if Pepsi wants this exclusive.

BBDO asks for one day to give ABC an answer—which is common industry practice. We've already signed on to be a sponsor of "Live Aid," but the ABC price for the broadcast is something close to outrageous.

This is, after all, a charity event. The performers are donating their time. The crews and producers and suppliers are giving it their all and being reimbursed only for out-of-pocket costs. MTV is not going to earn dollar one for all its efforts. And the independent stations are at least contributing several minutes of free ad time each hour to the "Live Aid" organizers so they can entice corporate sponsors.

And ABC? Well, ABC's going to clean up. The relative pittance they're paying the "Live Aid" organizers for broadcasting rights compared to the price they're asking for commercial time will yield them a handsome profit.

While we're debating the wisdom of becoming an ABC sponsor, ABC calls—before our one day is up—to say, "Sorry, we signed Coke this morning."

Somehow this doesn't seem a smart way to handle a major advertiser like Pepsi. But we're still very, very committed to "Live Aid."

You give me a good cause, the promise that you'll deliver the proceeds to the people who really need it, and a chance to reach hundreds of millions of thirsty consumers—I'll be there.

Coke now sees that giving millions to ABC for commercial time on "Live Aid" may not be a brilliant move. They figure out that they may be paying mostly for the privilege of giving the TV audience a good look at Pepsi signs. Not surprisingly, they cancel their ABC sponsorship. ABC calls to see if we're interested once again.

BBDO passes along my message: You've got to be kidding!

Philadelphia in August can be unbelievably hot. Fill an open-air stadium, add television lights, and you have the makings of some world-class thirsts. To relieve those thirsts, Jay's people have Pepsi—and Pepsi cups—everywhere you look.

But when I see those cups on Phil Collins's piano, even I am surprised. And when Phil comes out and takes a swig, I can just imagine my friends at Coke breathing a sigh of relief that they backed out of the ABC deal.

Backstage, Jay Coleman is being his usual ebullient self, collaring performers and pitching wild notions that happen to make great sense. Today, he has a Big Idea: After "Live Aid," the only way to outdo Michael Jackson and Lionel Richie is to create superstar marriages. The more improbable the match-up, the more Jay likes it. The idea is to get performers who have sworn they will *never* endorse products to make little films that would work equally well as mini-documentaries or commercials.

Like, say, Tina Turner, David Bowie, and Mick Jagger.

We know Tina, and are, quite happily, sponsoring her exciting summer tour. And the Bowie-Jagger taped duet of "Dancing in the Streets" proves, they're a great combination. Add Tina Turner and . . .

Jay pitches this idea to Roger Davies, Tina's manager. Roger loves it and says that if Tina goes for it, he'll take it to Bowie and Jagger.

Jay wanders off and runs into Don Johnson. Most days, Don's an actor wearing pastel suits and outsmarting the bad guys on the set of *Miami Vice*. Here in Philadelphia he's a singer-songwriter—not performing yet, but on the way—who's hanging out with his pals. Would Don consider appearing in a Pepsi commercial? Would Don *sing* in one? It's an intriguing idea, and Don wants to think about it. Which clearly leaves the door open for further discussion . . .

Bowie and Jagger don't want to do commercials.

Period.

And though Don Johnson, in the summer of 1985, is easily the most popular human being who doesn't wear socks, he is not yet a major rock star.

Michael Jackson . . . Lionel Richie . . . and . . .

Of course—Bruce Springsteen.

We know as well as the next guy that one of the many great things about Springsteen is his affinity for blue-collar America. Will he accept a large sum of money to endorse a product? Don't even bother asking. On the other hand, a certain tradition of excellence has been established in the Jackson and Richie commercials. We've demonstrated that it's possible to serve business interests and make a personal statement—indeed, that a personal and artistic statement is better for our company, anyway, than a hard-sell product endorsement. But Bruce feels he can make personal statements quite satisfactorily by himself, thank you. We hunker down and think some more.

Someone suggests Madonna. Madonna may be very talented, but after those pictures in *Penthouse* and *Playboy*, who cares?

Someone suggests Prince. Prince may be very talented—but in 1985 his biggest achievement may have been to sit in a restaurant while his bodyguards muscle photographers.

Someone suggests Eddie Murphy. Well, I loved *Beverly Hills Cop* and *Trading Places*—but Eddie Murphy's done an in-concert special on HBO that's *unbelievably* raunchy, right?

"No, Dad," my son says. "Eddie Murphy's *great*!"

So I call for the Eddie Murphy HBO special and watch it. Two seconds in, I'm groping for something stronger than Pepsi, because some of his language is so far over the line that, as funny as Eddie Murphy can be, I would never be able to sign him.

What if Don Kendall or Wayne Calloway asks—as Vic Bonomo did when we signed Michael Jackson—for a sample of his work? No way can I let anyone in PepsiCo management see this show—not, anyway, without a cardiologist in attendance. On the other hand . . . Aaron likes him. And everybody else talks about him all the time. So I tell myself: Roger, you're forty years old—maybe it's you.

I watch the HBO special again. No change. Doesn't matter who listens to it. Even a twenty-year-old assistant brand manager whose Walkman earphones are welded to his head wouldn't recommend signing *this* Eddie Murphy to do commercials. Then I get an idea.

Okay, so Eddie Murphy is completely unacceptable as the Eddie Murphy in the HBO special. But Eddie Murphy is a sensational *mimic*. And Eddie Murphy is working up a new career as a *singer*.

We can't get Bruce Springsteen? Eddie Murphy can be Bruce Springsteen. Michael Jackson won't do commercials again? Eddie Murphy can be Michael Jackson. Eddie Murphy can also be Prince. Hell, Eddie Murphy can even be Madonna.

And while we're at it, Eddie Murphy can be Bill Cosby. Doing Coke commercials. Well, parodies of Coke commercials, anyway.

Mostly, though, I think of the mystery we can create with Eddie. We might, for example, announce that Pepsi has searched far and wide for a rock star of the magnitude of Michael and Lionel—but we've simply been unable to find anyone who's up to that standard. So, we'll say, we've embarked on the biggest talent search in history. And we'll unveil the winner in our commercials on Grammy night, giving everyone the chance to compare the performer *we* think will be tomorrow's biggest star against this year's most acclaimed performers.

Of course, the hottest new singing star in the country will be . . . Eddie Murphy. When viewers see Eddie doing Bruce or Michael or Prince or Madonna, they'll groan, all right—and then they'll grin at the irreverence. Suddenly Eddie's HBO special doesn't seem so awful. I'm even willing to pay him a sum that—though I'll never get used to so many zeroes—no longer seems unthinkable.

Eddie likes the idea. I'm sure he doesn't hate all those zeroes.

But it's not the right time for him to do a Pepsi spot—he's got too many movie projects on the boards.

But wait! Somebody *is* hot—so hot that we run to the trivia books to see what other group has had *five* top-ten records in a single year. Okay, so the leader has an earring. Okay, so they're English. That didn't hold the Beatles back. But . . . *Wham?*

Still, 20 million teenaged girls think they're a big idea. Not, admittedly, as big as Michael or Lionel, but definitely hot enough for us to think about. And because nothing else is coming around, we do begin to play Wham's records and tap our feet to the beat. Sometimes we even hum.

Wham wants to play our tune too. George Michael, the brains, beauty, and earring of the duo, gets so enthused, in fact, that he offers to write us—well, *sell* us—a new song. How much will all this cost?

Sit back—Wham doesn't even want to *talk* about the money part of the deal. Nope, the important thing is creative agreement. They want to be comfortable with us. And they want us to get comfortable with them. This makes me suspicious. On the other hand, they're not asking for any money up-front. They're going to write the song, and then we'll talk.

Well, you know what happens. A month goes by. Two. Three. We get nervous. George Michael keeps putting us off. He's been *so* busy he hasn't had time to write our song—but he's getting to it any day now. That's not good enough. We start to look around.

Which brings us back to Don Johnson. And the big question: Can he sing?

The old show-biz saw holds that singers can often make the transition to acting, but actors have much more difficulty becoming credible singers. Phil Dusenberry can cite any number of tragedies that have occurred because overzealous producers have forgotten—or worse, willfully violated—this rule. Though he'd love to do a commercial that zeroes in on the pastel palette of *Miami Vice*, he's inclined to pass on the idea of asking Don Johnson to sing.

"But Walter Yetnikoff's given him a record deal," I point out, and if the president of CBS Records says Don can sing, I'll take it on faith.

So I call Walter.

"Can Don sing?" I ask.

"He's . . . musical," Walter says. "He has a good musical sense."

"Can he sing?"

"Look, I gave him one and a half million to make a record and a video."

"Walter, can he *sing?*"

"Yeah, he can. He's actually pretty good—and he's so popular I'll make a fortune."

He probably will. But just to be on the safe side, Phil, Jay, and I fly down to Florida and spend two extremely pleasant hours with Don. We leave feeling confident that Don can do a lot more than just collar villains.

A week goes by. Don sends up word that he'd like to do the commercial—but he's not so sure it's the right vehicle for his solo singing debut. Okay. We go back to our "Live Aid" concept: staging unlikely duets. Don Johnson and . . . sure—Tina Turner.

Don loves the idea. Tina's manager loves the idea. But 1985 has been such a great comeback year for Tina that he doesn't want to risk over-exposing her in a commercial in '86. (Later, Tina does do a terrific series of duet commercials for Pepsi-Cola International—but these are shown only outside the United States.) In desperation, Jay calls Skip Brittingham, Don's lawyer.

"How can we save this?" Jay asks. "Who's Don willing to sing with?"

"Hmmm. How about Whitney Houston?"

Whitney Houston's a great idea. She's young and attractive and gifted. If you've heard her, you know she's going to be around for a while. A fine choice.

But this is just in the idea stage. Don can say no. Jay calls Whitney Houston's manager.

"I can't believe you're calling me," the manager says. "Guess what I have here on my desk—a contract from Diet Coke."

"Signed?"

"Not yet."

"Pardon my asking," Jay says, "but what's the deal?"

The manager tells him. Jay suppresses a whistle. These are not Pepsi numbers, not by a long shot. Looks like Julio Iglesias has cleaned the Coke boys out.

"Give me twenty-four hours," Jay says.

"Why?"

"Because maybe I can double it."

It turns out to be both our and Jay Coleman's misfortune that he's recently closed a lot of deals on our behalf. A few weeks earlier, he had suggested we sign Michael J. Fox.

I liked *Back to the Future*—as did about 100 million other people—and I'm not blind to the fact that Michael gets 21,000 fan letters a week. I asked my son, Aaron, about Michael J. Fox.

His reaction was: *"You* know Michael J. Fox, Dad?"

Well, not personally yet, but I saw an opportunity to raise the old dad's stature, so we signed Michael.

Around the same time, I suggested that we sign Billy Crystal. Billy was no longer doing *Saturday Night Live,* but kids—and just about everybody else—were still going around saying, "You look maahvelous," his signature line. One of those kids was my son. So we signed Billy to deliver that line to our newly designed package for Diet Pepsi.

Now Jay's on the phone to one of my colleagues suggesting we sign yet another performer. He can't guarantee that Don will sing with her. If Don won't, though, Jay is sure that we can find something for Whitney to do. But on this day, my colleague has a very predictable reaction.

"What do you think this is, Jay, the William Morris Agency?"

"It's not a lot of money," Jay says.

"The money's not the issue. If Don vetoes singing with her, we've got to get him someone else. On top of that we'll have Wham, Michael J. Fox, Billy Crystal, and Whitney Houston, solo. How many show-biz personalities do we *need?*"

"I can't possibly get Don's approval in the next twenty-four hours," Jay says.

So we pass. Whitney Houston signs with the Coca-Cola Company—and makes some absolutely terrific commercials for Diet Coke. (Memo to Coke: I'm *still* waiting for a thank-you note.)

Which puts us back at square one with Don Johnson—again. A good time for Don to save the day by suggesting Glenn Frey.

This is an inspired idea. Glenn was the powerhouse lead singer of The Eagles, he's carved out a new career on his own, and his "You Belong to the City" is one of the reasons that the *Miami Vice* album is selling in the millions. Glenn will not only sing with Don and compose the music, but if Don chooses not to sing, Glenn can carry the musical side of the spot himself. We're completely covered—if Don and Glenn will sign.

I tell my son about Glenn Frey. His eyes light up, but he says nothing. I press for his reaction. He wonders out loud whether I shouldn't be paying him for all this advice I'm getting.

"Maybe I should see what Coke would offer me," he says.

My look says that's not funny—though it was—and we laugh about it together.

"Glenn's cool, Dad—and Don Johnson's supercool," Aaron finally informs me, "but Wham isn't."

Wham isn't?

Meanwhile, back in England—this is like a tennis match, isn't it?—Wham reviews the concepts we've sent over one last time, approves them, and because George Michael hasn't gotten around to writing that song he promised, we agree to use a single from their new album. We agree on money and a filming date. Then we hire Joe Pytka, a very classy and expensive director, to immortalize the group. These are, we now think, going to be excellent commercials.

One is sort of a "Wham Across America" documentary—the group flying from concert to concert, jamming on the plane, running onstage in different cities, escaping in tanks or something afterward. It's a nice concept—particularly if you *like* to spend a bloody fortune.

The second idea is more reasonable, more on the lines of "Wham in Your Neighborhood." In this commercial, Wham's bus breaks down. They get out, and in the distance they hear music. Not just any music—*their* music. They follow it to a barn, where high school kids are having a dance. Naturally, this dance doesn't become less exciting when the group shows up.

I really would, however, like to see what George Michael's signature looks like, so I send our lawyer, Clay Small, to London to close the deal.

As soon as he arrives, the deal begins to sail south. But then, how was I supposed to know English lawyers like to shout so much? And who would have thought terms that looked so clear one week would turn so murky the next?

The song that was part of the deal? Now Wham wants an additional $500,000 for it. And now they want to know just how many times we plan to run the commercial—because they are suddenly very, very concerned about the dreaded phenomenon of overexposure. So concerned that they want the right to kill the commercial outright if they don't like—get this—the final edit.

Maybe I could have handled all this if Wham had thrown this curve early on. But based on the understanding that the major terms had already been worked out, we have already booked Joe Pytka and set a date for filming. In about two weeks we're going to have to pay Pytka and his crew a small fortune—whether they come to our set or loll on the beach.

Clay calls. "These people are completely unreasonable," he says. "This doesn't feel good."

I have been down this road before. I'm not doing it again—not, anyway, with Wham. So I just let the deal . . . fall through. And, happily, we sign Don and Glenn.

It is now January of 1986, and we are thirty days away from our bottlers' convention and advertising premiere. Every commercial has been shot—with the happy exception of Wham's. And, oh, yes, the Don-and-Glenn spot.

Fortunately, the concept, as those who have seen the Johnson-Frey commercial know, is no problem. We just take "Wham in Your Neighborhood" and give Don and Glenn a vehicle more appropriate to their characters—a black Ferrari. And because it's Don Johnson, we make the young mechanic who fixes his stalled car a girl. When she kisses him, girls across America will, we hope, be reaching for Pepsis to refresh their suddenly parched lips. But a day without creative turmoil is—at Pepsi, anyway—a day without life.

This year's crisis is about time. Don shoots *Miami Vice* all week—and all hours of the day and night. Glenn is acting in a movie in Chicago. That leaves weekends. So, each Friday, we send the Pepsi plane to Chicago, where, at the end of the day, Glenn tumbles aboard for a subsonic flight to his second job in Miami. Ridley Scott directs Glenn and Don all day Saturday, Saturday night, and all day Sunday. Then the plane flies Glenn back to Chicago. And people think stars don't do anything for their money!

Ridley Scott wraps our most expensive commercial yet—all that weekend night shooting at rates the unions call, correctly, "golden time"—in two weeks, and the film is shipped to New York, where it joins nineteen other commercials that BBDO and J. Walter Thompson are readying for the bottlers' convention.

They make steady progress, but not, it turns out, steady enough. For Don Johnson reveals during this period that he, too, is a perfectionist; he cares a lot about this spot and wants it to be a real event. Normally—if "normal" ever existed around here— we'd be happy to accommodate him. But this is exam time and prom night all rolled together, and we just can't send Don every single version. And, because of some confusion about just what it is Don wants to see, we don't send him an almost-final edit until three days before he's to romance the bottlers and the press at the premiere.

Don suggests eight or ten small changes. Phil Dusenberry says he'll think about them and may well make them all—but not until after the premiere. It's not, after all, as if these are going on the air right away. This time, thank God, we've got a whole month separating the advertising premiere and the night of the Grammy Awards, when we first show our most "leading edge" commercials on network TV.

The advertising premiere is in San Francisco on Saturday evening, with a press conference on Saturday afternoon. On Thursday, Don is in Miami making his television show. On Thursday afternoon, Don's agent calls us—in San Francisco, where we're rehearsing our presentations—to say that the Johnson-Frey commercial must not be shown at the premiere. By now, you know what my reaction will be to that. If necessary, we'll meet in court. But this doesn't sound like Don Johnson to me.

Don's agent has a second thought. You guessed it—more money. A little bonus. "Tell him no damn way," I say to Alan.

Alan's already communicated that message, but is more than happy to do so again.

The agent's demand for more money also doesn't sound like Don Johnson to me, so we send the Pepsi plane to Miami to pick Don up anyway.

Friday night I come back to my hotel to find messages from Don and Skip Brittingham, his attorney. Now I begin to panic— am I really about to learn, at the eleventh hour, that Don's going to pull a no-show?—but I know Skip to be a reasonable guy, so I call him. No answer. I try for an hour. It's twelve-thirty A.M.— three-thirty A.M. in Miami. What now?

Why not call? It's Don Johnson. He's probably up.

He is. He films all Friday night. And, his aide says, he really wants to talk to me. He'll call me when he's finished shooting—if that's okay with me.

"How late will that be?" I ask.

"Could be another hour."

"Sure, I'll wait up."

At one-thirty A.M.—four-thirty A.M. in Miami—Don calls.

"What the hell, Roger," he says. "You think you own the night out there?"

"*You* should talk, Don."

"Well, we're almost done," he says. "Hey, thanks for sending the plane."

That's nice. He plans to come.

"Look, I don't think I've been treated right by you guys. I want this thing to be really good-looking and stylish, and I don't think you've used the best takes. I'll grant you, it's ninety percent there—but I don't want this shown tomorrow until we change it."

"Don, I'll change it, but I physically can't do it by tomorrow afternoon."

"And what's this about my agent supposedly coming back to you for more money? I'm not trying to get more money out of Pepsi. Why did Pottasch say that?"

"Wait a minute. Alan said it because your agent tried to do it. I don't know if he admitted it to you or not."

"No. Of course not. Because he didn't do it."

"He did it with Dusenberry and he did it with Pottasch—two different times."

"Well, let's not argue about that," he says. "Let's talk about the commercial. I don't care if you show it to the bottlers, but I don't think we should show it to the press until it's right."

"Why not? It's close enough."

"If they don't like it, they'll pan it. And those little changes might make the difference."

"Don, they're not film critics. They're not going to be in a darkened theater. They're going to see it once, in a club. Two minutes, it's over."

There's a pause, the first in our conversation.

"I don't know," Don says at last. "I'll think about it."

"Don, I share your concerns. I want to make it perfect, too— but hell, it's *already* fabulous. It could be the best we've done yet. It's got a look all its own. And it's got style to burn."

Another pause.

"If we don't show this commercial at the press conference tomorrow," I continue, "they'll assume there was something wrong with it and really be ready to tear it apart—so I don't think we really have the option of pulling it. My option is to cancel the press conference. Which I'm willing to do—if you'll commit to doing another one with the rest of the guys the day before the Grammys. Those are my only two windows."

"Roger, I would—but I can't. *Miami Vice* could have me tied up then."

"Then," I say, "I'm in one hell of a box."

"Look, Roger, there are two changes I *really* care about. They're both audio. I told Phil about them. One is when Glenn and I walk into the school dance and I say, 'Hello, girls.' And somebody goes, 'Oh, there's Don Johnson.' Well, that's corny. And the other's at the end, when the girl mechanic puts her dirty hand on my jacket and Glenn says, 'Mr. Cool.' If, when he saw her handprint, he just said 'Cool,' it'd be a lot better."

I wonder: Has Phil made these changes? Can we fudge them somehow? There's got to be something we can do.

"Don, if Phil didn't make the changes, we'll find a way to bleep those lines out."

"Hey, it's almost five A.M., Roger. I gotta get to the plane."

"See you later, Don. Get some rest."

We hang up. He's coming.

I call Alan Pottasch. It's nearly two A.M. here in San Francisco, but I don't see why I should be the only one not getting any sleep. He tells me that Phil's already made those changes.

Two years ago, when I was playing junior film mogul, I'd have probably been standing outside the editing room waiting to see Phil's latest edit. This year, Phil and Alan have their act so well coordinated that when I do poke my face into their business, everything's been taken care of. What a difference twenty-four months makes!

I assume that Don will show up at our convention head-quarters, the Fairmont Hotel, around eleven A.M. What would surprise him most? Well, I know what would surprise me—seeing the president of the company standing at the door, waiting for me. So I do it.

Don's limo pulls up. A darkened window goes down. "Hey, pal, climb in."

Clearly, a night on the company plane with a steward making up Don's bed right after takeoff and squeezing him fresh juice in the morning hasn't rubbed our star the wrong way.

"I hope you don't think I've been a creep about this commercial," Don says. "It's just that I'm three thousand miles away with all this stuff going on and I don't hear from anybody for a day or two. So I begin to wonder what the hell is going on. It's my *career*, you know."

"Don't worry about it. I knew what your motivation was."

"Okay, right. But tell me—was I the most difficult person Pepsi's ever worked with?"

"Don, you never touched Joan Crawford in her prime," I say. "She required toasted French bread, slightly burned on top, in her hotel room—not that she ever ate it. Also in her hotel room, she had to have seven packs of cigarettes, four closed, three opened. She required a licensed engineer on duty, and she had to know the number of steps from her room to the elevator. She . . ."

But Don's laughing too hard for me to go on. And, I figure, he's probably thinking: You know, maybe I've been too easy on this guy—I could have been a much bigger S.O.B., after all.

The press conference is held at a small club. The format's simple: Show a commercial; bring the star out; fire away.

The first commercial shows Billy Crystal telling our new Diet Pepsi can—"you little twelve-ounce beauty"—that it looks "maahvelous."

We don't prompt our stars. "I used to play here," Billy Crystal says, when he takes the stage to lead off the celebrity phase of the afternoon. "Wasn't that the *strangest* opening act?"

Question time. No one seems to have any. "The answer is Curt Flood," Billy says.

"Do you drink the stuff?" a reporter asks.

"Yes. I've been sworn to say yes."

"Why'd you do this commercial?"

"I'm making a bat mitzvah for my daughter this spring. And the band is so *expensive* . . ."

A half-second pause.

Billy peers over the podium at the reporters. "So, how are you guys doing—working?"

"Will you do more Pepsi commercials?"

Alan Pottasch steps forward and says no, not this year.

Billy turns to Alan. "Why? Wasn't I good, Alan?"

Somehow, Alan recovers sufficiently to lead a round of applause for Billy.

Now the Michael J. Fox commercial comes on. In it, Michael's bored with studying and thirsty. But he doesn't have change for the Pepsi machine. He's left his textbook, *The Power of Suggestion,* on top of the library's photocopying machine, though, and is stunned to see the machine produce a color picture of a can of Pepsi. Michael tears the paper—and hears the Pepsi fizzing. He rolls it up, holds it to his mouth—and drinks.

Refreshed, he tosses the "can" into the trash—and it rattles with the sound of aluminum on steel.

Michael J. Fox, without prompting, comes out with a can of Diet Pepsi. He opens it, sips, coughs.

"What *is* this stuff?" he says.

Well, you can't get much looser than that.

"How old are you?" someone asks.

"Twenty-four—how about you?"

"Ever do any commercials before this?"

"Yeah, in Canada, for a tile cleaner. 'Look at him scrub!'"

"How is this commercial different?"

"It's creative," Michael says. "I don't have a film coming out this year, so this is like my mini-movie for the year."

"Okay, but why Pepsi?"

"Metamusil hasn't gotten in touch. And Pepsi's a classy company—they do classy ads. I'm pretty happy with the way mine turned out."

When Michael J. Fox steps off the stage, I'm stunned by how real and unspoiled he is. Out of curiosity, I ask him if his actor friends have given him a hard time about doing a commercial. "Yeah," he says. "A lot of them called me to say what a big mistake I was making. I told them, 'Hey, my kids are going to college.'"

But Don Johnson and Glenn Frey top everybody. Don's wearing a double-breasted sharkskin suit, an open shirt, no socks, and loafers. Glenn has a tie, a blazer, socks—he could pass for a regular person.

"Does this commercialize Sonny Crockett?" a reporter asks, referring to Don's character on *Miami Vice*.

"I thought," Don says, "that he was pretty commercial to start with. This is just a little film about style."

"What won't you sell?"

Don gets a funny look.

"I like this product," he says. "Considering some of the liquid refreshment I've reached for in the past, I would have done a lot better to reach for a Pepsi more often."

"Glenn, do you feel constrained writing for a commercial?"

"No. I wish all the songs I have to write were only a minute," Glenn says.

"Is that why you did this?"

"No. I wanted to work with Ridley Scott . . . and hang out with Don."

"And make a little movie," Don adds. "An intensified moment."

"One more question," Alan Pottasch says.

"Are you guys using Pepsi?" a reporter shouts. "Or is Pepsi using you?"

Don Johnson laughs. Then he gives an answer that sums up the day with perfect Sonny Crockett bluntness. "Are you kidding?" Don says, pointing to the cameras. "*We're* having a good time using *you*!"

The bottlers' convention goes off like the spectacular Grucci fireworks display we shot off over the bay that night.

Everybody's really up. We've just finished the best growth year in our history—and it looks as if 1986 will blow past even that milestone. Once again, Alan's a hit with the advertising. And the added luster of Billy Crystal, Michael J. Fox, Glenn Frey, and Don Johnson joining Alan on stage after each of their commercials doesn't do anything to dampen our enthusiasm.

I announce that we're going to roll national with three more Slice flavors, each with 10 percent juice and each in diet and regular versions. And, for the first time in public, I share my outrageous goal for the brand: Slice as the third-biggest trademark in the industry. An annual sales volume of 500 million cases—over $2 *billion* a year at retail.

And once again, the "New Generation" advertising gets great press coverage. The *Today* show puts us on—twice—in February alone.

After we premiered five of the new commercials on the Grammy Awards telecast—including a sizzling two-minute version of Don Johnson's style and Glenn Frey's music—critics proclaim Pepsi advertising the sweep'em-up award winner.

And not long afterward, we were informed that Pepsi had been voted another, most special award—from the "4 A's," the foremost association of advertising agency people in the country. The award was a new one, never granted before. It's for the company that, over the years, has had the most consistent excellence in advertising in the country.

The Pepsi Generation was the winning advertising, and Pepsi-Cola was the winning company—for over twenty years of being the best.

As you can tell, I felt immensely proud that Pepsi was receiving that award. Not just for myself—I'm a relative newcomer here—but for all those who truly made it happen, and for the folks who were there at the beginning.

People like Don Kendall, who would be retiring not two weeks before the award was to be presented.

And Alan Pottasch, who, if I have my way, will *never* retire.

And all the wonderfully creative and dedicated people at BBDO who have directed the creation of our advertising for more than twenty-three years: Allen Rosenshine, Phil Dusenberry, and, yes, in the early days, John Bergin.

For though John Bergin had worked hard at Coke's advertising agency these past several years—I'm told that "Coke Is It," which was great advertising, was his baby—he was at the ceremony.

As chairman of the "4 A's" committee that voted us the honor, he was, you see, presenting the award.

CHAPTER 16

Clear Sailing

In what is euphemistically called "spare time," a lot of executives I know like to read about naval warfare. Having seen how long it takes for battleships to turn, I understand their interest. For most of these men, running a business is very much like turning a battleship—once strategic decisions in slow-moving, machinery-driven businesses are made, they're very hard to adjust.

Pepsi generates less paperwork than any company I'm aware of, but, like every other executive I know, I don't have enough time to read for pleasure. And when I do have some time for myself, the books I read tend to relate in some way to the work I do. So I, too, read history—mostly military history.

I'm not a big fan of battle books. I prefer military history that's insightful about strategy—or that *is* strategy, plain and simple. A copy of *The Art of War*, a small Chinese classic reintroduced by James Clavell, sits on my desk as a constant reminder that good ideas, properly utilized, are worth as much as heavy weapons. And if I can clear some time, I may even—to the certain puzzlement and probable consternation of my friends and associates—try to plow through Mao Tse-tung's book about guerrilla warfare.

Recently, however, my reading's been more traditional. And what's more traditional than English military history? Even here, however, there are surprises. I found one not long ago when I was reading *The Great War and Modern Memory,* Paul Fussell's book about the British experience in World War I.

Fussell's aim is to show how this war, which flat-out eliminated a generation of English males, was *so* horrifying that the only way it could be dealt with was through the conventions of literature, movies, and myths—that is, as the English *remembered* war, not how this one was *actually* experienced. And more: "Every war is alike in the way its early stages replay elements of the preceding war. Everyone fighting a modern war tends to think of it in terms of the last one he knows anything about."

That paragraph struck me with particular force. And a certain irony.

For as I come to the end of *this* book, I realize that the story I've told here is not just the story of my two passions: superior execution in the basics of our business, and a constant thrusting toward novelty and entertainment in our advertising.

This book describes a cycle. Two different cycles, really—Coke's and Pepsi's.

The Coca-Cola Company is like Fussell's England, circa 1914–1918. Coke continues to react to Pepsi as it has for the last two decades of the eighty-eight years we've been each other's primary competitor. To Coke, we're an upstart who may come close to victory at times, but we simply *can't* displace Coke's mythic dominance because . . . well, because everybody knows that just *isn't* in the script.

What happens when reality changes the script?

At Pepsi—the big company that acts like a little company—we take to our offices and . . . think. Not very dramatic. Damned unpleasant work. But somebody's got to do it—particularly if the way you plan to get to the top is via shrewdness, originality, surprise, creativity.

At Coke—the big company that regards itself as bigger than life—the tendency is to stand tall. Not just to show that it can flex its muscles, but to pump them up, to make them bigger and bigger and bigger.

In this corner, brains.

In that corner, brawn.

Obviously, that's an overdrawn comparison. Coke executives are not only tough competitors but smart ones too. Still, the most basic truth about the psychology that underlies the corporate culture of the Coca-Cola Company is that the men who run it perceive Coke's reality as unchanging. Domination in the past. Leadership in the present. Supremacy forever. And so Coke executives would probably say Coke shouldn't be discussed in terms of cycles at all; if you want to chart Coke, they'd say, just draw an unending straight line high above the competition, now and forevermore, amen.

I can understand why they'd think that. And, perhaps, need to think it now more than ever. For in their one big experiment with change—New Coke—the men who run Coke discovered that Americans will tolerate anything from Coke *except* change.

That's exactly why I think Coke *is* in a cycle—an endless cycle with a lot of running in Atlanta just to stay in place.

But life is about nothing if not change. Which brings us to Pepsi's cycle.

In each of the three years I've been president of Pepsi USA, there is a repetitive pattern. I like to think of it as a skyrocket. We introduce new products. Spruce up our imagery. Pack as much entertainment value as we can into our advertising. Then we launch it.

If we've prepared it correctly, it throws off different colors and effects as it goes higher and higher—and it doesn't burn out for a whole year. And while it's shooting higher and higher, we pretend we've never made anything beautiful before and look for new ways to build the next one.

And the following year, we launch another skyrocket. More new products. Freshly scrubbed imagery. And even more entertainment value crammed into our advertising.

For three years, we've put on fireworks shows that have titillated, amused, and delighted our loyal customers—and, I am pleased to note, an ever-growing number of our competitor's once-loyal customers. Now people have come to *expect* us to surprise them with flares, whistles, and magic. And because we like pleasing people, we'll keep trying to make our business more entertaining year after year.

But now that we're in the entertainment business as well as the soft drink business, I've learned something about our cycle that they probably don't teach at business school—and that we didn't need to know when I was a pup at General Mills and Frito-Lay.

There are, as someone has pointed out, only seven great stories in literature. The great storytellers are those who know how to combine them, dress them up, and present them as though they've never been told before.

Translated into business terms, this means that even the most enlightened Cola Warriors can't help but "replay elements of the preceding war."

We've come to understand that. And, instead of denying it or wildly looking for some new craze to ride, we've decided that it might be okay, after all, to replay history a bit. Particularly if we consciously *choose* to replay it.

Two caveats: The aspect of our history that we replay *must* be true to our character. And, because our boredom threshold is just as low as yours, it must be *fun*.

Pepsi's character has, for the longest time, been Underdog. It's a thrilling character to play—given a choice, who'd choose to be Goliath over David?—and, as I hope I've shown in these pages, we don't have to be great actors to play it. For no matter how big and successful we get—and no matter how fast the plot changes each year—temperamentally, the role is still ours. Best of all, our competitor doesn't seem to want it.

Coke *can't* want it, really. As the Cola Wars of 1985 proved beyond all argument, the people who run Coca-Cola—and the people who will come after this particular group of executives—have to be caretakers of the greatest trademark in American history. Even if it's no longer necessarily the most potent trademark in America.

But that's their problem. Mine, this year, is to make sure that Pepsi gains more ground in restaurants and vending machines. To support our new Slice flavors as they go national. And to make sure my old nemesis, Diet Pepsi advertising, works for real this time around.

And, of course, to do what only a company president can do: take the leadership role in charting a strategic direction for our business in the coming year.

For in 1987, once again, we're trying to reinvent the wheel. Along the way, though, two things I never *ever* thought would come to pass have indeed transpired. One involves growth. Not the invention of a new product in our R&D lab—a process I love like no other—but an effort to acquire another soft drink company. The other is something I swore never to do: We're going to step in the same stream twice.

I think that second move is risky. I don't think, however, that I'm exactly replaying elements of the preceding war. If we can combine underdog strategy and the creativity of a hugely talented performer—and get a fraction of the good luck we had last time those came together—I think we're going to make history all over again.

Business first.

In the spring of 1985, the chairman of the Philip Morris

Company talked—at some length—in a securities analyst's report about his strategic priorities for his business. Now at PepsiCo, we do not usually pore over reports of the Philip Morris Company. But Philip Morris had, in 1978, paid a whopping $520 million for 7-Up.

And just eight years later, in a thorough discussion of his corporate priorities, its chairman never *once* mentioned 7-Up.

Impossible for Bob Beeby, the president of Pepsi-Cola International, to ignore that omission. Particularly because a lot of our international bottlers also are 7-Up bottlers. If we owned 7-Up's international business, we'd reach critical mass in a number of countries. So the Pepsi-Cola International division approached Philip Morris. Would they sell us 7-Up's overseas operation for a reasonable price?

Word came back. No, but they'd sell us the whole company— the third-largest soft drink in America and that overseas business—for a reasonable price. Well, this was something else. Something a great deal better.

For one thing, 7-Up is a unique product, a brand with a special position in the consumer's mind. Although its sales have been sinking lately, a lot of the fault lies with its management. If it were managed by a company that understood better how to market soft drinks—like, say, PepsiCo—it might do much, much better.

And 7-Up is not just a brand; it's a business organization. In addition to the critical mass 7-Up would offer Pepsi overseas, we'd also get a second bottling and distribution system in most of America. Only 20 percent of the 7-Up bottlers in the United States are also Pepsi bottlers. The other 80 percent of the 7-Up bottlers, if brought into our system, would be like a second Pepsi USA army—and anyone who can have two armies in the soft drink battle with Coke has to think seriously about the proposition.

In January 1986 we made a deal to buy 7-Up for $380 million. Now, who knows how good a deal this might have been—there are many ways to analyze cost versus return. But here's a simple one that says quite a lot: Dividing the price we had agreed to pay by the number of cases of 7-Up that were sold in 1985, we would have bought 7-Up at 63 cents a case.

Here's another way to analyze that deal. With the addition of 7-Up, Pepsi would gain about 7 share points. We'd be just a few share points shy of the Coca-Cola Company—within striking distance.

You may imagine the consternation this caused in Atlanta. Particularly because our 7-Up deal had been so skillfully and quietly orchestrated by Fred Meils, Pepsi USA's chief financial officer, that our competitors—including, I do believe, our friends at Coke—didn't know it was happening until a day or so before they read it in the papers. Anyway, who'd have believed it if the news did leak out? Pepsi just doesn't, as we all know, acquire soft drink companies.

Coke forgot that, at Pepsi, we have only one rule: to change the rules of the game, again and again.

And so Coke tried to play a more expensive game. Catch-up.

Just one month later, the Coca-Cola Company agreed to buy Dr Pepper, America's fourth-largest soft drink company. Its owners put up $30 million in equity for the company and took on $170 million in debt in a leveraged buyout two years earlier. For the privilege of taking it over, Coke would pay *$470 million.* What would Coke get for that hefty price?

Well, they'd get Dr Pepper itself, a spicy cola that, Coke insists, wouldn't compete with *its* new spicy cola, Cherry Coke.

It would get a bottling system in which 40 percent of Dr Pepper bottlers *already* bottle Coke—and in which 30 percent of the rest bottle *Pepsi.*

And the per-case cost? Analysts estimate that Dr Pepper sold 467 million cases in 1985. Having looked at their prospectus and broken down their figures using other sources, I think they actually did closer to 330 million cases that year. If my figures are right, Coke agreed to pay $1.42 a case for Dr Pepper—about two and a quarter times more per case than we agreed to pay for 7-Up.

But however much duplication Dr Pepper would have brought to the Coke system, whatever problems they might have had working with Pepsi bottlers, and however pricey the purchase might have been, Coke could have gotten something the gentlemen in Atlanta find very important.

Bragging rights.

With this purchase, Coke would have protected its leadership position—at least for a while.

As I write, the 7-Up and Dr Pepper purchases have been challenged by the government. I suppose they may not in fact be consummated at all. The Federal Trade Commission seems to consider the acquisitions to be anti-competitive. I don't see why. After all, is there a more competitive consumer-product industry in the country than soft drinks? Haven't the commissioners heard and read all about the Cola Wars?

I would have thought they had. And I would have thought they'd see that the battles between Pepsi and Coke have been very good indeed for consumers; the retail cost per ounce of our soft drinks is as low today as it was ten years ago.

It'll be no surprise to you, I'm certain, to learn that I hoped a way could have been found for Pepsi to purchase both the international and the domestic divisions of 7-Up. But it may surprise you to learn that I had hoped Coke's Dr Pepper deal would go through as well.

As for 7-Up, it is, as I've said, a failing brand, and I would have liked to help save it. Then, too, it would be a shame for Coke to lose Dr Pepper. Why? Because any time they want to pay $470 million for the privilege of saying they're number one, I have to regard that as another Pepsi victory.

Well, that's the business side of things at the moment. That's the steak—now here's the sizzle.

In the fall of 1985 we were asked if we wanted to be the sole soft drink sponsor of the 1986 Goodwill Games, an international athletic competition.

Organized by the USSR Sports Committee and Ted Turner, one of America's most colorful entrepreneurs, the Goodwill Games seemed like an excellent idea. And with cable television available in more and more of America, we felt that Ted Turner's network, CNN, and his SuperStation, WTBS, would be able to deliver a significant audience.

There was also a personal reason to become involved with this two-week-long athletic competition in Moscow. Don Kendall—who opened Russia to American consumer products when he persuaded the Soviets to build Pepsi bottling plants there—was retiring in May 1986. Going to Moscow with the great internationalist himself was an opportunity that might never come again.

In December 1985 the Russians had an idea. They communicated it to Turner's people. And Turner's people passed it on to us.

The Russians, you see, knew all about Pepsi advertising. They thought we had an in with every great American performer. And so, as long as we were sponsoring the Goodwill Games and bringing a planeload of Pepsi bottlers and employees to Moscow, why didn't we also bring Michael Jackson?

I remember exactly what I said to Richard Blossom when he told me of this request.

"You've got to be nuts."

In the spring of 1986, with the advertising premiere behind me, Slice rolling out its new flavors all around me, and the Goodwill Games making my summer look like all the fun I needed to round out my year, I went off to India for a week to attend a conference of the worldwide Young Presidents' Organization.

I was invited by Mohan Murjani, the young fashion entrepreneur of Gloria Vanderbilt fame and, lately, the driving force behind Coca-Cola clothes. Never mind the fact that we're about to bring out our own line of Pepsi New Generation fashions with a Murjani competitor, V.F. Corporation, the makers of Lee jeans. Mohan and I are friends, and we and our wives had a fascinating time in India.

When I returned, I had a stack of phone messages. And a blinking light on my phone.

"Yes?"

"Roger, it's Jay Coleman," Patti says.

"Oh, God, not today."

"He seems awfully excited about something."

"He *always* is. Tell him . . ."

"He says he *has* to talk to you."

I groan. But I take the call.

"Roger, are you sitting down?"

"Yeah—in a very distant time zone too."

"I know, I *should* ask you about your trip, but I got a call you're not gonna believe. It was from Frank Dileo and John Branca—*Michael Jackson wants to make more Pepsi commercials!*"

After New Coke, I thought I was pretty unshockable. But I have to tell you, this news jolts me.

"Michael's got a new album coming out, and he's going to do a tour," Jay continues, "and they want to make a major deal for him."

"What did you say?"

"The obvious—that we all thought Michael couldn't stand it the last time."

"What did they say?"

"That it wasn't true. Back then, he was forced into the Victory tour and the 'New Generation' commercials, but he's all on his own now—and he *wants* to do this."

"Why? He doesn't need the money."

"They had an answer for that too," Jay says. "Michael's definitely not averse to making more money—but what really gets him going is the idea of topping himself."

Topping himself? "Thriller" sold 40 million records. Springsteen's "Born in the USA," the next record to roll across America like an evangelical crusade, sold maybe 15 million. It's very, very unlikely that anybody—ever—will do what Michael did with "Thriller."

Another thought crowds all that out: "Michael Jackson topping himself" can be interpreted in various ways.

One meaning it *can't* have is that Michael will come cheaper than $5 million.

"What did they say about price?" I ask.

"First let me tell you what they said about sponsorship. They're talking a worldwide deal. Concerts, tours, public appearances, commercials—the whole ball of wax."

"What did they say about price?" I ask again.

He tells me—but I can't tell you, our contract prohibits it. Let's just say that somehow I've gotten used to numbers with lots of zeroes behind them, but that it's considerably less than the $15 million reported in the press. And he tells me that Dileo and Branca are going to be in New York. We can fly back to Los Angeles with them, talk over the deal, and go meet Michael at his home to hear directly what he'd like to do.

On our airplane with Dileo and Branca, Jay, Clay Small, and I have very little difficulty becoming enthused over the prospect of tying up with Michael once again. We have a great time rehashing the events and the characters of the Victory tour—and can actually laugh now about all the misunderstandings, late-night phone calls, and courier-delivered videotape edits of the Jacksons' commercials. The business discussion—the guts of what will be included in the deal—goes smoothly. Which leaves me with two questions.

One I can answer: Does Michael Jackson really want to be with Pepsi again? I'll know that soon enough, when we arrive at his home.

And one I can't answer: *Will* Michael Jackson be as hot in 1987 as he was in 1984?

I do know this: Michael Jackson and Frank Dileo have done a terrific job of controlling Michael's image. For two years he's been practically off the air—writing some thirty new songs and working up a new act and look. No more "bandleader" outfits, no more moonwalking.

And all that time, he's made no noteworthy public appearances save his dedicated involvement with "USA for Africa." He's given no interviews. Faded—deliberately—so effectively that, when he comes back, we're bound to be surprised.

Will he be as hot as he was?

I could, perhaps, hear the new album, see sketches of the new costumes, watch a preview of the new act. But even then I wouldn't be able to guess if Michael could sell 5 million, 10, 15—or 40 million—records in the years to come. And neither, with certainty, can anyone else.

So the question "Will Michael Jackson be as hot in '87 as in '84?" isn't something that can be answered before the fact. But on the basis of Michael's track record, I'm certainly inclined to roll some dice with him.

All this, however, is so much intellectualizing. The fact is, I like Michael. And I haven't talked to him for a couple of years. Why not do the smart thing—listen to what he has to say?

Michael Jackson walks confidently into his living room. His voice is no longer a faint whisper. He's still shy—but much more assertive. He actually seems glad to see us.

"Michael, I don't want to rehash the past, but after all we went through, I'm a little surprised that Jay and I are here," I say. "I know there were mistakes made, but I think they were made on both sides. This time, if we work together, I want you to know that we're much better at it. We've had a lot more experience with talent. And what we've learned is this: Stars like you and Lionel and Michael J. Fox, Billy Crystal, Glenn Frey, and Don Johnson have a great deal more to offer than just their faces in our commercials. You've got creative vision and we're idiots if we don't take advantage of that. That's why we want a longer-term deal this time—not for commercials, because that *would* overexpose you, and us with you—but so you can consult with us. Maybe, if it's appropriate and it's something you want to do, you could direct or co-direct a commercial."

This makes sense to Michael, who comments knowledgeably about the Pepsi commercials each of those stars has done. He also discusses the need for a creative partnership to bring new excitement to the public.

Then I tell him our idea for his 1987 commercials. He sparks to it.

I can't tell you about it here—suspense is half the fun, after all—but it's an enormously difficult idea to pull off. It needs Michael Jackson—and an absolutely first-rate director—to have a chance of succeeding. But no one has ever done anything like it before, and if we can make it happen, it will be gangbusters.

Michael's reaction to the idea? "Roger," he says, "This time we're going to set the world on fire!"

He didn't, I assure you, mean that literally.

And then there's this other idea I have. When I describe it to him, it stirs something in Michael's soul—because it will benefit millions of other souls. But that, too, is something for the future.

In early May 1986 we hold a press conference to announce our second deal with Michael Jackson. It's a multiyear creative partnership: international and American tours, a worldwide advertising campaign starring Michael, and other activities not yet made public.

The news conference is held at the Red Parrot Club in New York—and highlights are later sent by satellite hookup to hundreds of reporters in other cities. It's an event, and is handled that way.

That week, Coca-Cola also holds a little event: Coke's one-hundredth birthday celebration in Atlanta. Thousands of their bottlers and employees from all over the world swarm through the city to celebrate their astoundingly successful first century. Celebrities entertain them. Politicians applaud them. The public enjoys the spectacle, and the spectacular parade through the streets of Atlanta.

For that week, the Cola Wars are suspended—even for me.

Pepsi-Cola's signing of Michael Jackson, our deal to buy 7-Up, Coke's deal to buy Dr Pepper, and Coca-Cola's celebration of its hundredth birthday are nice symbols for me precisely because they *don't* return us quite to where we started.

Once again, both Pepsi and Coke are trying to make some history—but the game's just different enough now to make it even more interesting.

To be sure, the pressure's still on—but we like it that way. And the stakes are higher, but that's fine, too.

If we win . . . well, by now, both of us know that neither Pepsi nor Coke wins decisively in this game. There will always be other battles on other fronts keeping us too busy to celebrate.

And if we fail . . . well, we've both failed before and picked ourselves up off the floor.

As I see it, the important thing in all this for Pepsi is that we must keep demonstrating that we have the capacity to surprise you. By its very nature, the soft drink business forces us to reinvigorate our business year after year. Given that, it's crucial that we not only deliver refreshment that America prefers, but clever and amusing surprises that America comes to love.

The way we do all that best at Pepsi USA, as I hope these pages have shown, is first and foremost by surprising ourselves—by coming into the office, morning after morning, with the sense that anything we want to do is possible.

And it's amazing how original you can be—and how much fun you can have—when you've got that mind-set working for you.

We're committed to constantly changing the rules of the game. To thinking and planning and acting like number two—no matter how successful we are. But we have a goal—leadership in our industry—and a map to get there. And, best of all, we can see ourselves having a hell of a good time on the way.

Will we make it?

Stay tuned.

EPILOGUE

"AMERICA'S CHOICE"

This time last year, I was spending a great deal of my evening and weekend time staring at the tiny screen of a MacIntosh computer. Somehow, this seemingly innocuous activity came to be seen by the folks at Coca-Cola in Atlanta not only as the writing of a book but as the firing of another Pepsi salvo in the never-ending Cola Wars—a salvo that in Coke's view was particularly reprehensible in its audacity.

I realized at the time, of course, that writing a book might entail some personal risk. After all, most of the events Jesse Kornbluth and I would write about were quite current, and most of the central characters in our story were still on the job. But I was quite unprepared to hear through an intermediary that according to a Coca-Cola functionary, by writing this book I had actually "crossed over the line of death."

To this date, I'm still not quite sure how to interpret that. But inasmuch as I've survived another year of the Cola Wars, I suppose it was merely a particularly colorful warning that our friendly competitor intended to go on the offensive. On the other hand, I have considered starting my car by remote control in the morning.

In the soft drink industry, nothing stays the same for very long. When you think about it, that should come as no surprise. It's a natural result of intense competition. But of all the events that have taken place in the Cola Wars during the last twelve months, two—one bad and one good—stand out in my mind as most significant from the viewpoint of lessons learned.

The bad has to do with the events surrounding Wendy's restaurant chain's decision to abandon Pepsi after a seventeen-year relationship. The good—and this may seem strange coming from me—is the success Coca-Cola enjoyed in its efforts to re-establish Old Coke in the aftermath of the New Coke fiasco.

First, the bad. Late one afternoon, Pepsi Public Relations Director Becky Madeira walks into my office. This is not the brash, amusing Becky you met some chapters ago, back when we were countering the introduction of New Coke. This is a nervous and anxious Becky, in a new role: bearer of bad tidings.

But not just bad tidings—more like unbelievable.

Becky informs me that calls are coming in from reporters. There's going to be a press conference. Scheduled for ten A.M. tomorrow. By Coke. Something to do with Wendy's. Wendy's is dropping Pepsi to take on Coke. What's our reaction?

What's our reaction? Impossible. Pepsi has been part of Wendy's success ever since Wendy's founder, Dave Thomas, opened his first restaurant in Columbus, Ohio, seventeen years ago.

Don Kendall plays golf with Wendy's founder. In 1985, Wendy's made Pepsi its "supplier of the year." Moreover, not ten months ago, they signed a new, five-year, tight-as-a-drum contract to serve Pepsi in every one of their company-owned restaurants. No, this Coke press conference, it's got to be about something else. They're feeding misinformation to throw us off. Just to be sure, I call Don Kendall.

Don Kendall gives the press rumors even less credibility than I do. Kendall and Thomas have been friends for a long time. "Dave Thomas isn't that kind of guy. If he had a problem with us, he'd pick up the phone and tell us about it. Besides, he and I are going fishing next week—with our families."

But then Becky tells me *The Wall Street Journal* has called with a scoop. The press conference tomorrow is to be a joint Coke-Wendy's press conference. We're out, they're in. How could this happen?

The next morning, at the press conference, we see some of the answer. On the platform are three former executives of the Pepsi fountain beverage division—men who are now in the top management echelons of Coke's fountain business. Clearly, we are being sent a message. And the message is this: The Cola Wars have gone nuclear. The principle of honoring and fulfilling a contract, it seems, is out the window.

Our response? Not if we can help it. We sue Coca-Cola for

"tortious interference in a contractual relationship." We sue Wendy's for repudiating their contract with us. And Wendy's sues us, claiming that we breached the same contract, presumably because we're insistent that the terms of our contract be fulfilled. Meanwhile, Wendy's says it will continue to serve Pepsi in its company-owned restaurants. Apparently, it's worth the effort to fight for what you believe in.

In a way, fighting for what you believe in may also be the lesson from the other major Cola War happening of the last twelve months—Coke's efforts to re-establish Old Coke after the debacle of the New.

We'd always expected that national attention on Coke would continue for a while once the Coca-Cola Company bit the bullet and brought back the product it had abandoned in the spring of 1985. And we assumed there'd be a kind of halo around Old Coke that we'd have to live with for a while, after which things would settle down, with consumers recognizing that Classic was the same old Coke that didn't, for most cola lovers, taste as good as Pepsi.

That, anyway, is what we expected. But by the fall of '86, it was obvious that things weren't turning out that way. More than fifteen months after its return was forced by the American public, Old Coke was still flying high. Its sales curve was on an upward trend, its image on a higher plane. And Pepsi sales were beginning to feel the heat.

Why? Well, one reason was we were preoccupied at the time with introducing a billion-dollar product called Slice. And another—more important—reason appeared to be that precisely one year after the wild summer of New Coke–Old Coke, the company's management had gotten its act together—in fact, it had a whole new act, with a new cast of characters.

Coke's reshuffling of key executives was the by-product of the mergers-and-acquisitions craze, which is the biggest continuing story in American business. For when Beatrice Foods was purchased by Kohlberg Kravis Roberts and Company, Coca-Cola got an opportunity to buy Beatrice's Coke bottling plants. Coke took it. At about that same time, Jack Lupton, the largest independent Coke bottler in America, and other Coke bottlers decided to sell their plants. Coke bought them, too. But the price of taking control of those operations was steep: $2.7 billion.

That's a lot of debt to take on in any business. So Coke hit upon a less-painful way to take control of those bottling operations—spin them off into a separate company. This would require the largest stock offering in American history. No problem: The Coke name was magic. Only there turned out to be a big problem. In its preliminary announcement, Coke priced the offering at $22.50 a share. Wall Street thought that was a little high—like about $7 a share more than it ought to have been. Nobody bit. So when the public was formally invited to buy into Coke's bottling operations, the price was closer to the figure that Wall Street wanted.

Coke's restructuring did more than wipe the new debt off the balance sheet. It allowed Brian Dyson, president of Coke USA, to search for new dragons to slay as president of the newly formed Coca-Cola Enterprises bottling company. At Coke USA, his replacement was Ed Mellett, who was, you'll recall, once a top executive at Pepsi. Sergio Zyman, Coke's senior vice president of marketing and another graduate of the Pepsi executive team, was off "pursuing other interests." In his place at Coke's marketing helm was John Reid.

The announced strategy of this new team was to build the power of Coke's cola business by using New Coke as an "attack" brand. Its target: Pepsi's strength in the youth market. Classic Coke, meanwhile, would continue to be marketed as a drink that embodied all that was good about the American way of life. Its line became "Red, White, and You," followed by "Coke's a Part of Your Life." New Coke went on the air with "Catch the Wave." Its spokesman was a New Wave, computer-generated personality by the name of Max Headroom. His mission was to counter the galaxy of "New Generation" stars who'd helped establish Pepsi's leading-edge imagery.

Not a bad strategy. But we didn't consider it a real threat to Pepsi's momentum in the marketplace. Old Coke's advertising, we believed, would serve merely to re-enforce a position it already owned in the consumer's mind—and Pepsi had clearly done well competing against that position. New Coke, moreover, was a discredited failure, a dog. Not matter how good the commercials might be, Coke was wasting its money.

As it happened, we knew that Coke was signing Max Headroom before Coke announced it. A friend of mine in the entertainment industry told us all about it. He even brought us tapes of Max's British television show, in case we wanted to preempt Coke's move by creating a Max Headroom character of our own. Now, this might sound funny from the guy who signed Michael Jackson twice, but Max Headroom seemed too strange for a mainstream product. The more Coke ran these commercials, we figured, the more they'd turn consumers off.

We were both right and wrong. The Max Headroom commercials weren't a turnoff—Video Storyboard voted them the best-remembered commercials of 1986. But they didn't help sales of New Coke; in two years, New Coke fell from eighteen share points to just one and a half.

And yet, what Headroom did for New Coke turned out not to be the point. What the Coca-Cola Company had unintentionally done was to make people forget about the New Coke–Old Coke business. In fact, it was as if New Coke didn't exist! Instead, Coke had—at enormous expense and with huge embarrassment—stumbled onto a way to graft contemporary edge onto Old Coke's traditional appeal.

Clearly, it was time for Pepsi to react.

Our marketing plan for 1987 was pretty well set by then. With much fanfare—and even more expense—we were to ride the crest of Michael Jackson's return to glory. But it was obvious by the beginning of 1987 that our traditional way of releasing music-oriented commercials—a premiere on the Grammy telecast, followed by a saturation campaign—wasn't going to be possible for the second round of our Jackson commercials.

This wasn't because Michael was being his old perfectionist self and blocking the completion of the commercials. This time around, Michael was totally cooperative—and his face was all over the commercials. The problem was Michael's album. It didn't exist—in finished form, anyway. Not that Michael wasn't working on it. On the contrary, he was working too hard. He'd write and record a batch of songs—and then reject them. And then he'd start the process all over again. At this rate, there was no way he'd have the record out before the summer of 1987.

The delay made me impatient. I knew how good those commercials looked. And how much good they could do. And, after all, I was the one who'd announced that Michael would be back with Pepsi in '87. But before I could hit the subclinical level of neurotic distress where I seemed to live in the winter of '84, the bluebird of common sense came to rest on my shoulder. This wise creature taught me that one sure way to guarantee failure would be to air the commercials before Michael's fans had a chance to hear the album and see his new look. It taught me that

I was powerless to change the situation. And, given my conviction that the gods do drink Pepsi, the bluebird reminded me, this delay might be a blessing in disguise.

So I took to waiting. Confidently. Comfortably. Calmly. But I'd be lying if I said I didn't have a sleepless night every once in a while.

While I waited, the blessing in disguise materialized. Pepsi USA's president, Ron Tidmore, and Mike Lorelli, Ron's new senior vice president of marketing, pulled together a new marketing plan. Its target: every consumer. Its goal: Remind America that Pepsi is not only the choice of the new generation, but the preferred taste of every generation. Its name: America's Choice.

As they did in the years of the Pepsi Challenge, consumers would have an opportunity to "let their taste decide" by stepping up to one of the thousands of taste-test booths throughout the country. Americans would vote with their palates to determine which cola was, in fact, "America's choice."

Was there any question in our minds who'd win? As Bronson Pinchot, our chosen spokesperson for our America's Choice campaign, would say, "Don't be reedeecoolus!" For one very simple reason, we knew Pepsi would win: Victory claims based on results at taste-test booths aren't permitted in television advertising. All that's allowed are the results of independently conducted in-home research. And that research—undertaken well before the America's Choice ads went on the air—clearly supported consumer preference for the taste of Pepsi over Classic Coke.

That campaign would nicely buttress our Michael J. Fox commercial and a "Top Gun" commercial that about five million buyers of the videocassette of that movie found at the head of the tape. A few more leading-edge surprises are never to be despised. But which ones?

In 1985, you'll recall, Jay Coleman went to "Live Aid" with the idea of arranging some superstar partnerships. His great idea then was a Pepsi commercial with Mick Jagger, David Bowie, and Tina Turner. That couldn't be put together, but we did get Tina Turner to do some commercials for our international division. They were thrilling and effective, and so we thought they'd be a good bonus for our post–Labor Day efforts. Tina would be going on tour in September, so we agreed to coordinate our efforts—we'd sponsor the tour and put her commercials on American television.

Then a curious thing happened. Jay Coleman was talking to David Bowie's manager, and it turned out that two years had made a great difference in Bowie's attitude about commercials— now he'd love to do a duet with Tina Turner. This pleased us. And we were pleased again when Bowie agreed that we should sponsor his tour, too. That gave us America's Choice in the early part of the summer, David Bowie–Tina Turner commercials on the air in July, Bowie on tour in July, and Tina Turner crisscrossing the country in September.

Was I still nervous about Michael Jackson? With all this good stuff in the pipeline, not nearly as much as our friends in Atlanta would probably have liked.

Meanwhile, remember Savannah Classic Cola? That was going to be another product that, like Slice, was going to have no direct competitor—it was, you'll recall, our version of Old Coke. We were going to introduce it around Labor Day, 1985. But Coke cut us off at the pass by bringing the old formula back.

Savannah was the brainchild of Dan Clark, Research Director John Almash, and Brenda Barnes, the marketing director of brand Pepsi. It was a good idea at the time. And, we decided, it was a good idea even after Coke brought back Merchandise 7X.

This time, though, we weren't thinking of Savannah Classic Cola as a Coke clone. Maybe, we thought, we'd bring it out in a diet version. Why? Well, you'll recall that Diet Coke has a very different taste than Coke. It's built around a completely different principle: the "absence of negatives." Its purpose is not to offend, which is why it tastes more like a cream soda than a cola. That left a big marketing hole for the soft drink that could taste more like regular Coke—yet with just a fraction of Coke's calories. How few? As we'd learned from the success of Diet Slice, which has about 10 calories, a calorie-conscious public wasn't wedded to a 1-calorie diet drink. A few more calories were fine, so long as there was a big taste dividend.

Savannah became Project Rambo and, in turn, Jake's. Jake's 15-Calorie Cola, just so everybody knew what they were getting. And to give Jake's a down-home feeling, we decided it shouldn't be another new product from Pepsi—it should come from a separate company, with its own general manager and a fun, small-town approach to business. A young, enterprising product manager, Marc Johnson, got the nod, and he set about implementing this plan. Soon there were Jake's pencils (the flat kind that you sharpen with a knife), a Jake's neon sign (the slogan on it reads: "Jake's is real good"), and a private joke on the side of the can (inspired by LSMFT on the old cigarette packs—Lucky Strike Means Fine Tobacco—Jake's says FCMGT, or Fifteen Calories Mean Great Taste).

As I write, it's too early to tell if Jake's is going to be big enough to roll nationwide as a flanker to Diet Coke. This much we do know: Among cola drinkers, the taste of Jake's beats Diet Coke—by a lot.

There's one more product introduction I ought to tell you about. We know it will work. It's Ice Mountain. Bottling location: Mount Zircon, Maine. Calories: none. Additives: none. The product? You guessed it—water.

Pepsi? Water? Well, Americans drink nearly 6 billion gallons a year of the stuff. Industry sales hover around $1 billion. And we are in the refreshment beverage business, after all. And we surely do like surprises.

When I finished this book last year, I looked back and assessed what the Cola Wars meant. I wouldn't mind standing on that assessment: Coke is rising again, but Pepsi is rising faster. This year, honesty compels me to say that I'm impressed by Coke's comeback. But I'm not worried about it. For as I write, hundreds of thousands of consumers have been stepping up to our America's Choice booths, comparing the taste of Pepsi to Classic Coke, and picking Pepsi over Coke 62% of the time.

But last year, Coke bottlers were fighting for their lives after the debacle of New Coke. Their trademark was, for the first time in a century, suddenly in danger of being incredibly devalued. Their backs were, quite literally, to the wall.

It's not easy to beat people with that much at stake. But what you can do is never forget is that no victory is permanent. Ours wasn't. We knew it wouldn't be. Our future success will be based on taking the offensive over and over again.

Meanwhile, there's a great lesson to be learned from Coke. You can make gigantic mistakes—and still recover. You can think the grass is greener in somebody else's formula—and still find your way home. You can take risks and fail—and not get killed.

And something else. It may sound funny coming from me, but Coke's success in re-establishing Old Coke may be one of the best things that's happened to Pepsi in the last year. To understand my meaning, you've got to look at it this way: Nothing that's ever happened at Pepsi—no event, no marketing idea, no leader—has done more to improve our quality control, keep our product price modest, or enhance the drive of our people than our intense battle with Coke. If the Coca-Cola Company didn't exist, we'd pray for someone to invent it. And on the other side of the fence, I'm sure the folks at Coke would say that nothing contributes as much to the present-day success of the Coca-Cola Company than the men and women of Pepsi.

Sound strange? It shouldn't. Competition is almost always the force driving the achievements of every soldier who's engaged in a war where no victory, however sweet, is ever permanent; no wounds, however public, are irreversible; and no one, absolutely no one, owns the right to a single future sale.

But enough. I hear the bell ringing again.

Are you ready for the next round?

We are.

Index

G

H

I